Inequality

Inequality

The Political Economy of Income Distribution

FOLKE DOVRING

PRAEGER

New York
Westport, Connecticut
London

HC
110
I5
D68
1991

Library of Congress Cataloging-in-Publication Data

Dovring, Folke
  Inequality : the political economy of income distribution / Folke Dovring.
    p. cm.
  Includes bibliographical references and index.
  ISBN 0-275-93963-4 (alk. paper)
  1. Income distribution—United States.   2. Income distribution.
I. Title.
HC110.I5D68 1991
339.2′0973—dc20   90-27556

British Library Cataloguing in Publication Data is available.

Copyright © 1991 by Folke Dovring

All rights reserved. No portion of this book may be reproduced, by any process or technique, without the express written consent of the publisher.

Library of Congress Catalog Card Number: 90-27556
ISBN: 0-275-93963-4

First published in 1991

Praeger Publishers, One Madison Avenue, New York, NY 10010
An imprint of Greenwood Publishing Group, Inc.

Printed in the United States of America

The paper used in this book complies with the Permanent Paper Standard issued by the National Information Standards Organization (Z39.48–1984).

10 9 8 7 6 5 4 3 2 1

Contents

Tables and Figures	vii
Preface	ix
1 Overview	1
2 Meanings and Causes	5
3 Measurement	29
4 The United States	47
5 Across the World	67
6 Economic Growth and Development	87
7 Consequences for Society	105
8 What Is New in the United States?	123
9 To Turn the Trends	141
Appendix I *Population and Distributed Good: The Problem of a Companion Function*	151

Appendix II	*The Exponential Functions*	159
References		163
Index		181

Tables and Figures

TABLES

3.1	Deciles, Quartiles, and Medians, at Selected Levels of Inequality	37
3.1a	Inter-Quartile Ratios, Inter-Decile Ratios, and Logarithmic Ratios	38
3.2	Percent of Total Income Going to the Lower One-Tenth, Lower One-Fourth, Lower Half, Upper Half, Upper One-Fourth, and Upper One-Tenth of the Population, at Selected Levels of Inequality	40
A.1	Negative Exponential Function and Companion Function	154

FIGURES

3.1	Lorenz's Curve	32
3.2	Examples of Exponential Functions, Interval Frequencies, Percent of Total per Interval of One-Tenth Average Size	39
6.1	Theoretical Examples of Sector Changes Covering a Fifty-Year Period	90

A.1	Negative Exponential Function and Companion Function for Distribution of the Good	153
A.2	Negative Exponential Functions for Three Logarithmic Bases	156

Preface

With rising numbers of homeless children, a trillion-dollar national debt at high interest, and increasing environmental damage, the economy of the United States is now in worse shape than it was ten years ago. If the recent crisis of communism is not to be followed by a severe crisis of capitalism, something serious must be done about the economy of the richest country in the world. There are several facets to our economic quandary. A large part centers around the distribution of income and wealth, which has become visibly more unequal in the last few years. This book endeavors to explain the facts and the problems of economic distributions to the general public.

The trouble with facts is that there are so many of them. Although this was recently expressed by a prominent astronomer, it applies to economic data just as much as to the stars. There is indeed a great wealth of information about economic distributions, as on many other economic topics. To avoid repelling the reader with a surfeit of statistics, data will be cited mainly as signposts to lend some reality to the explanation of economic changes. Some of the facts will change even as this book goes to print, but the explanations should nonetheless apply to the foreseeable future as well.

Inequality

1
Overview

"Life is unfair," is a truism often repeated. This applies to many things. Closest to the political mind are the inequalities of income and wealth, which continue to figure prominently in nearly all acceptance speeches at party conventions nominating candidates for president: Equal opportunity is as American as apple pie. In terms of individual justice or injustice, inequalities of income are easy to grasp. As agents in the workings of the national economy, however, these inequalities are far below the surface of ordinary debate. This book will focus on income inequalities in terms of political economy. This means the economy of the whole polity—the wider society within which inequalities occur and work their effects.

Economic distributions conjure up a wide array of problems: of meaning, measurement, explanation, and policy prescription. The topic should be at the forefront of our current political debate, for economic inequality has been growing in the United States for some time, and very evidently so in the 1980s.

Distribution almost always means some degree of inequality. This turns out to be ambiguous. Inequality can be good or bad depending on a host of intricate connections with nearly all facets of economy and society. Income, wealth, size of firms, size of communities—all functioning entities in society can be, and are, of unequal size. As a consequence, they control different sized parts of the whole that is distributed among them. This includes the control of the creation and allocation of human capital.

The meaning of inequality touches on many factors, both individual and collective. Among them are incentives to exertion; reward for effort; the resources to realize one's potential; welfare, both individual and collective; and power within society—power to maintain one's private sphere versus the power of great wealth to coerce or enforce the will of the rich and the economically powerful. Money power often tends to infringe on ballot power. James Madison, the principal author of the U.S. Constitution, warned against the possible misuse of money power.

Rewards and incentives can be individual, within the existing system: If you work harder and better than the next person in the same occupation, you should be better paid. This would be true if the system were unambiguously geared toward individual justice without any interference from group egoism, patronage, or Mafia solidarity. Regardless, the incentives and rewards can depend on how entire strata of society fare in the distribution of the pie of production to which all are contributing, directly or indirectly. If there is not equal pay for equal effort, then the reward to an individual may be dwarfed by the reward for being in a favored category. Economic theory says that we get the worth of what we produce; however, daily experience tells us that any such a theory is imperfect. It is in part a tautology, for the existing distributions contribute to deciding what we are worth in the market sense.

How much inequality is right for maintaining both incentive and reward, while also maintaining a healthy balance in society? Too much or too little spoils the balance. This basic fact of life is what economists should keep in mind when they try to explain economic margins and economic marginality. There must be some inequality of income because there has to be some motivation to excel and to seek the kind of occupation where one does one's best. However, too much inequality will hurt society as well as many individuals if economic advantages are too concentrated, leaving many people without any realistic hope. In the extreme case, the distribution is unsound if those at its lower end are forced to accept wages that are below the real cost of producing and reproducing their kind of labor. Concentration of economic power in a few hands also limits the opportunity for change. What is the right balance? The question is often asked but seldom answered with any confidence. It is easy to see that the United States now has more inequality than is healthy if the nation is to get the best out of all its human resources. When the trend is toward increasing inequality, it is evidently heading in the wrong direction. We must pay attention to trends no less than to the level of inequality.

This book will elucidate the problems of economic inequality by refining the concepts and the reasoning, and by applying a consistent system for measuring inequality. Measurement should have been the special province of economists, but until recently they could not agree on a system of measurement (Kuznets 1965). Armed with these tools of concept and measurement, we will seek to discover what has happened to income distributions in modern times in the United States and across the world. The findings should give some perspective to the debate about current and prospective national economic and social policy, industrial and trade policy, and taxation.

The basic explanation of economic inequality was put forth nearly two centuries ago by David Ricardo, (1817, 1819, 1821) in his classical formulation of the theory of rent. Unending debates since then, from Karl Marx to members of the Hoover Institution, have stirred up much dust, but when the dust settles, Ricardo's concept of rent still comes out as the primary idea around which economic inequalities can be explained. The political nature of economic distributions has been highlighted by a social science generalist who focuses on politics: Harold D. Lasswell ([1936] 1950). His formula of "who gets what, when, how" places the question in a rigorous conceptual framework that is among the starting points for explanations of inequality.

Ricardo's concept, like economics as a whole, is based on scarcity as a steering force. This concerns the economy first of all, but it also affects other facets of society. Scarcity makes scarce goods and services high-priced both in money terms and in terms of other societal rewards. This tends to remove the scarce goods from the command of the more disadvantaged groups in society and to concentrate them in the hands of the rich and the powerful. If there were total affluence, nothing would be scarce, and there could be no inequality of distribution. The air we breathe used to be free for all, at least within the same air quality zone: There could be no rich or poor in the access to atmospheric oxygen. However, air pollution tends to destroy even this kind of equality, as the least polluted areas are at the command of those who who can pay the most for them. In remote antiquity, the case was similar with many other natural resources. Human ingenuity in older times led, above all, to more food production and hence to larger populations, which became increasingly unequal as other resources remained more restricted.

The experience of primitive resource abundance got a new lease on life in the Western hemisphere following the geographic discoveries. The North American frontier experience was a breeding ground for economic and political democracy. The same force was frustrated in Latin America because its institutions were patterned on Old World scarcity and inequality. Similar problems also took root in the South of the United States with the slavery economy. Here, the logic of scarcity was inverted: Bondage (as in parts of the Old World) was a response to the scarcity of labor. The history of bondage and labor freedom in Europe, including Russia, reflects this paradox (Dovring 1965). The same has been true until recently in parts of Brazil, for instance.

The American experience with abundant land was paralleled later in the country's unexpected abundance of petroleum and natural gas. Again, as in the Old World, resource owners sought relief from the cheapening of abundant resources by promoting intentionally designed overuse, leading to social waste, and hence contrived scarcity (Dovring 1984b). Contrived scarcity turns the relation between rich and poor into a class conflict rather than a matter of economic rationality.

From the New Deal until recently, public policy in the United States to some extent tended to favor less economic inequality among the population, as should be expected from economic development and affluence. In the 1980s, however, this trend was reversed. Tax reform also has moved the trend in the wrong direction, without achieving the consequences for the sake of which it was advanced. An already disturbing tendency toward plutocracy in the nation's political and social life has been furthered by official policy on the mistaken assumption that this would maximize economic growth. Mistaken ideas of so-called conservatism have, in fact, led the nation into a direction that, if pursued, could well mean the end of democracy as well as of sustained economic growth.

It will become clear to the reader that the trend toward more inequality is part of a general decay syndrome in U.S. society. The last chapter in this book sets forth some ideas about how these adverse trends may be reversed, which will necessitate a much more active role of the federal government to foster renewed growth, full employment, and full education.

2

Meanings and Causes

Economic distributions determine the rewards for ability and effort, as well as welfare and power. The reward is only in part allocated to people according to what they may be worth as producers. It also reflects the use of capital, the ownership of which may or may not be deserved. In modern times, the classical dichotomy of labor versus capital has been complicated by the increasing importance of human capital, which also is not necessarily deserved. Rent (in the wide sense), accruing to both conventional and human capital is an important instrument of distribution.

Distributions can be discussed in terms of both justice and efficiency. These two criteria do not always lead to the same conclusion, but they overlap to a large extent. In common understanding, just distributions will reward hard work, competence, inventiveness, and initiative. They will also protect the weak or temporarily unfortunate individuals against hardships that may not be their fault and that might otherwise destroy their ability to make their contributions to society in the future. Just distributions should also protect against extreme concentrations of economic and political power. In extreme cases, unjust distributions may be highly detrimental to society as well as to many individuals.

Justice is a subjective concept; it is what an individual feels to be reasonable and fair. When such a feeling is widely accepted in society, this may be said to express a primary *social contract*; and as such, to gain a measure of objective validity, at least in a functional sense (Rawls 1971). This formulation of justice has provoked wide debate (Nozick 1974; Daniels 1975), often to the point of the concept's rejection (for example;

Bronfenbrenner 1986). This conflict brings to mind the different formulations of the "golden rule" in Jewish, Christian, and Chinese traditions. The different value placed on the individual in European and in Far Eastern cultures, for instance, also reminds us that one person's justice may be another's folly. One way or the other, every society needs to determine their own concept of justice in order to function in a consistent manner.

The question of justice focuses primarily on individuals—what they are thought to deserve. Parallel, and less subjective, is the question of aggregate welfare or social utility. This is a separate concept, but does not necessarily conflict with the notion of justice. Utilitarian theory has mainly concentrated on the *sum of utility* for all individuals, as did the early welfare theory of C. A. Pigou. In this book, we will emphasize aggregate effects on society as a whole, which may be qualitatively different, and greater than, the sum of effects on individuals. Welfare is, then, not merely a matter of compassion but also of a society at peace with itself, and in command of all its resources.

Income distributions affect the access to economic opportunity, which is a matter both of justice and of social utility. In our "diploma-mill" society, access to opportunity depends on access to institutions of formal education. Even if everyone were to get some comparable measure of education, the resulting diplomas would still have different effects in granting access to careers affording high economic rewards, depending on what seat of learning has issued the diploma. Opportunity is not merely a matter of reward or failure for individuals; it also concerns society's access to its entire potential talent pool. Such access is blocked when the gifted poor are held back and the mediocre offspring of the rich are favored beyond their ability.

Economic inequality also affects power. Income means not only the opportunity to consume and invest, including investment in one's own or one's family's human capital. Income also means economic power, which is eventually translated into political power. Increased economic power to one group may impose special constraints on the whole course of economic change, and thus can impinge positively or negatively on the power as well as the welfare of other groups.

Income distribution can also influence the rate and direction of economic expansion. This is not just a matter of standard economic theory. It also depends on special forces that may influence the amount of investment versus prestige consumption, for instance. Thus, it can influence the demand schedules for essential supplies such as housing and quality food, and create demand schedules for nonessential goods and services such as fur coats and cosmetic surgery. The various forces that affect income distribution often conflict with each other (Dugger 1987).

IMPERFECT JUSTICE

"To each as they deserve" appears to be a basic tenet of what passes for economic conservatism. It may be an ideal, but as pure theory it is too good to be true. It is, in a sense, a logical circle for it assumes that justice is what markets dole out. Even on such a "conservative" assumption, we would have to admit that distributive justice is as imperfect as the markets themselves.

Perfect markets would assume perfect people. We have not met anyone who would answer this description. As early as 1920, Pigou found that economic theory was unable to explain unemployment, which is one of the pervasive causes of economic inequality. Blaming unemployment on "market imperfections" means, implicitly, that we recognize standard economic theory as a construct full of half-truths, because it fails to include a great many of the factors that determine what is actually going on in a country's economy. There are different types of market forces, as we shall discuss near the end of this chapter. There is also the productivity paradox of punishing progress, on which we shall also elaborate.

Imperfections in the distribution of income can be individual or systemic. If we only look at individual imperfections, we can easily recognize that some people are overpaid and some underpaid merely because those who decide about salaries and other economic advantages are fallible and make mistakes, whether knowingly or not. It is too easy to dismiss this by saying that individual mistakes occur randomly and are equally distributed between underpayment and overpayment. This might let the mistakes cancel each other in the statistical sense, leaving the average outcome close to ideal. Even if this were so, however—and this is not self-evident—it would still be relevant only if we disregarded the qualitative effects on society of the under- and overpayments. Both the underpaid and the overpaid people represent some damage done to society as a whole, for both cases represent a less-than-optimal use of resources. For society as a whole, the underpayments and overpayments do not cancel each other. Instead, they sum to a loss of efficiency, an effect that is larger than the sum of either the under- or overpayments.

For individual mistakes, there is, of course, no general remedy. They could certainly be reduced if public morality laid greater emphasis on competence and integrity among those who have the privilege to decide about the economic fates of other people. Systemic injustices are another matter, however. They may be remedied or mitigated by changes in social systems. Most, if not all, systemic injustices can be traced to rent in the broad sense—the special return to scarce resources. Some recent theories of economic inequality have tended to place less importance on the *factor shares*: how much of the income that can be distributed goes to capital and how much to labor (Blinder 1974; Atkinson 1975; Sampson 1984).

This classical distinction previously went a long way to explain inequality of individual or family income, since most capital returns went to the upper income strata in society. This trend has now been modified in two ways. For one thing, large amounts of capital returns from industrial stocks and bonds now go to people of all income classes as pensions, by way of pension funds investing in securities. For another, there is now increasingly more rent going to human capital. Labor is no longer a single factor of production but rather many different factors, some of which are more scarce than either land or capital. How far this overrides individual probabilities, and how far it can be said to be justified, is in fact a large part of the modern problem of distribution.

RENT

Rent is many things, including more than the classical case of land, reflecting the relative scarcity of lands of varying natural productivity. A special case is *quasi rent*, an accounting concept on the border between rent and profit, which we must distinguish from the regular cases of rent. Rent also accrues to site values, scarce competence, and the even scarcer *star positions* or *positional goods* in the public and para-public sectors of entertainment, politics, and economic leadership. In a wider sense, all differences in individual ability (whether hereditary or acquired) also lead to rent; the extent again depends on scarcity. Rent can also be traced to many cases of social discrimination. This includes sex bias, ethnicity, class barriers, family ties, and organizations of the Mafia type. Sometimes any and all such distorting forces are summarized as "history" (Roemer 1987). To understand what is occurring, we should first look at the classical theory of rent.

In economics, we distinguish between rent and profit (for example; Montani 1975). The distinction is not always as clear as we might want it to be, and we shall have to comment on gray areas of transition between rent and profit. For the moment, let us state that profit is a way of recouping outlays in capital formation, including a normal rate of return to capital. The size of the profit also varies depending on the skill in handling resources of all kinds. In this way profit may also be said to reflect what the profit takers deserve. That is true in principle, and on the condition that profits do not also include varieties of rent. An inclusion of rent among profits may be accidental or contrived. When rent and profit occur side by side, as they often do, the distinction between the two can be maintained only at the cost of rigorous analysis.

Rent originally referred to land for agricultural production, but the concept has been widened to embrace other input factors that may be scarce in a rigid kind of way, such as qualified labor, star positions in society, groups favored by discrimination, international comparative advantage, and protection rent in international economic relations. There are various other refinements to the original concept, such as economic rent (as distinct from contract rent) and monopoly rent. How rent relates to market equilibrium is a complicated problem whose answer depends in part on how far we accept existing institutions and existing power positions as given, or whether we reject some of them as unjustified or unnecessary.

RICARDO

The theory of rent, which modern-day economists still use, came to us from David Ricardo ([1817], 1821). In Ricardo's time, farming was still the dominant economic activity, and the rich classes in England received a large part of their income from farm rents. Ricardo explained that rent on land is purely a matter of distribution of the proceeds from the use of a resource that is scarce. When good land is abundant and available for the asking, rent will not be paid for its use. Rather than pay rent, farmers will move on to free land elsewhere. All the proceeds from free land come to the people who do the productive work on it. Secondarily, some returns will also come to people who supply intermediate production goods to the land users, but this does not represent rent.

When land of the highest quality becomes scarce, Ricardo explained, some people will find it necessary to cultivate land of lesser natural fertility. These people will then receive less reward for their efforts at cultivation than the cultivators of land of the highest quality. This means that rent begins to accrue to the holders of the highest quality land, and it becomes possible for landowners to lease the land to someone else to cultivate, charging as rent the difference in product from the highest quality land over the less fertile land now also being used in production. However, even if the owners continue to cultivate the highest quality land themselves, they nonetheless now receive some implicit rent among their income. Their cultivation efforts cannot be priced more highly than the same efforts of those who cultivate the land of lesser fertility. In a market sense, the reward for efforts in cultivating land should be what is received by those who cultivate the least fertile class of land that must be cultivated in order to produce all the food that society needs. As increasingly lower qualities of land are brought into cultivation, the reward for cultivation falls as well. This will continue until the level of reward for cultivation has come down to a minimum subsistence level below which the cultivator cannot work and survive.

An important tenet of Ricardo's theory is that rent is not produced separately from other returns to scarce resources. Rent is purely a matter of distribution of the proceeds of production, and this distribution is a function of the scarcity of land. The more the need for food leads to cultivation of land of lower quality, the greater the amount of the proceeds of production that will become rent to landowners, whether they cultivate the land themselves or not. Thus, population increase will lead to increasing inequality among landowners, and between landowners and other members of society. This will be true unless man-made productivity rises fast enough to offset the increasing density of population so that the supply of food (at a given cost level) keeps in step with the demand for food.

In Ricardo's time, rent theory was well illustrated in some of the countries of recent settlement, foremost the United States. In England itself, scarcity of land was a fact of life long before Ricardo's time, but the process was more complex than he describes; we will come back to this in Chapter 5.

Rent payments are not only a consequence of the unequal distribution of property; they also contribute to this inequality. Those who receive rent payments are also the people best placed to increase their landholdings by reinvesting savings from rental income. In market economies, much of the rent-producing lands tend to accumulate in the hands of people who are not working farmers. Concentration of ownership in rent-paying land is often a mainstay of economic inequality in countries where there is a high degree of inequality of income and wealth. Concentration of the ownership to property—of all kinds—in the hands of some groups in society is a source of economic class formation, even in advanced countries (Harris 1978).

Ricardo emphasized that rising rents benefit individual landowners but harm society as a whole. The level of rent versus profit has been the subject of continuing debate (Esfahani 1987; Gibson and Esfahani 1983). Rising rents are a symptom of increasing scarcity of land, which leads to higher prices for produce. Conversely, falling rents indicate that land is becoming less scarce. This can happen because of the settling of vast expanses of virgin land, but it can also reflect vigorously rising productivity. Either way, falling rents will stimulate the economy as a whole, while disadvantaging individual landowners. The latter consequence became evident in the United States when men like Thomas Jefferson and James Madison nearly went bankrupt in old age; their Virginia estates lost in value because of the westward expansion of farm settlement, a United States success story that Jefferson and Madison had done much to facilitate.

ECONOMIC RENT

Ricardo did not pursue the overall consequences of the rent-paying system in much detail, but his general explanation still holds. Basically, Ricardo limited his concept of rent to agricultural land because of its "original and indestructible powers" to produce (Ricardo 1817, 1821, Chapter 2). We now recognize that these powers are neither as original nor as indestructible as they appeared in England in Ricardo's time (Dovring 1983). However, this only makes it easier to apply the rent concept to other resources.

Forms of capital other than farmland would not produce rent, in Ricardo's thinking, but only profits, which were thought to depend on how economic skills were applied. Only toward the end of his chapter on rent did Ricardo admit to a borderline concept. Rent can also accrue to capital invested in land when the scarcity of land, and the consequent scarcity of raw produce, leads to the use of more capital spent on the good land than on the poorer land, and in such a way that the return to additional capital on the former earns a higher rate of return than that earned by similar capital invested in the latter. This difference in the rate of return to capital, when caused by differences in land fertility, also constitutes rent according to Ricardo.

More than a century after Ricardo, the concepts concerning rent were refined by Joan Robinson (Robinson 1933). She distinguished between contract rent, which is what resource (or asset) owners charge for the use of what they lease out, and economic rent, which is the return over and above any supply cost for the assets as well as for all other factors of production. Economic rent comes close to what Ricardo had in mind, even though he did not make the distinction explicitly.

In the sense advanced by Robinson, the rent concept is applicable to all cases in which production leads to more output value than the sum of the minimum supply costs of all factors of production, including a reasonable return to entrepreneurship. Rent is not produced independently of the products, but its extent can be obscured by the ways in which it is distributed among factors of production. As we shall argue, in the rest of this chapter, all factors may be more or less scarce just as land may be scarce, and the rent will be distributed accordingly. We shall also argue that scarcity can be natural (as in the case of overpopulation), or contrived, when it is the result of privilege, class politics, or market manipulation.

Robinson also contributed the insight that some other material can be as perpetual as land; for instance, steel when it is recycled (Robinson 1961). This reinforces the case for using the concept of rent to refer to all kinds of resources, especially since land is not as perpetual a resource as was thought in Ricardo's time. The built environment, immaterial property, and labor in many circumstances may all earn rent even though they are not perpetual. A country can earn rent because its natural resources give it a comparative advantage, but also by political contrivance, as *protection rent* (Lane 1979). Before going over several applied cases of rent, we must explain a related concept called *quasi rent*.

QUASI RENT

Quasi rent is an "as if" case. Returns that are, in part or entirely, of a different kind than rent are treated in the same way because the supply cost cannot be readily estimated. To a very large extent, quasi rent is calculated to show the value of fixed assets, especially land fixtures in both urban and rural areas. This is because the value of fixtures is often difficult to establish by other means than by inference from the returns they generate. Many buildings and other fixtures were put in place in the past when the value of money was different from what it is at the time of appraisal. Updating the value of partly depreciated assets is among the greatest difficulties in economic accounting. The older fixtures are now *sunk costs*. Their original cost is now irrelevant. Of interest instead is their productive value in the present and the near future, and estimating value becomes an exercise in rent computation. This is basically how land is valued—on the basis of rent, capitalized by means of the normal rate of return to money and securities.

Quasi rent is usually a mixture of rent and profit. We call it quasi rent because the fixtures always have some supply cost, or at least some replacement cost. To this extent we will have normal capital return. Elements of rent have now become impossible to distinguish because of difficulties in estimating rates of physical depreciation and also because of changes in the value of money and the relative prices of the investment goods used to establish the fixtures. This is also why some people use the term quasi rent in many other cases of economic rent. In the following discussion, we use the term *rent* whenever it appears evident that the rate of return exceeds reasonably calculated supply costs for a resource to which high returns accrue.

Quasi rent in real estate improvements can, to some extent, be self-reinforcing, for the investments already in place can discourage further investments of the same kind. This is a braking factor that in turn helps to prop up the value of investments already in place. Risk and uncertainty further reinforce this braking effect. Adding to the building capital usually means assuming some risk. This tends to be greater the more the demand for a given type of building is already filled by the existing building inventory. This phenomenon also has parallels in types of assets other than real estate improvements.

Quasi rent is of some importance in farmland, but is much more important in urban real estate and other nonfarm property. In these classes of real estate, fixed investments in manufactured capital are a much larger proportion of the entire asset value than for farms. What was said above about quasi rent on land investments, therefore, has much larger consequences for nonfarm real estate than for farmland. The gray area between rent and profit is also wider for nonfarm real estate. This is because for nonfarm property, rent in the restricted sense depends not so much on any natural property of the soil as much as—and in fact, mainly—on location.

SITE VALUE

Land can produce economic returns in other ways than by the inherent productive powers of soils, rocks, and groundwater. Foremost are the differences in economic advantage stemming from site or location. This is immediately evident in urban areas. In large cities, centrally located building ground commands very high prices. Ordinary residential areas in the outskirts of the cities also have much higher land values than the farmland from which they were once developed.

Such economic advantages due to location are not gifts of nature but rather the result of economic activity by society as a whole. Location values come about by the ways in which the built environment in cities and villages has been created and continues to be developed. Society also contributes in the way the overall economic landscape is shaped up. This gift of society, location value, is also more vulnerable to economic change than farmland. Location values have been created by the building up of fixed investments, and can therefore be reduced or destroyed by attrition and obsolescence in these investments, and eventually in the whole economic landscape. The borderline between what society contributes and what an individual contributes to the value of property is often fluid.

Some of the differences in site value are returned to society through real estate taxation. It has been suggested that society could recoup even more of the rent from site values by way of taxation (for example, by Henry George [1879] and his followers). However, such a policy, if directed at entire property values and not just site values, risks introducing high rigidities in fixed costs. The viable part of Georgist taxation proposals concentrates on taxing site value without the fixture values (Gaffney 1973), and has achieved limited application.

With all these qualifications, it is evident that site values are nowadays a large source of rental income. Rent originates from site values in the same way as from farmland: as a reflection of scarcity. With high site values, such scarcity is almost definitional, and certainly inevitable. The very nature of the advantage from central location points to relative scarcity as a normal trait. Increasing differentiation of site values contributes to making city growth a source of income inequality (Haworth, Long, and Rasmussen 1978). Even though site value rent is conceptually quite similar to farmland value rent, it is often even more difficult to distinguish it from quasi rent on the buildings that occupy most of the high-value sites.

SURPLUS VALUE AND THE PRICE OF LABOR

The theory of rent was further refined by Karl Marx. His most important addition to classical theory was the concept of *monopoly rent*, to which we shall return. Marx applied this term mainly to primary products. In a wider sense, however, and without using the term *rent*, Marx applied what amounts to the same basic concept to the general distribution of proceeds between labor and capital, under the category of *surplus value*.

In Marxist economics, a large part of all economic inequality comes from the appropriation by capital owners of all "surplus value" (*Mehrwert*). The capital owners can do this because capital is scarce and labor abundant, as was the case when Marx wrote. The issue of dividing factor shares between labor and capital has remained central to income distribution theory (Osberg 1984, ch. 5).

Surplus value is, in fact, a variant of the same concept as land rent. Since rent is a residual over minimum supply cost, the concept should apply whenever the market drives the price of any category of labor down toward the replacement cost of that kind of labor. For a time, the market can even drive the price of such labor down below its replacement cost. This can be done with seeming impunity whenever the kind of labor in question is becoming obsolete. If a particular kind of labor will continue to be necessary to the economy, its underpayment (below minimum replacement cost) will, of course, affect not only welfare but also continued labor supply. In modern times, we have begun to recognize that the minimum supply cost of labor includes costs of schooling and medical care.

Anything produced in excess of the minimum supply cost of factors of production (and among these costs are also those of capital and management) is available for distribution as rent or quasi rent. Only obsolescent labor can be used at wages below its replacement cost, for such labor is similar to part-depreciated investments: It has only opportunity value, and nothing more. In a pure market sense, then, no injustice would be done by the low pricing of labor with low opportunity value. The consequences for society as a whole are a different matter, however, as we shall discuss in Chapter 7. Opportunities forgone by such low pricing include, of course, those of retraining for new skills. Current-day Marxist writers usually emphasize class conflicts but generally do not identify surplus value as a variety of rent (for example, Dixon 1981).

In capitalist theory, the initial answer is the same as in Marxist theory: Surplus value should indeed go to capital, the scarce resource. The surplus value is then usually regarded as profit, which is implicitly thought of as deserved since it is the outcome of unhampered market processes. These processes value capital at its opportunity cost, which is equal to the capitalized value of the returns to it—another logical circle.

Capitalist practice, in principle, provides a way out. Sparing use of capital when it is very scarce, and the corresponding intensive use of cheap labor when that is abundant, will in time lead to a more rapid accumulation of capital, rendering the capital henceforth less scarce and the labor less abundant. The success stories of economic reconstruction in Germany and Japan after World War II are good examples of this process taking place over relatively short spans of time. The accumulation of capital will eventually be slowed down somewhat, and more of the value available for distribution will begin to go to labor as wages. In turn, increased wage incomes will then stimulate more production by way of increased demand for consumer goods. Some of this has actually occurred, but in a more complicated way than could be derived from Marxist or early capitalist theory. Rent to qualified labor reflects the differentiation of the labor market into many special markets, and income distribution will therefore also become more complicated.

RENT TO QUALIFIED LABOR

When rent keeps accruing to may kinds of tangible capital, this tends to depress the earnings of rank-and-file workers if they constitute a single, undifferentiated labor pool with some excess supply over total demand. In such a pool, individuals will be entirely mobile and interchangeable. This was the concept of Ricardo's scarcity effect: The people who did the farm work were essentially an undifferentiated labor pool, in contrast to land, which earned rent according to a scale of different natural productivities. This is also how we can understand Marx's theory that surplus value always accrues to the owners of capital according to the productivity levels of the capital goods. Labor, as long as it is in excess supply with no important differences of quality, will always be depressed toward the minimum wages that are necessary for the workers to survive and reproduce workers of the same general, nondescript quality. Labor will be paid the amount of its replacement cost, and no more. When all the surplus value accrues to the capitalist, this surplus value represents a general case of rent.

The process of holding rank-and-file workers down to minimum subsistence wages has not occurred in recent times. On the contrary, in capitalist countries most workers are paid wages that are considerably higher than the replacement cost of labor, even when one includes the cost of modern-day education and training as part of the replacement cost. The higher cost of training is often—and correctly, in principle—classified as *human capital formation*, even though the realities are often hard to pin down (Lucas 1977).

Higher real wages are reflected in a rising share of the wage bill in national product accounts, among other things. In the United States, labor's share of national product was about two-thirds in the 1930s, and rose to about three-quarters in the much larger national product of the 1960s. The causes of such a distribution of the proceeds of production between labor and capital are not merely labor legislation and the clout of labor unions. Neither could have had quite this effect unless other economic forces pushed in the same direction.

One such economic force is nearly full employment. If the pool of unemployed workers is nearly empty, the owners of capital can no longer acquire all the rent. Instead, some of it begins to accrue to labor because labor in general has begun to be scarce (Giersch 1983). In much of the literature, residuals accruing to labor are termed quasi rent. We prefer the term rent, because there is no unknown or obsolete supply cost; what we see is return above known supply cost, which is analogous to rent on land.

The tendency for rent to accrue to labor is reinforced by the increasing differentiation of the labor force among worker categories with specialized skills. Skilled workers are not as interchangeable as were factory hands at the time Marx was writing. Among his contemporaries who defended the standpoint of the capitalists, some were cited as saying that "machine work is easy." Maybe this was true in the early days of industry, when technology was still in its infancy, and the owners of a factory under strike could go out and recruit strikebreakers among the unemployed people in the street. Nowadays, when a specialized, modern industrial establishment is under strike, the managers can no longer recruit strikebreakers as easily. The strikers have the advantage that their skills are relatively scarce. Even though many of them might be replaced by the recruitment of workers with somewhat similar (rather than identical) job qualifications, these other workers on the whole will already be employed elsewhere. Scarcity of specific skills now forces more of the rent to be shifted into labor wages. How high such rents to labor may rise depends in part on the stakes on the part of the employers in obtaining workers of the right caliber and competence.

This risk is in some proportion to the amount of investment per worker. The larger the ratio of capital per worker the more imperative it is to the employers to obtain the best workers money can buy. Examination of the wage scales in different industries will show that in general, the more capital-intensive industries pay the highest wages. For instance, Reagan's secretary of transportation's breaking of the air traffic controllers' union (August 1981) did not do away with the necessity to pay high wages for this scarce skill.

The general tendency for rent to accrue to specialized skills and jobs with high capital intensity has without doubt acted in favor of wage workers in general (see Schultz 1968). It has tended to make their wages higher in relation to the incomes of entrepreneurs and rentiers than would have been the case without this set of forces acting on the wage scales. To individual entrepreneurs, this has meant lower incomes in the short run, but to entrepreneurs as a class, the higher share going to labor has also meant higher aggregate demand for the goods they produce, and hence, in the long run has also meant more industrial opportunity and higher entrepreneurial incomes.

Thus, rents to skilled labor have tended to diminish some of the income inequalities in society. However, they have also tended to widen the income inequalities within the ranks of wage earners. At the bottom of the scale are people like the migrant farmhands, who earn no rent at all—they tend to be paid wages close to minimum subsistence or replacement cost, or even lower. In between, some semiskilled workers also tend to remain with lower wages than in the high-skill, capital-intensive industries. This is especially true in industries with low ratios of capital per worker. The sweatshops of the garment industry are an example, and have been tending toward worsening conditions in recent years as immigrant workers from low-income countries have made labor less scarce.

When a large part of the social product becomes wages, do not the wage differentials then represent justice in rewarding the better workers more? Not necessarily. Discrimination against women and ethnic minorities is a large exception and easy to spot. Even without such market imperfections, it is only the *ranking* of workers according to skill and quality that can be established with some confidence. The *scale of differences* may still be influenced by the scarcity conditions of the time and place. In other words, we agree that the better workers deserve higher pay, but we may not agree on how much more highly they should be paid. Neither would marginal product be entirely decisive, for this too may depend on the pricing of the outputs, which in turn may be influenced by the relative wages of labor categories. Only workers doing the same job are directly comparable; most are compared by way of prices.

A special case is that of risky occupations where wages typically are higher, especially for people who are not wealthy (Viscusi 1978). This is not a case of rent, however; rather, it is one of actuarial principles, as in insurance: Risk becomes part of the supply cost of labor.

RENT IN SCARCE OCCUPATIONS

We have argued that rent can accrue to all kinds of skilled labor whenever that kind of labor is in some sense scarce. To an even higher degree, the same is true of occupations that are scarce in themselves, no matter what skills are really needed to handle the positions. The critical circumstance here is not so much the actual quality of the person as the opportunity—by chance or otherwise—to occupy such a scarce position. Sometimes, such opportunity is referred to as "exploitation by human capital" (Tinbergen 1975). This is analogous to high site value. Exploitation is the part of the pay that exceeds the supply cost—however high it may be—of the kind of person who has the position. The supply cost of real human capital should, of course, earn profit.

This kind of rent represents a variety of monopoly rent. It applies above all to the stars of the entertainment industries (including spectator sports) and to the political elites. In both these groups, opportunities for prominent and high-paid positions are scarce because of the ways in which these activities are organized. To a lesser extent, the same can happen in other activities because of influence exercised by interest organizations, political patronage, or mafia-type groups, or because of discrimination by sex, race, or other criteria that are not relevant to skill. Any of those influences can create artificial scarcities of opportunity that then function as if there were a scarcity of competent labor, and can be translated into labor rents in ways that are not beneficial to economy and society as a whole, and often downright harmful to the common interest. The scarcity of prominent positions has been discussed as star effect (Dovring and Dovring 1971), and as positional goods (Hirsch 1976).

Concentration of opportunity in the entertainment industries, leading to star effect, is quite evident in the United States. In this large country, the markets are continent-wide, and the opportunities for star positions are only a few per million of the population. The public's attention span is limited, and it can only take in so many stars at a time. The firms that "own" the stars also have a material interest in getting their stars used to the maximum rather than searching for new talent. In a small country this effect is not so extreme, but it still operates, if to a lesser degree. The markets are smaller and also somewhat more protected against imports, if by no other means than by language barriers, as is evident in both print media and other entertainment. There can be relatively more star positions even though they cannot be as highly paid as in a large country. The level of pay is thus, to a large extent, a function of the size of the market rather than of talent. This is very evident also in the pay scales of star athletes: Their income soared when sports became televised.

In regard to the political elites, some basic facts were discussed by Lasswell ([1936] 1950). With cogent logic, Lasswell showed that "who gets what, when, how" depends critically on how efficiently the ruling elites are able to uphold their positions and to prevent counter-elites from emerging and calling into question the justifications of the former group. This presents an analogy with the collective landowner monopoly in Britain in the time of Ricardo.

Positional goods in politics tend to become more scarce with the passage of time because of population increase, among other things. There can be only one president of the United States at a time, and thus an individual's chance of coming into that position becomes less with every generation, and indeed every year. The same goes for other positions of power and prominence, from Senate, congressional and gubernatorial positions down to those of mayors and other chief administrators. The number of school principals is not increasing as fast as the number of teachers. In this case, the exceptional opportunity is rendered even more exceptional by the lingering preference for male individuals to fill such positions, even though the recruiting base among ordinary teachers has a female majority.

Business concentration in industry, commerce, and banking also tends to diminish the opportunities to command large economic resources. This has always been compounded by the tendency to recruit business leaders from the sons of business leaders. In recent times it has been rendered even more serious by the ever more extreme concentration of many business leaders on obtaining the maximum monetary income for themselves, to the exclusion of other business objectives. We shall return to this problem in Chapter 8.

All these kinds of limitations on access to prominent positions are violations of the principle of free competition. They lead to the formation of monopoly rents (Haworth et al. 1978). All this is now exacerbated by television, which represents a high degree of industrial concentration and has created a new economic aristocracy, projected also into the field of spectator sports, and again with top incomes occasioned not by talent alone but by its combination with the centralizing influence of the principal medium of diffusion.

The border line between entertainment and politics is far from sharp; rather, there is a wide gray area. U.S. politics has long been recognized as a form of spectator sport. Recently it has also begun to be invaded by elements from the regular entertainment world. This is evident in the application of the same kinds of marketing techniques that created the star quality of movie actors and actresses to the creation of political stars, especially in "the making of the president." Campaign "handlers," from H. Robin Haldeman to James Baker III, have endeavored to make appearances reign supreme over any reality that may lurk beneath the surface. Ultimately, the tendency to elect entertainment stars to high public office threatens to turn the tables on the public and render appearances more important than reality after the election as well. The opportunities for off-stage influence by still other entertainers may become serious distortions in the running of public affairs. One soberminded pragmatist, torn between loyalty and intellectual outrage, ended up warning against making public service a mere performance (Regan 1988). In a wider sense, concentrated market power (by monopoly or oligopoly) tends to generate excess profits that include an element of rent (Powell 1987).

ENTREPRENEURIAL EARNINGS AND MARKET POWER

The current ideology in capitalist economics maintains that entrepreneurs deserve the full amount that they appear to bring into the firm. If they deserve all they contribute, then a graduated income tax could be represented as "immoral" because it deprives them of some part of what they deserve.

There are, of course, accounting problems involved in showing what entrepreneurs contribute. If anything, extremely high managerial salaries may actually contribute to limiting how much the firm can produce within the constraints of its income. Apart from that, the logic that credits a successful business leader with all the excess profits of the firm is faulty. In economic analysis, taking into account the marginal principle, the entrepreneur should be credited only with the increment of earnings that is over and above what would have been brought in by his next best competitors had they not been eliminated from the competition; that would represent the analogy with lower grade land in Ricardo's analysis. To say that society really owes so much wealth to the high captains of industry (as argued in the novels of Ayn Rand and the publications of the Hoover Institution) is therefore misleading.

As argued earlier, the case instead presents a clear analogy to the star effect in entertainment and to positional goods in politics. The entrepreneur heading a very large firm also benefits from the paucity of such elevated positions. How much of the high entrepreneurial incomes are not really deserved at all became evident not long ago in comments about "golden parachutes" (very large sums of severance pay) being offered to some of the failures among the leaders of large business (Segal 1989).

The tendency for large amounts of wealth to continue to accumulate where they are already concentrated is also relevant here. Large capital gains as unearned income are commonplace. Only recently has it been pointed out that this is, in fact, a variety of economic rent (Shepherd 1989).

DISCRIMINATION

The major cases of discrimination are well known and need not be elaborated in much detail (Thurow 1975, ch. 7; Osberg 1984, ch. 7). We shall come back to them in later chapters. For individuals to be categorized by sex, "race" (a misnomer for subculture functioning as caste), national origin, religious affiliation, and so forth has led to, and still often leads to, their degradation or unjust treatment. Often this happens through arrangements of such long standing that they are mistaken for normal market forces. Most women working in low-wage occupations, and blacks, are often excluded from professions and trades that they therefore have less opportunity to learn; similar trends have the double negative impact on society of denying it the full use of all the talent pool and of promoting to important positions individuals who are not the best that could be obtained had the market been free of discriminatory biases. When a mediocre white male gets a position that a brilliant woman or minority man would handle better, we are all shortchanged, for we are less well served in this way. Even those who reap but modest positive rewards in this manner may in fact be more hurt by the damage done to the system than favored in their individual lives; many of them might be better off in a less prominent position and thus in a society rendered more prosperous by unbiased job recruitment. Only few individuals are really better off under discrimination, and these individuals are then in some sense social parasites. They may not all understand this fact, but this should not make us forgive them—for the knowledge of what goes on is available to anyone who wants it.

All this can be studied in a more extreme form in the case typified by the Mafia. Several groups of Italian origin (Mafia, camorra, and cosa nostra) took their origins as underground resistance movements against tyrannical monarchies, but after surviving in quite different political scenes, they degenerated into severe cases of social decay through their discrimination. The author of *The Godfather* (Mario Puzo) compellingly described the case in Sicily. For instance, the Mafia had to be served by an incompetent medical quack when they eliminated their competent physician because he was not sufficiently loyal. Such primitive discrimination in its obvious destructiveness often did no more than copy what traditional class society had done behind the screen of inherited institutions and hereditary positions of economic power. It is significant that when the late medieval population decline in Europe improved the conditions of the common people (because of less Ricardian rent when people became more scarce and land therefore less scarce), historians, who were inured to the viewpoint of the ruling classes, tended to focus on the impoverishment of privileged people (such as German robber barons) as if that were the whole story, and the increased well-being of the common people was easily overlooked.

Mafias have existed in many countries and for many reasons. The Ku Klux Klan in the South of the United States also originated as a resistance movement against an occupation regime resented as unjust because it was hard on the elite of the defeated South; what this did to the common people (both white and black) is held in as little focus as the prosperity of the common people in late medieval Europe.

Yet another case of Mafia-like discrimination can be seen in the communist parties in countries where they have attained power—and the recent collapses in Eastern Europe have only underlined the conclusion. Milovan Djilas did the world an immense service by pointing to these party organizations as a "new class" (Djilas 1957). The class egoism, no less than the ideological rigidity, of these party organizations has without any doubt retarded progress in the countries where they have held power. The hidden wealth of high communist elites came startlingly to light in the Eastern European revolutions of 1989. This aspect modifies our concept of income distribution in countries with political monopoly parties.

THE VALUE OF LABOR AT THE MARGIN OF USE

The analysis of wage scales given above often runs into opposition from economists who are steeped in the rigors of neoclassical analysis. Such economists usually focus attention on the short run and on short-term decisions that business leaders need to make. Then, they take the large parameters of the whole economy as given, because this is what leaders of individual businesses must do when they operate in the same environment as their competitors. Discussing the economy of the whole polity, many of these static assumptions cannot be upheld if the analysis is to be realistic.

In short-run business economics, one of the standard tools is the *production function*. By means of an articulate set of mathematical equations, production function analysis endeavors to show how much each factor of production contributes to production *at the margin*. This expression means that, assuming production is increased or reduced by some minor amount, how much does each additional unit of output cost in terms of each of the factors of production? Factors are sometimes simplified into three categories: land, labor, and capital. Often one of the three is differentiated into several factors, each with its own input figures and its own product at the margin. This is often done with capital, which can be fixed or variable, and either form can consist of several different classes of goods with nothing in common except their ability to be equated in terms of monetary cost. The production function analysis will show what difference it makes to production if expenses for a given factor, or for all factors, are increased or reduced. The firm can afford to pay for a unit of a factor what that unit produces at the margin. This applies also to labor, which can be taken as one factor or can be specified separately for any desired number of labor categories, among them management. The net product of an additional unit (such as an hour or a day) of labor, as specified, should then indicate the correct market price for a unit as specified.

As an aside, we may note that applied production function analysis almost always contradicts some basic assumptions of neoclassical economics, namely, that the economy is in equilibrium, working according to perfect knowledge. If these assumptions held, the production function analysis would show that all factors were equally productive at their respective margins of use. It would be logical that entrepreneurs making their dispositions of the financial means within their control would use factors in such a way that each would give the same marginal rate of return, which would be equal to their price. The firm would break even at the margin. Its rate of profit would include all the rents to factors before they reach their margins, as well as the fruits of superior skills in business leadership.

Actual production function analysis almost never shows this ideal balance in the use of factors. Nearly always, some factors are more productive and some less so at their respective margins of use. All this is computed in terms of current prices of both inputs and outputs. If constant prices are used in order to show changes over time, some element of counter-factual assumption is thrown into the calculation, and the results are then more difficult to interpret in real economic terms.

This lack of conformity to theoretical expectations means, of course, that the idealizing assumptions of neoclassical theory are seldom true. At best, the neoclassicists can claim that real conditions will consistently tend toward equilibrium. Since they almost never get there, we must conclude that new imbalances are continuously being thrown into the system by any of a host of circumstances, among them the lack of omniscience on the part of entrepreneurs.

Production function analysis is often useful to entrepreneurs because it makes it easier for them to change the factor mix in order to obtain higher net returns. However, in political economy, the results of production function analysis lead us around in a logical circle. Assuming all market prices and all supplies of production factors to be necessary just as they are would fly in the face of all that we know about the effects of discrimination, market manipulation, and similar phenomena. Because the market tends toward equilibrium, it also tends to lend a seeming justification to the injustices and inefficiencies of the system because it treats all market facts as just and inevitable. In this way, each factor is assumed to be worth its price at the margin of its use, which in turn is a consequence of its actual price on the market depending on scarcity, whether real or contrived.

For labor, the conclusion should be clear. Whenever a category of skilled labor has become artificially scarce because of discrimination, avoidance of competition, or star effect, the artificial scarcity will inevitably lead to high marginal products, and hence to high wages. The medical professions are a good example. Not long ago, the services of competent doctors were artificially scarce both because of rationing access to medical schools ("in the interest of quality" was the often-cited motivation), and because many functions that are now increasingly performed by paramedics and midwives were reserved for doctors. The latter arrangement renders the services of average doctors (those not accorded star status by virtue of specialization) less scarce, and hence lower priced, even as their productivity in real terms (as opposed to money terms) has gone up because they no longer perform as many low-level routines as before.

A major example concerns migrant farm workers. When a culture of poverty maintains a chronic oversupply of low-skilled workers, the marginal product of such workers—for example, migrant farmhands—will be low because employers can afford to hire them right up to the point of very low marginal return in money terms. In the meantime, the market prices of outputs (for example, fresh vegetables and fruits) adjust to the low labor cost. Both costs and prices become part of the competitive structure, both among firms within the country and between them and foreign suppliers (e.g., fresh produce imports from Mexico and the Caribbean islands). If low-skilled labor were more scarce in this country, it would be used more sparingly in labor-hire operations, it would have higher product value at the margin of use, and it would be paid higher wages. Each firm might remain as competitive as before, at least within the country and with regard to other firms using hired labor. The higher labor costs would be paid by consumers, who would adjust their choice of consumption items according to the different set of prices. It is not even certain that the prices of produce would be any higher across the board, for with less competition from large-scale labor-hire farm firms, small-scale self-employed producers might have a larger market share and a better chance to bring their superior use of labor (because of self-interest, which the wage workers do not have) to bear on production and prices. As a complication, food distributors do not always choose their supply sources on the basis of price alone. The large food store chains in particular attach much importance to a dependable supply and uniform quality, both of which tend to favor large-scale, wage-paying farm firms over small, family-run farms.

Rent as a distributive mechanism also operates in the international economic system. We may cite the two major instances of comparative advantage and protection rent.

COMPARATIVE ADVANTAGE

Classical economic theory emphasizes comparative advantage as an important factor in determining which countries will produce which goods for export, and in what proportion they will contribute to world trade. The easiest to grasp is the extreme case that has been called "vent for surplus" (Myint 1958). This occurs when a country is so well endowed with an easily exploited natural resource that it cannot use it all itself, and therefore is better off to export some of it, even at low prices. The vent-for-surplus country alone may not be able to fill all the international import demand for the article, so other countries may also produce that article for export, but at a lower rate of profit for themselves. The difference in the rate of profit is rent accruing to the holder of the cheaper variety of the resource. This is the same principle used in determining land rent according to Ricardo.

In our time, vent-for-surplus cases are found mainly in mineral wealth—especially oil in some favored countries, but also other minerals that are traded internationally. To a lesser extent it also applies to farmland, although nowadays less so than before.

Industry can also earn rent by comparative advantage because of superior technology or superior management—and often simply because of acting first. This may also function as if the producing resource were cheaper. Such advantages tend, however, to be of limited duration because of continuing technological and managerial progress, and may last only ten years or less nowadays.

In a free world market the rents accruing to bona fide comparative advantage would be regarded as legitimate, and indeed as beneficial. Rewarding technological comparative advantage tends to deliver the goods at lower costs and to promote continued progress. This should lead to greater efficiency in the use of resources worldwide. Institutional wage rates, and the protection of domestic industry, often hamper the working of comparative advantage.

The fact is often overlooked that perfect markets would require not only free movement of merchandise but also free movement of labor. But the world does not have a single labor market, for reasons too complex to go into here. The limits on labor movements are the chief reason for the trade restrictions between countries. To a large extent, their implied purpose is to protect underemployed labor. This means interfering with the international distribution of income.

PROTECTION RENT

In a world where trade and its protection are intended for narrow national advantage rather than international economic justice, national policy can reap advantages by making life more difficult for competitors. A classic case concerns the French military actions in the 1600s which rendered Dutch overseas trade more costly, thereby reserving to France a larger share of the trade with the Caribbean area, and its profits (Lane 1979). F. C. Lane has also related how Portugal's attempts at reserving the ocean-borne India trade for itself actually backfired by raising the cost of Portuguese trade to the point where Italian merchants again could make profits from the overland India trade. This was a case of protection rent accruing to the other party rather than to the country trying to secure it for itself. The case parallels other instances in which organized violence led to restoring threatened class privileges where market scarcities would have made the distribution of income less class-bound—the early use of firearms in Western Europe is a case in point (Pettengill 1981).

Colonial history probably includes many cases of protection rent, although the analysis may be difficult to perform. Certainly, the conflict between England and its North American colonies in the late 1700s centered around the channeling of trade profits through institutional interference with markets. The concept may also apply in some recent trade history. Japan, and possibly also South Korea, may be engaging in *adversary trade*, the purpose of which is not just to secure a larger part of the market but also to drive the competition out of the market altogether (Drucker 1989). This is certainly not new: Classical "dumping" in the 1920s and 1930s included an element of the same thing, if in less extreme form.

Reverse protection rent can also be traced in recent international economic relations. The United States, the United Kingdom, and the Soviet Union, because of their high military costs, have indirectly—and maybe even unwittingly—awarded reverse protection rent to countries with lower military costs, foremost West Germany and Japan (especially so in the 1950s and 1960s), but also some other European countries. The intelligent policy of Costa Rica in abolishing its army altogether, probably also awarded that country some reverse protection rent by securing lower costs for both export commodities and the goods used in domestic consumption.

RENT AND THE MARKET

Rent distributes the proceeds of production between factors. It does so based on criteria that do not reflect the worthiness of each factor considered in the abstract, but rather reflect some combination of inherent productivity and scarcity. (The relation of these two is sometimes a paradox, as we shall discuss later.) Ricardo said the same thing about farmland, and we have argued that the same also applies to other kinds of rent across the whole economy.

Resources are allocated by scarcity. We have already shown that scarcity can be real or contrived. The latter reflects injustices that tend to be cast in stone by institutions, such as inherited wealth and long-term vested interests. Artificial scarcity may be increased by intentional social waste, which is often contrived and perpetuated as a means of protecting property and other established interests (Dovring 1984b).

This leads us to a first approach to the general subject of market forces. (There will be occasion to discuss this again in Chapter 9.) For now, let us only point out that the general reference to market forces tends to confuse two things: one is the market as a type of mechanism that is efficient because of self-regulating tendencies, and the other is the specific market forces that are in place in a given society at a given time.

Market forces as a mechanism have much to commend them, for they are, in many ways, more efficient and less costly than the command controls of political authority. Like the many feedback mechanisms in living organisms, market mechanisms, operating through supply functions balancing demand functions by the medium of price signals, can steer the economic processes more directly and more predictably than any system of rationing cards. This is not to say that rationing may not be necessary in time of war, but in peacetime we generally prefer to live without it. Moreover, none of this is meant to say that markets can do everything that needs to be done: The handling of social overheads without government authority is a problem with many facets, not least the *free rider* problem, which is the market's way of undoing concerted action by society as a whole. The *free rider problem* is well exemplified by firms securing higher profits by cheating on, for instance, pollution control.

But all the positive things that can be said about markets refer to market forces as a type of control mechanism—control by the automatic and predictable interplay of market demands and supplies as mediated by prices. Reference to market forces does not, however, imply with any certainty *what* economic power positions will fill the entries of the market play. Even less does this indicate what these power positions ought to be in order to serve the best interests of society as a whole. Neoclassical theory generally disregards market distortions, of which there are a multitude in all countries.

Some of these distortions were discussed briefly earlier in this chapter. Others exist in the tax system and in the systems of property and of corporate business, none of which are gifts of nature but rather represent various past attempts at solving social conflicts. When such conflicts are solved by the economically stronger forces acting in their own perceived interests, the result may have a semblance of being "right." The resulting distributions of income and wealth then become their own apparent justification, because they determine the supply and demand functions, and ultimately the prices of goods and services as well. Those who maintain that existing economic distributions are right or just are merely opting for the status quo. In this manner, the principles of market economics are confused with principles of protecting class privileges or other arrangements serving the economically strong rather than the whole polity. A pervasive problem is whether the existing economic distributions will allow all that modern industry can produce to also be consumed (Dugger 1987).

THE PRODUCTIVITY PARADOX

Productivity is widely hailed as an engine of progress—which it is in its aggregate effects on the whole economy. Yet the effect on distribution is widely overlooked or misunderstood. When an individual or a firm improves productivity above the general level in the same industry, then they are rewarded by higher incomes, if only until the rest of the industry catches up. With whole industries it is different: the industry that improves its productivity faster than most other industries is in fact punished by falling terms of trade—falling prices for what it has to sell compared with the prices for what it has to buy.

This seemingly perverse reaction to productivity gains is, in fact, quite logical. Rising productivity should mean falling real costs, and this ought to lead to falling relative prices of output combined with a tendency toward overproduction. The latter can be remedied in highly concentrated industries by cutting back on output, perhaps in collusion with the few other firms in the same line of production. But for highly competitive industries such as agriculture and many services, a general rise in productivity is rather a scourge. It benefits society as a whole, but not the people closest to where the beneficial effects take shape. (We mentioned the case of physicians who actually got lower incomes when their productivity was increased through lower paid assistance.) The reaction of the Luddites in the early 1800s against the introduction of textile machines in fact had some logic to it—for textile workers, but not for the whole community that was going to benefit from the textile workers' loss of work.

The productivity paradox is one more reason not to assume without proof that markets can automatically take care of all economic problems. Defenses against lopsided effects of productivity gains are not unknown: The whole recent history of agricultural policy in the United States reflects the general problem posed by the productivity paradox. We should remember this lesson when analogous problems emerge elsewhere.

RENT AND DISTRIBUTION IN THE FUTURE

The new trends in economy and society evident in the 1980s render it necessary to reexamine the whole question of the rationale for economic distributions. If rents continue to increase, even if partly disguised as high salaries, this will prove to be important as both a symptom and a warning of possible new trends in distribution and their effects on the entire social fabric.

If anything serious is to be done about these basic societal problems—and if we wish to avoid moving in circles—we must first of all understand what has been and is going on, and why. Several of the following chapters (4 through 7) will endeavor to fill out the picture of the past and the present. These elements should help put some order into the debate about the recent past and the likely perspective for the long-term future, which is discussed in Chapter 8. First, we must examine the other facet of distribution theory: measurement, which is treated in Chapter 3.

3

Measurement

Chapter 2 focused on the meanings and causes of economic inequality. The discussion mainly concerned the directional effect of several social forces that influence inequality. These include the real forces of population pressure and increasing scarcity of vital resources or discovery of new resources, whether by finding new land and mineral deposits or new and more productive ways of using known resources. Varying technological standards for labor competence also influence scarcity. All such "natural" reasons for inequality are variously and to a considerable extent modified—usually in the direction of more inequality—by social forces reflecting particular interests operating in the past or the present that generate contrived scarity. Extreme instances occur in the concentration of opportunity in entertainment, politics, and business leadership, creating star positions or positional goods that lead to monopoly rents.

THE NEED FOR MEASUREMENT

All the types of indications summarized above are in themselves merely directional: They point to what is likely to increase or decrease inequality. We also need to measure inequality by degrees—how it may change over time and how it may vary between countries and regions. We should be able to measure the degree of inequality in the population as a whole, and also separately within several subsets of the population such as men and women; race and other discernible ethnic groupings; occupational and industrial groups; and so on. We need to measure changes over time as well as variations in space or across society.

Measurement must be done in comprehensive terms so that we can understand how the changes and the variations of inequality affect not just a single group in society, but all groups jointly as well as separately. We must understand how change in one group may affect all other groups. Over time, the sum of the incomes that are distributed will vary by economic expansion or contraction, either of which may be affected by the degree of inequality in their distribution. In the short run, distribution comes close to involving a limited good. If one group receives more income, there will be less to spare for others. The difference between the concept of economic expansion and its actual distributional effects is among the continuing controversies of economic development theory, as will be further discussed in chapters 6 and 7.

Until recently, there was no generally accepted system for measuring economic inequality. Some writers still refuse to accept any existing system for measuring inequality (for example, Bronfenbrenner 1986). We may distinguish two main approaches: tracing a function that describes a whole distribution and places its parts in mathematical relation to each other, and establishing single indicators that purport to characterize some important facet of inequality in a given population.

DISTRIBUTIVE FUNCTIONS

A function is a set of numbers that are in some distinctive way the consequence of another set. For instance, the level of income is inversely related to the number of people who have that level—the richer the people you investigate, the fewer they are, and vice versa. This general principle can be articulated into a distinctive function by establishing the rates at which higher levels of income are represented by smaller numbers of people who have that income, and at which lower levels are represented by greater numbers of people.

The first such function to be proposed was formulated by Vilfredo Pareto near the turn of the last century. According to Pareto, the logarithm of the number of people who have a certain income level or higher, varies with the logarithm of the income level in such a way that the function becomes a straight line on a logarithmic graph. This involves two constants, one of which defines the slope of the function (how quickly numbers decline with increasing income level) while the other constant defines where the distribution can begin—it cannot begin at zero in a logarithmic system, nor can anyone live on zero or near-zero income. The former constant, the slope factor, is a simple expression of the general degree of inequality in a given population. The steeper the slope, the less unequal the distribution, and vice versa.

The Pareto function was at first greeted with enthusiasm in many quarters, and numerous scholars still cling to it (Aigner and Goldberger 1970), if only to portray the distribution in the upper tail—which includes the rich, and perhaps the upper middle class. Pareto's formulation does not fit any real-world population along the whole range of income sizes. Even if the upper (high-income) part appears as a straight line, which in fact is doubtful in many cases, in any event the formulation only holds in the upper ranges of the distribution. Distribution among rich people may have been what most interested Pareto. He was an upper income Italian economist (and a former railway engineer) who wrote around 1900. At that time there was little in the way of statistics on poor people and often not much interest in them either—Italy was then a poor country with a very aristocratic social structure.

The failure of the Pareto function to meet the need for measurement of inequality soon became apparent, and the search was on for other systems. One formulation that appeared promising for a time was set forth by Robert Gibrat in France (Gibrat 1931). He had found some data sets on the size of French industrial firms in which the frequencies of various sizes were distributed lognormally. This means that the distribution was normal, with a bell-shaped curve of frequencies around the mean, not in natural numbers but in their logarithms. There is a special diagram paper (log-probability–scaled paper) on which the lognormal function can be drawn as a straight line. The height of the bell-shaped curve expresses the degree of inequality—the higher and sharper the curve, the fewer individuals who are either poor or rich, and the less inequality there is; and vice versa.

The lognormal function also became somewhat of a disappointment, although not to the same extent as the Pareto function. The lognormal function appears to portray many economic distributions in the middle three-quarters of their size groups. It often fails in the bottom 20 percent and the top 5 percent. These areas represent the poor and the rich, which are often the most interesting and certainly the most problematic components of most economic distributions. Much mathematical work has been spent on formulating adaptations by which the lognormal function might be made to portray entire distributions (Aitchison and Brown 1957). Recently it was suggested that earnings at entry into the labor force are lognormally distributed (Creedy 1985), so that deviations from lognormality stem from subsequent modifications. The lognormal function has also been read as reflecting an incentive model of wages (Pomanskiĭ 1985). The general result of a long debate is that the lognormal function does not deliver a single usable system for portraying and measuring economic inequalities.

A third distributive function which was proposed more recently is the exponential function and its transformed versions; these will be used in this book and will be described later in this chapter.

THE GINI INDEX AND OTHER SINGLE-VALUE INDICATORS

Short of a system for portraying whole functions, many scholars concentrate on a single indicator that migh reflect the essential degree of inequality in a distribution. Foremost among such indicators is the Gini index (from Corrado Gini, of Italy). It is based on Lorenz's curve, a widely used graphic device of which an example is shown in Figure 3.1.

Lorenz's curve depicts the relation between the distribution of the numbers (of income recipients, or other units in an economic system) and the aggregate of the good (such as income) that is distributed among them. The curve is drawn in the lower half of a quadratic graph, in which the diagonal represents the line that would reflect complete equality (in other words, the same percentages of numbers and of the good would always meet). Such complete equality is never found in the real world of economics. Instead, the curve is a concave line below the line of equality. How far below

Figure 3.1
Lorenz's Curve

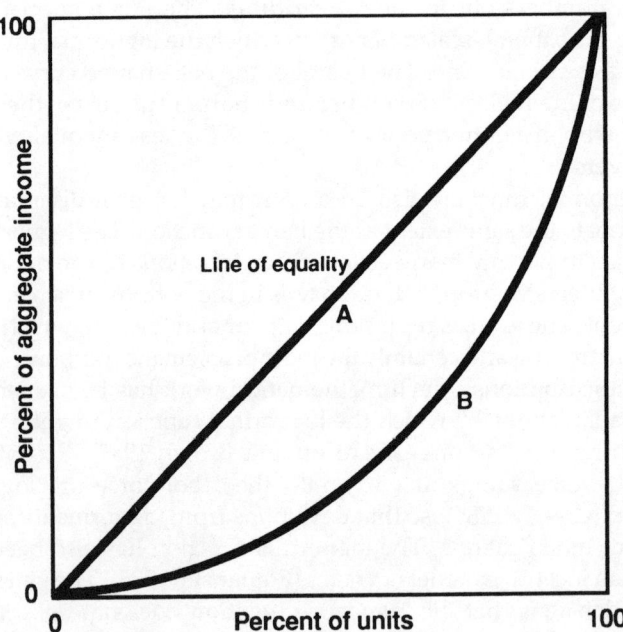

Note: The data used for this example are those for the untransformed exponential function where the median/average ratio = .693 and the Gini index = .51.

the line of equality this concave line falls is an expression of inequality: the lower the curve, the greater the degree of inequality. This visual impression is somewhat imprecise, and the value of Lorenz's curve for research on economic distributions was diminished when it was found that the curve can have different shapes; sometimes two curves even intersect. In such a case it is evident that the distributions are not the same even if their degree of inequality proves to be identical.

This is the main problem with Gini's index, which measures the proportion between the area between the line of equality and Lorenz's curve (field A on Figure 3.1) and the total lower triangle (field A plus field B). If the curve were one of complete equality, there would be no such area, and the index would be zero. In the other extreme—if one individual owned all the income—field A would equal field A plus field B, and the index would be 1.0 (for 100 percent). Gini's index is always some value larger than 0 and smaller than 1. Thus we find values such as .20 or .30. The higher the index, the more inequality there is in the population under study.

A weakness in the way the Gini index is often computed from census or survey data is that size intervals are assigned averages equal to their midpoints and that the last (open-ended) size group is assigned an average on somewhat arbitrary grounds (Sale 1974). These processes are not only inaccurate, the errors incurred are also not the same for all parts of a distribution, nor for different distributions as a whole.

The difficulty arising from the fact that Lorenz's curve can have different shapes even for the same degree of inequality is not reflected in the usual formulation of the Gini index. Many attempts have been made to improve on the system of measuring inequality by a single indicator. The Schutz index and the Theil index have been tried as improvements, and there are several other candidates for the best single-indicator index. A lengthy debate has led to the insight that no one single indicator is suited to analyze all types of distributions. For instance, cases where the distribution among low-income people is the main problem need a different treatment from those where the main focus concerns high-income individuals (Champernowne 1973; Saposnik 1988; Suppes 1988). The search for variant systems has continued until very recently (Slottje 1984; Berrebi and Silber 1987; Chakravarty 1988).

A further step in the search for refined analysis involves attempts at finding single-index measures that would allow us to identify underlying factors in the composition of the income, or in the population of income recipients (Shorrocks 1982, 1984; Satchell 1987; Silber 1989). The use of complicated algebra has increased, and with it the difficulty of following what happens along the distribution among the income-level subgroups.

It seems clear that single-value indicators assume some degree of consistency in the distribution to be portrayed (Esteban 1966), but it is precisely the absence of such conditons that often causes difficulties in the analysis.

However, a large amount of analytical work has been done using some form of the Gini index or a similar system. In the following discussion, results from such analyses will be cited, along with such reservations as the problems of the analyses render necessary.

For our purposes we will also use the most recently proposed system of distributive functions, namely the exponential function and its transformed version. This function can also be made to answer problems of irregular distributions.

THE EXPONENTIAL FUNCTIONS

The basic expression used here is the negative exponential function, which is the anti-logarithm of the natural logarithms:

$$y = e \exp -x \qquad (1)$$

where y is the percentage of the population remaining above size limit x, and the size limits are expressed as fractions and multiples of average size. $x = 1$ is average size.

This function, when drawn in semi-logarithmic scales, comes out as a straight line. It has some interesting properties; among other things, it is the only mathematical function that is its own first derivative. It often comes close to portraying entire distributions—from the lowest to the highest size levels—when the ratio of the median to the average (Me/Ave) is .693 (the natural logarithm for .5—the median size) or close to that value.

For the formulation in equation (1), it is easy to find the companion function for the distribution of the good:

$$z = y(1 + x) \qquad (2)$$

where z is the percentage of the good found above size limit x, while y and x are defined as in equation (1). Diagram representations of equations (1) and (2) are shown in Figure A.1.

When the Me/Ave differs substantially from .693, the formulation in equation (1) can be expanded by writing

$$y = e \exp -f(x) \qquad (3)$$

where the $f(x)$ is a function of x reflecting the degree to which the particular curve differs from the untransformed version of the exponential function. Under equation (3), the scale is either compressed in functions with Me/Ave over .693, which we call *high curves*, or stretched for *low curves* with Me/Ave below .693. In contrast to the untransformed exponential function, the high and low curves come out as curvilinear when scaled by x, but they can be made linear when scaled by $f(x)$ instead.

The function shown in equation (2) can also be expanded in ways analogous to those suggested in equation (3). Details of the computation of both high and low curves and their companion functions are shown in Appendix II.

There are three important requirements for analyses based on the exponential functions: The system of distributive functions that is used to portray economic distributions must be viable with regard to combining the distribution of the population and the distribution of the good; the system must be consistent in applying the same concept to all levels of inequality as well as across the entire range of income size groups within each function; and the function must be realistic in portraying distributions occurring in the real world.

By *viability* we mean that for each distribution of the population there must exist or be possible a distribution of the good (aggregate income or whatever), as explained in some detail in Appendix I. If this criterion is not met, a proposed distribution function cannot be taken seriously. Both the Pareto function and the lognormal function are, in fact, insufficient on this criterion. The untransformed exponential function does meet the criterion, as do the transformed functions as formulated.

Consistency means that the same mathematical formulations are used throughout, on all levels of inequality and on all levels of income within each function. This has not always been done in the literature to date—some analysts prefer a variety of expressions that are thought to meet ad hoc requirements of various statistical series. For instance, Pareto's log-linear function is clearly not applicable to the whole distribution. Usually, it can only apply to a minor portion at the upper end of the distribution at best; yet it is often taken seriously in applied analysis. The formulas shown in Appendix II and used in the following discussion meet the criterion of consistency, at least within the range of statistical variation that is usually represented in economic statistics. Only when the formulation is consistent throughout will it have any meaning in comparing the proportions between size groups with different income levels.

Realism has also been important for the choice of formulas in Appendix II. For instance, if a formulation that appeared to meet the criteria of consistency and viability tended to place the mode (the size of highest frequency) higher up on the scale of income sizes than is usually found in real-world data series, then such a formulation was rejected as not realistic.

To meet the three criteria, it is necessary to use formulations that are rather close to being exact, but they need not be absolutely so. It is sufficient if they are close to being exact—how close is sufficient will depend on how far one wants to pursue the analysis.

The calculations shown in Appendix II engage higher order equations; that is, equations operating with exponents on exponents. The reader of this chapter need not be aware of all the details in this procedure. However, some consequences of using these formulations must be explained in this chapter before they are applied to real-world statistics in the next two chapters.

MEDIANS AND OTHER FRACTIONS

To compare economic distributions with different degrees of inequality, standard fractions are often used. The most commonly used is the median (the size of income above and below which half the population of income recipients is found). When the median is expressed as a fraction of average size, Me/Ave becomes a convenient index of inequality. In the system of equations used for this book, Me/Ave is closely correlated with the a parameter (which expresses how the function at hand relates to the untransformed exponential function). The a parameter has been shown to be closely correlated with the Gini index (Dovring, Leuthold, and Karr 1974).

In addition to the median, the quartiles are widely used as inequality indicators. The first quartile is the income size under which is the lower 25 percent of the income recipients, while the third quartile is the size over which is the upper 25 percent. The second quartile is the median. One can also use any number of other fractions, or *fractiles*, such as selected deciles or percentiles. Table 3.1 shows the first and the ninth deciles, along with the first and third quartiles and the median, for selected levels of inequality. The ratios between these various fractiles, and the proportions between these ratios, can often be used to gain more knowledge about statistical series that otherwise appear not to give us all the information we need.

All the size limits shown in Table 3.1 are in terms of average size; thus, they are relative inequality indicators. We should note that economic distributions are almost always skewed to the left. Therefore, the median, as well as the first decile and the first quartile, are always lower than the average—the more this is the case, the greater the inequality of the distribution, and the inverse is also true. The third quartile is also below average in the more extremely unequal distributions, but in most of the distributions shown in Table 3.1, the third quartile is larger than the average. The same holds for the ninth decile in all the distributions shown in the table.

The first decile, the first quartile, and the median always rise with decreasing inequality, and vice versa. The third quartile reaches a maximum at $a = .693$ (which is also the median value here in the untransformed exponential function). The ninth decile reaches its highest value among the low-equality distributions, in the range close to $a = .50$.

Table 3.1
Deciles, Quartiles, and Medians, at Selected Levels of Inequality (each figure is a fraction or a multiple of average size)

1	2	3	4	5	6	7
a[1]	1 Decile[2]	1 Quartile[3]	Median[4]	3 Quartile[5]	9 Decile[6]	Gini Index[8]
.30	.015	.063	.202	.493	1.240	.82
.40	.032	.115	.331	.884	2.100	.75
.50	.054	.174	.476	1.178	2.495	.68
.60	.078	.231	.606	1.344	2.454	.60
.69315[7]	.105	.288	.693	1.386	2.303	.51
.75	.150	.372	.781	1.379	2.172	.46
.80	.213	.467	.843	1.349	2.025	.40
.85	.320	.587	.893	1.297	1.840	.34
.90	.499	.712	.934	1.225	1.610	.27

Source: Calculations based on the formulas shown in Appendix II.
[1] Reciprocal of the relative size at which the function at hand intersects the untransformed exponential function.
[2] Relative size under which is the lowest one-tenth of the population.
[3] Relative size under which is the lower one-fourth of the population.
[4] Relative size under and over which are the lower and upper halves of the population.
[5] Relative size over which is the upper one-fourth of the population.
[6] Relative size over which is the upper one-tenth of the population.
[7] Not an intersection value: This is the untransformed exponential function.
[8] Gini index = $(1-a)$ exp. .5642; .5642 is $=1/\sqrt{\pi}$.

Ratios between the quartiles and between the first and the ninth decile are shown in Table 3.1a. The table also shows the logarithmic ratio between these two sets of ratios. This logarithmic ratio becomes an important indicator for determining whether the distribution under study is a case of regular exponential function (transformed or not) or has some significant deviation from such a normative case. In the cases shown in the table, the logarithmic ratio is 1.96 in the untransformed exponential function and some of the variants close to the same, but at higher and lower levels of inequality this ratio gradually rises to the vicinity of 2.2. In other words, the logarithmic ratio is close to 2—meaning that the decile ratio is close to being the square of the quartile ratio. When this relation does not hold, we should look for the character of and reasons for a serious deviation from the regular exponential case.

As an example of an almost continuous function, we chose the data on U.S. household incomes in 1977—a benchmark year for projections (U.S. Department of Commerce 1980). For all households in 1977, we obtain a Me/Ave of .843, which is the same Me/Ave as for a = .80 in Table

Table 3.1a
Inter-Quartile Ratios, Inter-Decile Ratios, and Logarithmic Ratios (for the same a values as in Table 3.1)

a	Quartile Ratio[1]	Decile Ratio[2]	Logarithmic Ratio[3]
.30	7.83	82.67	2.14
.40	7.69	65.63	2.05
.50	6.77	46.20	2.01
.60	5.82	31.46	1.96
.693	4.82	21.85	1.96
.75	3.71	14.48	2.04
.80	2.89	9.51	2.12
.85	2.21	5.75	2.21
.90	1.72	3.21	2.21

[1] Third quartile divided by first quartile.
[2] Ninth decile divided by first decile.
[3] Logarithm of the decile ratio divided by the logarithm of the quartile ratio.

3.1. A comparison of the tabulated figures for $a = .80$ and the statistics for household incomes in 1977 shows close agreement.

The slope of the 1977 data differs, but only moderately, from that of the exponential function at $a = .80$. On a diagram or in regression analysis, the difference would be negligible.

Pursuing the analysis in Table 3.1a, we also get close agreement.

For comparison, Table 3.1 also shows Gini indexes for the levels of inequality shown in the table. They turn out to be a direct function of the a parameter in each function (see Table 3.1, footnote 8). Obviously, it varies inversely (the higher the a, the lower the degree of inequality, which is the obverse of the variation of the Gini index).

SIZE GROUP FREQUENCIES

The meaning of the inequality differences exemplified in Table 3.1 can to some extent be visualized by means of diagrams showing the frequency (of factors such as income recipients) within each of several size groups of standard scope (in this case, for instance, by size groups representing one-tenth of average size). Some examples are shown in Figure 3.2.

The highest curve shown in the figure, with $a = .87$ and Me/Ave = .911, is sharply dome-shaped, with quite low frequencies in the lowest size groups. It has a clearly articulated mode (point of highest frequency), which is close to the median size. The high size groups are again

Figure 3.2
Examples of Exponential Functions, Interval Frequencies (Density Function), Percent of Total per Interval of One-Tenth Average Size

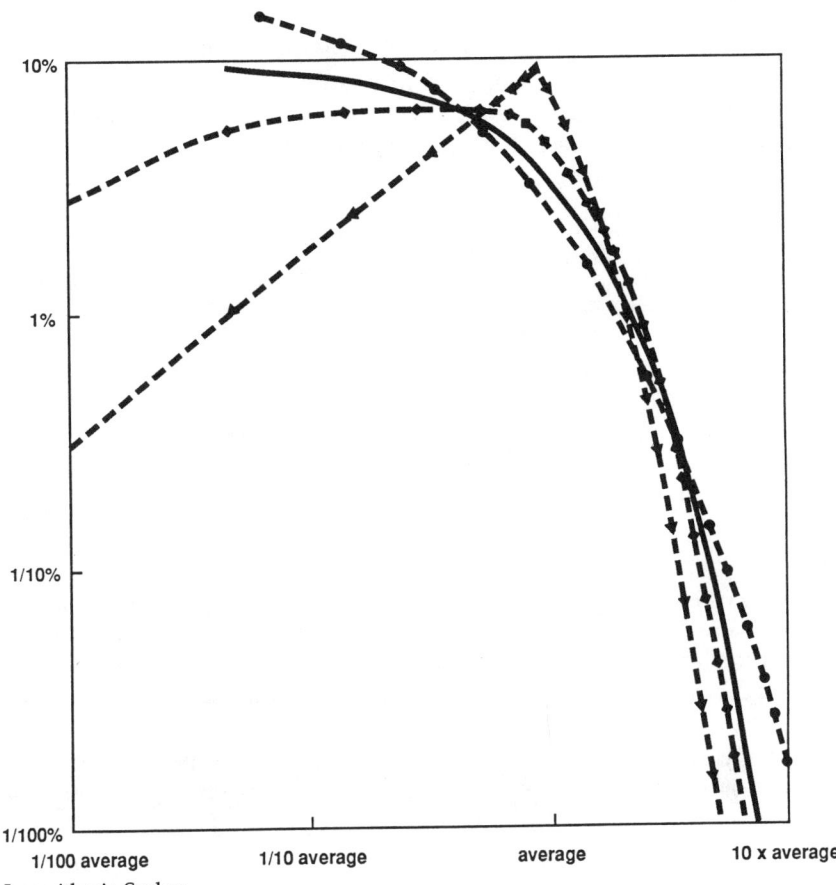

Logarithmic Scales:
Triangles: $a = .87$, Me/Ave $= .911$; Diamonds: $a = .77$, Me/Ave $= .801$; Full-drawn line: Untransformed exponential function, a and Me/Ave $= .693$; Circles: $a = .50$, Me/Ave $= .476$.

less frequent than in the other examples. The second example, with $a = .77$ and Me/Ave $= .801$, does not have a very clearly articulated mode. Instead, it has a plateau of several successive size groups with nearly the same frequency. The poor and the rich are somewhat more numerous than in the highest curve. The full-drawn curve, representing the untransformed exponential function, has no mode—the lowest size groups, however formulated, are always those with the largest frequency. Again, the poor and the rich are more numerous than in the previous two cases.

Finally, the figure also includes a low curve with $a = .50$ and Me/Ave $= .476$. This again has no mode, and it shows both the poor and the rich as more numerous than in all the preceding cases, leaving the middle income groups more weakly represented. All four curves come close to each other (because they intersect) in the size groups around .4 to .5 average size, and again in the range between two and a half and three and a half times average size. Evidently, any observations that focus on these volatile size groups can be deceptive for economic analysis. The consequences for welfare, both individual and social, will be discussed in the following chapters.

DISTRIBUTION OF TOTAL INCOME

How the good—total income, in this case—is distributed is in some ways more revealing than the distribution of income earners. Table 3.2 shows numbers to exemplify this aspect, chosen to represent the same levels of inequality as in Table 3.1.

As inequality declines, the differences become relatively larger in the lower income groups and relatively smaller in the upper ones. For instance,

Table 3.2
Percent of Total Income Going to the Lower One-Tenth, Lower One-Fourth, Lower Half, Upper Half, Upper One-Fourth, and Upper One-Tenth of the Population, at Selected Levels of Inequality

1	2	3	4	5	6	7
a^1	Lower One-Tenth	Lower One-Fourth	Lower Half	Upper Half	Upper One-Fourth	Upper One-Tenth
.30	.06	.62	2.9	97.1	88.3	77.5
.40	.10	1.00	6.2	93.8	76.8	62.4
.50	.29	1.37	9.5	90.5	65.0	47.0
.60	.37	2.50	12.4	87.6	62.2	40.0
.69315[2]	.52	3.42	15.3	84.7	59.2	33.0
.75	1.00	4.60	19.1	80.9	55.5	28.9
.80	1.45	6.70	22.7	77.3	50.1	26.7
.85	1.90	9.00	27.3	72.7	46.7	23.1
.90	3.70	11.50	34.6	65.4	40.5	19.7

Source: Calculations based on the formulas shown in Appendix II.
[1] Reciprocal of the relative size at which the function at hand intersects the untransformed exponential function.
[2] Not an intersection value: This is the untransformed exponential function.

when a rises from .75 to .85 (an the Me/Ave from .781 to .893), the lower one-tenth and the lower one-fourth nearly double their modest income shares. The lower half gains nearly 40 percent in its income share, while the upper half loses only about one-tenth of its much larger income share. Pigou's criterion for increased welfare is well illustrated here. The upper one-tenth of the income receivers loses only 5.8 percentage points of the total, which is just over one-fifth of the share still coming to this group at $a = .85$. The upper one-fourth of the income recipients loses 8.8 percentage points of the total, or just under one-sixth of the share it had at $a = .75$. Since the upper one-tenth is included in the upper one-fourth, subtractions allow us to show that the stratum from .75 to .90 (the 76th through the 90th percentiles) have fallen from 26.6 to 23.6 percent of total income, or 3 percentage points, which is 11 percent of their income share at $a = .75$. This is a smaller proportionate change in the income share than that experienced by the upper one-tenth. The percentiles between .50 and .75 (the 51th through 75th percentiles) gain but slightly, and the same is the case for those in the second fourth (counting from below).

Thus, we find that in the range of inequalities just analyzed, the shifts within the middle half are quite modest. Most of the changes are now located in the lowest and highest parts of the distribution. In other inequality ranges, this will be different. Moving from one inequality level to another will have a different incidence among the income size groups, and in different ways, depending on the scale of inequalities that we are analyzing.

On this level, too, we may use the 1977 data on U.S. household incomes. For the distribution of the income between size strata of income recipients, we obtain remarkably close agreement. The distribution of income among U.S. households in 1977 conforms closely to the transformed exponential functions at $a = .80$, Me/Ave $= .843$, corresponding to Gini index $= .40$.

DISCONTINUOUS DISTRIBUTIONS

The exponential functions we have discussed so far are continuous. With a given level of inequality, they reflect a single set of proportions between the various size groups of the distribution, as shown above. We may assume that a single set of variables (or a stable combination of variables, functioning as if it were a single set) decides the slope, and hence the variation, within the distribution. The untransformed exponential function may be assumed to reflect an unhampered, random walk of events, while the high and low curves each reflect a single set of circumstances causing the distribution to be different from that of an umhampered, random walk of events, and leading to a different but continuous slope of the function.

The U.S data on household incomes in 1977 would appear to represent this kind of theory for an income distribution, as closely as one can expect in the real world. In reality, many distributions are not continuous, as would follow from a single set of circumstances affecting the slope of the distribution. In the literature, problems of this kind are met with attempts at formulating compromise measures that will encompass the various modifying forces that affect the distribution at hand (for example, Ebert 1988 a & b).

Looking at discontinuous functions, we prefer to assume that the population itself is heterogenous. This is quite evident, for instance, in the case of farms classified by size, because here we often have different geographical environments in which the economic rationale for farms of differing sizes differs. Examples are not hard to come by, as for instance Nebraska (Corn Belt crop farms versus ranches in the western parts of the state), or New Zealand, where lowland and highland farms have such different qualities of land that a joint size distribution is perforce discontinuous.

Analogies to this among income distributions are often not as clear-cut, but they are often easy to demonstrate just the same. We can often show when the income of some population is distributed in a discontinuous way, that this reflects the heterogenous composition of the population itself. For instance, in the United States this is particularly evident in the category labeled "unrelated individuals," which includes both young people earning their first wages, middle-aged poor people, and widowed retirees on reduced incomes. These three categories do not receive their income from the same type of source, and hence would not be expected to have their incomes distributed in the same way, or reflected in a single, continuous function. If occasionally they do appear to be distributed in a continuous way—in some state, at some time, for instance—then this would be taken as a chance occurrence, and not something that we should expect from the situation.

Such distributions can still be analyzed to good advantage by aid of exponential functions. We may compute several fractiles, according to what seems to be the problem in each distribution. From a comparable table (such as that in Table 3.1) we can then find what degree of inequality, and hence what slope of the distribution, comes closest to the indicator found for each of the fractiles we have calculated. The following two chapters will make use of this device, where appropriate, both in order to characterize the general degree of inequality that dominates in a given distribution, and to show how the apparent degree of inequality varies along the distribution according to the different slope factor for its several parts.

Such an analysis will form a counterpart to the attempts made throughout the literature at decomposing Lorenz's curve in order to study sources and subgroups—meaning qualitative groups, not size groups—among the population (Satchell 1987).

MEASURING WHAT?

When we measure inequality of income, we must first define our concept of income. In nearly all statistics this is money income as reported in censuses, surveys, and tax data. This inevitably brings in some lack of precision. Conventional accounts of income, such as those of national product, of necessity use some simplifying assumptions. Similar assumptions are implied in any data on income specified in money terms. The value of money is far from being strictly comparable throughout the world, or even within a large country or between social classes.

Money income usually does not include estimates of the value of income in-kind, which is present at many levels. In advanced countries, the *second economy* of bartered goods and services operates as a tax haven, evading explicit money specification or documentation.

An even larger topic is the question of housework and other work that people perform for themselves and their immediate families. For such work, most of the time, specification of money's worth is not available. In an extreme expansion of this concept, a proponent of feminist economics has suggested the inclusion even of birthing and the care of children as work of economic value. This would raise the total of all income quite considerably. It would also change the relative positions of women and men in creating economic value (Waring 1988).

Valuation problems are severe when most of the efforts in question have no markets in which they might be sold. The economic value of children varies, of course, as the demographic controls in China emphasize. Different family systems, leading to endogenous versus exogenous fertility, render the problem quite different in both locale and time period (Nerlove, Razin, and Sadka, 1987).

Quite apart from valuation problems, inclusion of service rendered to oneself and one's own household—no matter how the system boundary is drawn on account of the family concept—risks diluting the problem of distribution. The more these services are included, the less the apparent difference between the rich and the poor. When all their self-produced wealth is included, the poor are not quite as poor as we might think. Inequalities are thus reduced in appearance.

In appearance only. This argument leads us back to the central role of money as an arbitrator of what is scarce. Our ability to do our own housework is not scarce in the market sense. Even though some things of economic consequence are not covered in money transactions, yet the goods and services that can only be obtained by spending money are in many ways critical to well-being. It does not help some people to be good housekeepers if lack of money excludes them from affordable housing—it takes a dwelling to do housework—or even from sufficient food. Household economy conveys little market power and even less political power. Social status and esteem are closely related to the command over others that money buys (Rainwater 1974). Thus far, the conventional money income concept is in fact better suited to bring out the real significance of economic distributions than any of the proposed modifications, including nonmoney income.

It is evident, however, that money income tends to conceal some price bias according to social class. The rich often spend carelessly and for reasons of prestige rather than for the real quality of goods and services, and thus may derive less real or conventional satisfaction from their consumption. They also may draw less on real resources than might appear from their money expenditures. At the other end of the scale, many poor people "buy expensively" for a different set of reasons: because of a short economic horizon, inability to await the best bargains, or exploitation by flea-market merchants and usurious moneylenders. The middle classes, on the whole, get the best value for their money by prudent spending, a good sense of timing, and distance from exploitive forces.

When the real distribution of consumption is investigated, this usually reveals somewhat less inequality in kind than in money (Roemer 1979). This observation cannot, on the whole, be applied to most of the statistics on incomes and their distribution, but we must keep it in mind when commenting on the consequences of income inequality. The conventional data on distribution must be treated as proxies for those on real inequality; however, this kind of observation has less bearing on the role of income inequalities in distributing political power.

MEASURING WHOM?

Statistics on income distribution always relate to some concept of who receives income. For instance, in the U.S. statistics, we get data on income of households, families, unrelated individuals, persons, and taxpayers. The indicators of inequality are often quite different for these different groups. How the groups are defined is evidently of some consequence for the appearance of inequality. For instance, unrelated individuals have a degree of inequality very different from that of families. However, when the families and the unrelated individuals are summed together, both their number and their degree of inequality come close to that of taxpayers, yet without coinciding entirely with that fiscal concept, in which the definition of income is also somewhat different from that of the census statistics.

It should be evident that the choice of definition for the population will depend, among other things, on the purpose of the analysis. Income of persons, irrespective of how they are grouped in families or households, will be significant if we want to study the degree of justice in the distribution of reward for effort. It is principally here, for instance, that we are told something about the differences between the wages of women and men. Data on households, families, and unrelated individuals, by contrast, will tell us more about the welfare effects of the distribution of individual incomes, both earned and unearned. Taxpayer statistics, finally, enable us to follow the modifications in both reward and welfare that derive from the fiscal system of the country, state, or community.

A pervasive shortcoming in all such income statistics is that they almost always measure income and its distribution at some juncture, such as a census or tax year. They do not tell us how lifetime incomes are distributed. Common sense tells us that lifetime incomes should be somewhat less unequal than appears from the "snapshot" data of individual years. A few spot inquiries have confirmed this (Duncan et al. 1984). The conclusions are far from unequivocal, as will be discussed in Chapter 4. Comparisons with human wealth still show more variation in lifetime earnings than in human wealth. Estimating the present value remains problematic when lifetime earnings are differently distributed over time (Lillard 1977). To be valid, calculations of lifetime earnings should incorporate data on differences in mortality as well as discount rate differences (Moss 1978). Statistical research to improve this kind of inquiry is still going on (David 1985).

To calculate lifetime incomes from snapshot data would be rather problematic even with the application of sophisticated tools of mathematical transition theory. The reason is analogous to the situation in demography where the concept of *cohort fertility* turns out to be academic despite its improved precision over crude vital rates, simply because cohort fertility histories are only available ex post, as each cohort of women completes its reproductive life. They cannot be made up ex ante, for we do not know how much the women entering the fertile phase of their lives are going to reproduce. Similarly, any ever so accurate compilations of what an individual's or family's lifetime income may have been in the past really do not tell us what can be expected in the future, for here we would have to work with some array of assumptions or hypotheses concerning ongoing and upcoming changes in distributive inequality, as well as considering other relevant economic changes in the future.

There is no way out of this general difficulty. We simply will have to use the snapshot data as proxies for lifetime statistics, keeping in mind that the real differences are different and usually smaller than the apparent ones (see Creedy 1985, chapter 9 and page 72 on age profiles).

TRENDS VERSUS LEVELS

The many ways in which a given level of inequality can be interpreted also point to the need for attention to observable trends of inequality. This refers both to inequality as a whole and to specifics such as wage differences by sex or ethnic group. How we are moving may in fact be more important than where we are. Establishing trends with confidence is in no way simpler than establishing levels of inequality at any one time, for demographic and other social changes may cause variations in some of the basic concepts such as the family or household. The dynamics of income distribution will be more revealing about the role of distribution within the wider fabric of economy and society. Few as they are, any indications on the distribution of consumption should also be used in comprehensive analysis (see Roemer 1979; Fichtenbaum 1985).

4

The United States

Is the United States a country of high or low inequality? The answer, in part, depends on one's viewpoint. As we shall see, the question of trends is more compelling than the level of inequality: The reversal of a long-term trend, away from declining and into rising inequality, is more meaningful than static measurement at any given time or under any particular definition.

The static measurement depends in part on how the population is defined. No one expects little children to have an adult income, and no one expects all adults to have the same level of income. It is a truism that incomes usually rise from youth through middle life and then fall off at retirement, when family responsibilities (other than for health care) are also on the decline. Some inequality between families should thus be expected as a consequence of the logic of the life cycle.

The balance of the "correct" degree of inequality will depend on what we expect society to accomplish, both for its members and for the nation as a whole. One of the myths about the United States is that inherited wealth is of secondary importance to earned wealth. "Shirtsleeves to shirtsleeves in three generations" has been cited as a family cycle working against permanent economic class formation, but actually, some class barriers are more rigid than the adage would let us expect (Rothman 1978). They may be more important to power than to welfare.

The historical record will show that the United States at the start of independent history was not particularly egalitarian. Plantations in the South and wealthy merchant houses in the Northeast stood so high above the income levels of ordinary people, and controlled such a substantial portion of all the money income as conventionally understood, that the income distribution must have been rather unequal. From the Civil War to the end of the nineteenth century, inequality appears to have increased even further. From that time to the end of World War II and several years beyond, however, inequality in this country was much reduced, in ways we will try to sketch in this chapter. Today the pressing problem is that the trend has turned again: Income distribution in the United States has become visibly more unequal at least since the 1970s.

Chapter 5 will present some international comparisons. The United States will be compared to several other countries on both high and low levels of per capita income. We should be skeptical about any too close comparisons unless we can rest assured that the populations are defined in the same way, which is often not certain. Again, comparing trends is more important than comparing levels of inequality. In this chapter we will concentrate on differences over time. Despite all the statistical difficulties it is possible to show that certain trends remain the same no matter how the populations and other statistical base data are defined.

INEQUALITY AMONG WHOM?

How much inequality we find often depends on the statistical framework. This will be evident when we compare inequality measures for several concepts of population that exist side by side at the same time, and even from the same statistical source. As before, we use as a measure of inequality the ratio of median to arithmetic mean (Me/Ave), which is a close proxy for the Gini index as shown in Chapter 3—with the scale inverted, the higher Me/Ave denotes the lower degrees of inequality.

For the year 1979 we can cite five different such ratios, four of them from the 1980 Census of Population and one from Internal Revenue Service data on income tax returns. Depending on what we examine, we get:

Households	.829
Families	.862
Unrelated individuals	.721
Persons	.720
Tax returns	.762

By any measurement, these differences in apparent inequality are huge. Moving upward, the Me/Ave could never exceed 1.00; practically speaking, it is seldom much over .900. In the downward direction, anything below .700 would be called large inequality.

Let us first see how these population concepts relate to each other quantitatively. Households in the 1980 Census numbered 80.6 million, families numbered 59.2 million, unrelated individuals numbered 30.0 million, and "persons 15 years and over" with income were counted at 147.2 million. Individual tax returns for 1979 were 92.7 million, of which 92.2 million had an adjusted gross income. If one adds together the families and the unrelated individuals in the census, then the number comes close to that of the tax returns, and the inequality indicators are also relatively close, even though such grouping involves some problems due to different size classes being used in the published census data for families and for unrelated individuals.

On aggregate income, both census and tax data are tolerably close to the income sums of the national accounts. The sums of income of households, of families plus unrelated individuals, and of persons are about the same; they could not be exactly the same since they are estimated from samples. This common amount is close to the "disposable personal income" in the 1979 national accounts, which is about three-quarters of the "national income of persons" in the same accounts, and about 85 percent of total (before-tax) personal income. The total of "adjusted gross income" of individual tax returns comes to less than 90 percent of the census income totals. "Statutory adjustments" in the tax statistics account for only a minor part of the difference. Even so, the returns include some income that is not counted in national accounts, such as capital gains.

When the inequality indicators differ so much as a function of how a population is defined, it becomes interesting to examine the way in which some of the populations are composed. In particular, the figures for persons are telling, for here we systematically get separate data for women and men, as well as for black and white persons. Looking first at the sexes, we find that the average of .720 for all persons 15 years and over with some income differentiates as .806 for males and .760 for females. Thus, there was less inequality within each sex than there was in the whole population. This reflects the much higher income level among men than among women. Women's average income was 62 percent of the general average, and men's average was 135 percent of the general average; the women's average income was merely 46 percent of the average for men. Obviously, the labor market is far from integrated. The circumstances making for unequal incomes were not the same for men and for women. Any meaningful analysis must keep in mind such market imperfections. They will variously influence our reading of statistics about income inequality. The example also shows that data for a large, heterogenous population may mask differences between parts of that population. In this case, the differences between the incomes of men and women are a larger source of inequality than anything occurring among the members of the same sex.

Data on persons according to color at first reveal somewhat less difference than those by sex. The Me/Ave for all persons, .720, differentiates here as .722 for white persons and .755 for black persons. Since the whites are a large majority, they should be close to the general average. When black persons have less income inequality than white persons, this is worth noting.

Even more remarkable are the data by both color and sex. The average for all male persons, .806, differentiates as .812 for white males and .805 for black males. Among female persons, the Me/Ave of .760 divides up as .762 for white females and .745 for black females. The lower average ratio for black women points also to differences in the shape of the distribution. In dollar averages, the incomes of white women were 44 percent of those for white men, but black women earned 64.5 percent of the income of black men. Black persons received 66 percent of the income of white persons, with black males receiving 61.5 percent as much as white males while black females had 89 percent of the income of white females. The income distribution for black women had about the same slope as that for white women in the lower and middle income ranges, but differed markedly in the upper ranges. In the very highest bracket shown in the statistics ($50,000 and over) there were proportionately (but not absolutely) more black than white women—apparently, these were well-paid singers and actresses.

The generally lesser income difference between white and black women compared to the inequality among men is, of course, related to the much lower absolute level of income among women, who include many individuals on minimal incomes. White women had much lower incomes than black men in three consecutive censuses (1960, 1970, and 1980).

Census data for households and families come close to agreeing with some version of the exponential function—the fractiles are close to what should be expected to agree with each Me/Ave according to Table 3.1. The same is true, to a lesser extent, about the data on income of persons. The data on unrelated individuals show much more variable slopes, with both low and high fractiles differing remarkably from what should be expected according to the normative indications in Table 3.1. This is not surprising, since the unrelated individuals category includes many different social and economic situations.

The tax return data also differ from the exponential functions at both ends of the distribution. At the low end, large numbers of tax-exempt people mean that this part of the distribution is truncated, in comparison with what would have been obtained if all the low-income people had to file tax returns. At the high end, we also might expect deviations due to the various tax avoidance strategies (both legal and illegal) used by many high-income people.

Specifications show that several income categories other than wages are concentrated in the upper income strata, while wages dominate heavily in the lower and middle income groups. Wages generally leave less opportunity for tax avoidance.

LONG-TERM TRENDS

Before the coming of national income estimates in the late 1920s, information about incomes and their distribution is scanty and somewhat uncertain as to how it should be understood. A few "signpost data" may be quoted.

Calculations for the year 1798 show the newly formed U.S. republic as a society with large economic differences between the rich and the common people. The data are primarily for property rather than income, and here we always expect larger differences (and more inequality) than for incomes. One set of data on housing values has, however, been interpreted as also reflecting incomes (Soltow 1985, 1987). The size classes shown in the data are few, and interpolation is therefore uncertain. The indications point to a Me/Ave in the vicinity of .45, denoting substantial inequality. Data on wealth from 1860 hint at the possibility that inequality had become somewhat greater than in 1798, but this conclusion does not appear certain (Soltow 1984).

Apart from the uncertainties in statistical estimates that are based on samples, there is also the question of whether wealth was assessed on comparable levels in all parts of the country. In the new settlements of the Midwest, land values were still low in the presence of large amounts of raw unoccupied land. Rent, therefore, accrued to the landowning farmers, making their real incomes higher than one would expect from the amount of wealth these people possessed. In the older farming areas, especially those near the cities and containing orchards, dairy farms, and hay crops for city draft power, land values had already risen more than at the frontier. In any event, the broad strata of U.S. society, outside the circles of the very rich, was more egalitarian than the overall estimates would indicate (Williamson and Lindert 1980).

A set of comprehensive data for 1891 refers directly to income and its distribution (Spahr [1896], 1970). The data include only three size classes, one of which contains 88 percent of the families. Interpolation is, therefore, very uncertain. The slope of the distribution may have been somewhat uneven, so that relative inequality may actually have been lower among the lower income size classes than among the higher ones. As far as the evidence goes, inequality may have been somewhat larger than in 1860.

The next major set of data refers to 1910 (King 1915). Here we are offered a large number of size groups as well as separate data for single men, single women, and families. The series as a whole shows a Me/Ave of .74 and, thus, much less inequality than in any of the sources from the 1800s. The slope appears to be highly irregular. The first decile and the first quartile seem to belong in a distribution with less inequality than the Me/Ave, while the third quartile and the ninth decile seem to represent more inequality.

Such discontinuity should not surprise us in an economy where only 60 percent of the income went to labor (including self-employed labor) while 40 percent was capital income. The rate of interest was 6 percent or higher, with a rather stable long-term value of money. The matter can be further elucidated by separately analyzing the data on single persons. These are all concentrated in the lower income-size classes. Their average income was less than 60 percent of the general average of the whole population (including families). The average income for single persons was less than half that for the subset labeled families. These single-income recipients were about 35 percent of all income recipients, or 9.67 million. Of these, 7.86 million were single men and 1.81 million were single women. The income of single individuals was evidently composed mainly of wages, and the distribution among them was also much less unequal than among the total population. For single men and women together, the Me/Ave was almost .90, which agrees with detailed wage data from the 1800s (Williamson and Lindert 1980). When the data for single men and single women are analyzed separately, both series show even less inequality, with Me/Ave exceeding .90 in both groups. Women's wages were lower than those of men, but the difference was smaller than in recent times. Single women earned almost three-quarters as much as single men. This also reflects the lower labor force participation among women compared to later times. The degree of inequality was also somewhat lower among the women. This may reflect a narrower set of wage-earning opportunities for women than for men. In both series, the other fractiles show inequality indicators close to that of the Me/Ave.

The data on families only, numbering some 18.3 million, still show a profile similar to that of the total series (including also single persons), but the Me/Ave is lower, at .65, as should be expected when a large part of the wage-earning population is now excluded. The low and the high fractiles again point to a variable slope, indicating a heterogenous population. The slope shows that high incomes were proportionately more numerous than the median would indicate, while the low incomes were less than indicated. The truncating effect may also contribute to this because extremely low incomes would not be livable.

A coherent statistical series begins with 1929 (U.S. Department of Commerce, 1975, ch. G; cf. Leven et al., 1934). Data are shown for families and unattached individuals, and for families only. Incomes are given in current dollars for each year from 1935–1936 to 1964, and in 1950 dollars for each year from 1929 to 1957. In 1929, unattached individuals were less than one-quarter of the total for families and unattached individuals, thus resulting in a lower proportion than in 1910. The series in 1950 dollars has more detail and allows more analysis. Data on male and female persons begin in 1944.

For families and unattached individuals, the Me/Ave in 1929 comes to .693, with the lower fractiles somewhat higher and the higher ones somewhat lower than would be expected from the exponential function; thus, it is a similar situation as in 1910, but less extreme.

By 1950, a dramatic shift had taken place. The Me/Ave for families and unrelated individuals had risen to .833. Unrelated individuals were reported as only 18 percent of the total of families and unrelated individuals. The lower fractiles come out somewhat higher than would be expected from the exponential function, pointing to somewhat fewer poor people. The high fractiles are again much higher, indicating the continued existence of numerous very-high-income people, more than would be predicted by the part of the distribution that was dominated by wages. This was, however, also less extreme than before. Data for 1964 show only small changes over 1950—the Me/Ave now comes to .839.

The changes are, to some extent, illustrated by tabulations showing how much income went to each fifth of the population, and to the upper 5 percent (U.S. Department of Commerce 1975). The upper 5 percent of the income recipients had 31 percent of the income in 1929. This figure fell to 26.5 percent in 1935–1936, and then to about 21 percent around 1950 and about 20 percent of the now much larger income sum, with small variations, from the early 1950s to 1964.

The highest fifth of the population (which includes the top 5 percent) received 54.4 percent of all the income in 1929. This figure fell to 44.5 percent in the early 1950s, and then rose to 45.5 percent in the early 1960s. Subtraction will show that the next highest 15 percent of the population (from 80 to 95 percent) held their income share steady at about 25 percent of the total income through the whole period 1929–1964. The fourth fifth (from 60 to 80 percent) gained very slightly. The largest gain was in the middle fifth (from 40 to 60 percent), which rose from 14 to 16.5 percent of the much larger income sum. The second fifth (from 20 to 40 percent) improved its income share by one-tenth, from 10 to 11 percent of the larger income total, while the bottom fifth moved slowly back and forth in the range of 4 to 5 percent of aggregate income.

Thus, the net change in income distribution of the Depression years, the years of World War II, and the early postwar period was a strengthening of the middle income strata. The poor gained somewhat, but mainly on account of the rising general level of income; their relative position changed but little, and may in fact have deteriorated somewhat because of the changed composition of the stream of production and consumption (see Jencks et al. 1972, ch. 1.).

A separate set of tables focuses on the top 1 percent of the income recipients (U.S. Department of Commerce 1975). This class of rich people received about 15 percent of the income in 1913. Their share fell below 13 percent in the latter part of the World War I years and the early 1920s, and then rose to 14.67 percent in 1929. It fell to less than 9 percent in the late 1940s.

The trends from 1947 to 1960 were summarized in a report for the 1960 Census (Miller 1966). Both the Gini ratios and the shares of income going to the top 20 and top 5 percent of the population were standardized for the 1960 population weights, whereupon they showed less variation than in the actual data for each year—in the unweighted data, there was a slight tendency for the Gini ratio to go down, which would indicate reduced inequality; but this was mainly among rural families who were more unequal to begin with. Thus, the years from the end of World War II to the early 1960s were a period of remarkable stability in income distribution in the United States. Other analyses also show little change from the 1940s to the 1960s (Budd 1970).

Welfare programs and transfers in kind are thought by some to have reduced inequality even further between 1962 and 1972 (Browning 1976). However, other analysts have interpreted the net effect of such programs as "losing ground" for the poor in this country (Murray 1984).

The reversal of the trend—in other words, a shift toward more inequality—seems to have begun in the 1970s. It was foreshadowed by the rise in the proportion of unrelated individuals to families, which rose slowly in the 1930s and then more rapidly, and is now again one-third of the number of families and unrelated individuals, just as in 1910. At present there is much more inequality of income in the United States than in the 1950s and 1960s. Details will be discussed further on.

MEANING OF LONG-TERM TRENDS

The long-term trends from the late 1700s up to the 1960s are in essential agreement with the economic theory of rent, as explained in Chapter 2. For the 1800s, we need to focus on three main factors: the abundance of raw land for settler agriculture, the scarcity of capital for urban industry and trade, and the plantation–slavery economy of the South. In the late 1800s there was also an abundance of recent immigrants available to work for low wages. Moreover, in the 1920s through the 1960s, there was an abundance of fossil energy sources as well.

For most of the 1800s, the seeming paradox of great inequality amid an abundance of land for farming is explained by the dichotomy of city versus country existence. In a country where incomes of the common people were foremost those of independent family farmers working on land with very low market value, and where wages in the towns were generally higher than those in Europe, there were good markets for both imported merchandise and domestic manufactures. There was, therefore, a general scarcity of capital other than farmland. This explains the very high capital returns in urban industry and commerce. The same also led to wider disparities between the wages for skilled and unskilled labor (Williamson and Lindert 1980, chs. 6, 10). The high capital returns must have included large amounts of rent, and the wages of skilled labor much less so.

In the plantation South, labor was artificially abundant, first through slavery and later through special arrangements under Reconstruction. Hence, economic rent to landowners was high in that region. The plantation system was destroyed during the Civil War but largely reconstructed in the 1870s, with de facto bondage for many black people. These arrangements lasted, with variations, until the mechanization of cotton production and the subsequent breakup of the segregation system in the 1960s.

However, the appearance of a highly unequal society in the 1800s is somewhat deceptive. In most of the country, most people lived with only a moderate dispersion of income (Williamson and Lindert 1980).

Scarcity of capital in manufacturing and commerce continued as a concomitant of rapid economic expansion. After 1870, with the natural population increase beginning to slow, increased immigration resupplied the urban labor force and helped keep wages to levels at which profits in industry could remain high. From around the turn of the century, the incipient maturity of the industrial system and a slowdown of population growth led to decreases in income inequality even as inequality in wealth continued to be very great. The trend toward less inequality of income that is visible in the 1910 statistics accelerated during World War I when there was nearly full employment. Even with some reversal of the trend in the 1920s, the 1929 data still show less inequality than in 1910.

This sequence of events is reflected in the changes in interest rates (Dovring 1984a). Through the late 1800s, these had remained generally around 6 percent. There was a sharp reduction under the war economy of World War I, and then a partial resumption (but only to a 4-5 percent level, in real terms) in the 1920s. From the Depression onward, and into the 1950s, real interest rates (adjusted for inflation) were actually negative, signaling an abundance of capital—a prerequisite for higher real wages.

The long-term process is essentially in agreement with Simon Kuznets' observation of the inverted U-shape of the long-term changes in inequality —increasing inequality in the early stages of development followed by a decrease in later stages, as will be discussed in Chapter 6. As of the 1960s, the United States had arrived at a much lesser degree of inequality than in any previous period except the very first stage of colonization. This relatively favorable state of affairs had remained more or less constant, with but slight variations, for about three or four decades. This stability at the interim of falling and rising inequality, might call for a theoretical explanation of its own. In any event, the renewed rise in inequality from the 1970s onward has not been explained by any theory to date.

Amid all this was the 1960s "war on poverty." Some analysts think the effort had a measure of success—not all the changes of real income are reflected in conventional statistics (Plotnick and Skidmore 1975; Browning 1976). Some of this progress, such as it was, again became watered down during the 1980s, compounding the changes that had occurred independently of policy, as we shall discuss later in this chapter and more completely in Chapter 8.

Let us now look at some of the obvious sources of inequality, such as sex discrimination, farm versus nonfarm income disparity, black-white income disparity, state and city differentials, and lifetime incomes.

SEX DISCRIMINATION

When women have much lower incomes than men, overall and in most occupations, this is an important factor in both the general level of inequality and its changes. In part, at least, it presents a paradox.

Women's earnings were always lower than those of men, although not to the same degree in earlier periods as in recent times. The 1910 data show less sex disparity of incomes than later statistics. Even in the 1800s there are indications that this kind of income inequality may have been relatively modest—teachers' salaries were somewhat lower than those of common laborers, but not by much (Williamson and Lindert 1980). The teachers were, of course, mainly women. After 1919, the wage differences between women and men widened considerably at the same time that women began increasingly to participate in the wage-earning labor force. This may have meant less scarcity of female labor, and hence less ability to retain any rent. The wide disparity has persisted, with only a modest reduction recently.

A detailed analysis by a demographer working for the federal government showed that up to 1980, women's wages were much lower across the board than men's wages, foremost because women were employed mainly in low-wage occupations (Rytina 1982). Even in the higher wage occupations, women earned less than men. This may, however, have been influenced by age distribution—women have tended to come into those occupations only relatively recently. Even several years later, women were far behind in levels of earnings, despite some improvements (O'Neill 1987).

Meanwhile, the trend toward less inequality in family income up to 1970 was furthered by women's increased participation in the labor force (Treas 1987). This change during the postwar years may have contributed to making it only seem that income inequality was less a problem than before.

FARM VERSUS NONFARM DISPARITY

Part of the early disparity of income in the United States was due to the difference in income level between farm people and the urban population. In part, this disparity may have been deceptive, because farmers enjoyed amenities and in-kind incomes not available in the cities. Nonetheless, we must admit that there was a large gap between average farm incomes and average urban incomes. The influence of this gap on general income inequality necessarily diminished with time as farmers decreased as a proportion of the population—down to half in the 1870s, one-fourth around 1930, and only a few percent recently.

In the 1950s, the gap between farm incomes and those of other people was still wide. It was widest in the East (both the Northeast and Southeast), where it was on the order of four-tenths to one. In much of the Midwest, the gap was about six-tenths to one. In the Pacific region, there was hardly any gap at all, despite a large inequality within the agricultural population of that region with its large farms and numerous wage workers.

These differences by region are likely to reflect settlement history. The eastern states were settled at a time when many farmers lived in a semisubsistence economy and therefore were not fully integrated into the urban economy. Comparison of farm incomes to city wages was, therefore, not fully relevant. The same was less true in the Midwest, where farms were generally larger to begin with, and where they were also more directly linked to the wider market economy early on. In the Pacific states, settlement began with mining and city building; the farm economy was built up subsequently, and was almost completely integrated into the general economy from the start—there was never an agricultural surplus population.

The influence of settlement history on the farm versus urban income gap has parallels elsewhere in the world. Most of the Old World had farm settlement antedating the modern expansion of the city sector. Such areas long retained agricultural surplus population and hence a gap between farm and urban incomes. The same is seen in parts of Latin America, which to a large extent inherited South European institutions. Chile, for instance, with early European settlement (as Latin America goes), had a wide farm–nonfarm income gap even in recent times. Argentina, with a more recent history of farm settlement (other than extensive cattle ranches), shows much less income disparity in recent times than Chile. Australia and New Zealand, latecomers to modern settlement, never had much of a semisubsistence farm system; their agriculture was linked to world markets from the start, and they have had a positive income disparity (in other words, farm incomes higher than urban incomes) in recent times.

The influence of farm incomes on general income inequality in the United States was strengthened by the inequality of farm size, which tended to be the widest in the same states where the general income disparity was among the widest, even after the farm sector had dwindled to a minority (Dovring 1973). Farm size has also been a prosperity factor. The farm sector has generally been the most prosperous (for all its people) in locations where farms were of moderate size (Goldschmidt 1978), which has generally been the case when inequality of both farm size and farm incomes was also moderate.

The connection between farm income inequality and levels of inequality by states, leads into the subject of race discrimination, because inequality at the state level is generally the largest in the same states where the nonwhite population has been (and still is) the largest—foremost, the plantation states of the Deep South.

BLACK-WHITE INEQUALITY AND STATE DIFFERENTIALS

The influence of race discrimination on general income distribution has been documented many times. Its influence on state income disparities has been shown to be strong. Despite some improvement in recent times, most of the inherited black–white income disparity persists, with negative consequences also for white workers; only employers are the winners (Reich 1981). Urban slum formation has contributed to making a more or less permanent underclass, consisting mainly of blacks (*Chicago Tribune* staff 1986).

In the 1960s, the racial composition of the population was the major reason for state differentials in income inequality, although somewhat less so in 1959 than in 1949 (Al-Samarrie and Miller 1967; see also Aigner and Heins 1967). The Gini index generally declined in the South, except in West Virginia and the District of Columbia. The South consistently had the widest income inequality of all the regions in the United States; the North had the least, with the West in an intermediary range. In the South, the widest inequality was found in Mississippi, which had one of the largest black populations.

A second analysis of the 1960 Census found age distribution more significant than the black–white composition of the population (Conlisk 1967). Possibly, the northward migration of black people had also changed the age composition in the South. Further studies using county data still found a strong influence on inequality from the black–white composition of the population in most southern states, the exceptions being Florida and Maryland (Farbman 1973). Analysis of state-level inequality over time (1949, 1959, and 1969) showed some influence of race but more so from the rate of economic development of each state (Jonish and Kau 1973).

At the state level, the percent of the population that was nonwhite was always found to be significant, along with age distribution; there was some improvement in inequality overtime, although it was slower in the 1960s than in the 1950s (Sale 1974).

A special study of the Louisiana parishes (of which here were sixty-four) showed movement toward less inequality both in the 1950s and the 1960s, but with notable exceptions associated with higher proportions of nonwhite population, higher proportions of elderly persons, and lower levels of educational attainment (Rice and Sale 1975).

County-level data showed that the black–white composition of the population related positively to wide income inequality not only in the South but also in eastern states (Foley 1977). Economic expansion, on the other hand, related positively with declining income inequality. The conclusion has been reiterated several times. Sometimes it is emphasized that state-level analysis tends to confirm Kuznets' hypothesis on the connection between advanced economic development and declining inequality of income (Ruthenberg and Stano 1977; Grasso and Sharkansky 1980). More recently it was found that the connection between income inequality and income level holds up only to a point, after which the trend reverses, as has been the case in recent years in the country as a whole (Nelson 1984).

CITIES AND INEQUALITY

Urban areas are, on the whole, more highly structured than rural areas, and this might be expected to carry over into a more unequal income distribution. There is some evidence of this, but it is not entirely unequivocal. One inquiry found that city size as such did not explain variance in income, but that more was explained by industrial diversification, percent of population that was nonwhite, and the general income level. These factors explained two-fifths of the income variance (Betz 1972). Other researchers found that high population density is positively related to large income inequality (Foley 1977). Another study found that larger cities have more inequality, which may be due in part to the presence of more households with female heads (Long, Rasmussen, and Haworth 1977).

The issue is rendered more complex because of the definitions of city and urban area. The affluence of the automobile age, which accompanied the moderate level of income inequality in the 1950s and 1960s, is also associated with urban sprawl, suburbanization, and large exurban settlements in rural areas adjacent to cities. While this trend can be said to reflect a certain type of affluence, it also absorbs some of the new prosperity in a way that calls into question whether the increase in real welfare is proportionate to the additional income. At the low end of the scale, the process might render many of the poor even poorer in real terms (Jencks et al. 1972).

LIFETIME INCOME

Most of the statistics on income distribution are snapshot data covering one year at a time. Evidently, this allows the chance inclusion of more cases of very low and very high incomes than would be the case in statistics of lifetime incomes, if such were available. The snapshot data have a built-in tendency to exaggerate the degree of inequality. Specifically, they will exaggerate the shares of the poor and the extremely rich in the social structure. The problem was dealt with briefly in Chapter 3. Here we may add some of the attempts to solve this statistical problem in the United States.

One official inquiry covering the years 1956–1972 described average yearly incomes and lifetime incomes of men in the United States (U.S. Department of Commerce 1974). Distribution by size classes was not given; moreover, the estimates of lifetime income reflect past experience, and do not include any attempt at estimating the effect of new trends in the economy. It is evident that the gap between incomes of men with only elementary schooling and those with higher education (specifically, those with four- or five-year college degrees) diminished over the years covered. This gives an interesting indication that some types of inequality may have continued going down, even as the general degree of inequality flattened out in those years. The same indication also warns us not to exaggerate the possible difference in inequality between yearly incomes and lifetime incomes.

This inquiry was conducted at the time when the reduction of inequality had flattened out, and before the opposite trend had begun to show. In the same general period another inquiry was started, based on a sample of 5,000 families, beginning in 1968 and continuing through 1982 (Duncan et al. 1984). It was found that the distribution of lifetime family incomes was less unequal than it would appear from data for single years. Specifically, the population of poor people showed high turnover rates. A surprisingly large part of the population had experienced poverty at one time or another, but relatively few remained poor all their lives. The conclusion could have been anticipated in principle but not to the precise extent shown by this inquiry. The comment was made that "income distribution" as such is misleading, and that the debate should be shifted toward income dynamics, because in the United States, with its high degree of social mobility, only relatively few people are left behind in permanent poverty (Lilla 1984). This comment apparently focuses on welfare rather than on the nation's use of its human resources.

For what they were worth, the comments were already becoming obsolete as they were being published. The shift toward more income inequality in the United States was in full swing in the early 1980s. This shift cannot help but affect income dynamics. As shown in Chapter 3 (and

Figure 3.2), inequalities have very different meanings for income dynamics depending on the level of inequality that is there to begin with. Inequalities with Me/Ave around .90 have strong middle classes and relatively few poor and rich; the chances of advancement upward from below are statistically quite good, while further advancement upward from middle-income status toward great riches is relatively scarce. Already around Me/Ave of about .80, these proportions shift significantly, and there will now be many more poor and quite a few more rich people, while the middle classes will begin to weaken. At Me/Ave around .70, the same is even more so, with size frequencies sloping down all the way: The statistical chance of moving up from poverty is now much less because there are fewer middle-class positions into which to move and more poor people waiting to move up. High riches, on the other hand, are now relatively less uncommon.

These distinctions are important, for it is within this range of inequalities—between .70 and .90—that recent changes have been taking place. The matter is further complicated because the 1968–1982 inquiry (which was headquartered in Michigan) specifically investigated families, which is the population with the least inequality, as we saw already in the first examples in this chapter. The recent rise in the numbers of unrelated individuals reflects, among other things, an inability to form or remain in a family, which is often a consequence of economic failure.

We may also note that much of the reduction in inequality for families and households (1930–1970) was due to a greater labor force participation by women. Their inexplicably low wages contributed to reducing the inequality of family incomes because they made the two-earner family a more frequent feature. The undeserved disadvantages of women and of black men were not explained—nor explained away—in the Michigan study. They would be more clearly reflected in statistics on unrelated individuals, persons, and taxpayers. Unrelated individuals have the greatest degree of inequality in the United States and their share in the population has been increasing in recent times. Single men and women were about one-third of the income recipients in 1910, but only about 18 percent in the 1940s and 1950s. Now they are approaching the same proportion as in 1910.

Analyzing family incomes also obscures what is, in fact, the largest inequality problem in this country: sex discrimination. The proportions of this problem were touched on briefly in the above discussion and will be discussed in more detail in Chapter 8. When sex discrimination is submerged in the family concept, this also conceals or ignores the fact that we have at least two very distinct inequality problems: those of welfare and justice. Data examining families and households mainly address the question of the welfare effects of inequality, while those on individuals come much closer to illustrating the justice problem and its ramifications into incentive, including the incentive to form human capital. Besides, the welfare function of family units has been shown to be an extremely complex issue, with ramifications into fertility, and an issue where much depends on the assumptions made by researchers (Nerlove et al. 1987).

THE GREAT SHIFT BACKWARDS

Let us first look at the bare bones of the data, and then proceed to explain some of their direct meaning. The further implications of these data in the United States will be discussed in more detail in Chapter 8. Recent data published in *Current Population Reports* (U.S. Department of Commerce, 1988) show that inequality of household and personal income has changed considerably in recent years. Me/Ave of household income changed from .894 in 1967 to .843 in 1977, and dropped to .808 in 1987.

"Household" is a composite concept, which has changed somewhat in size and composition over the 1970s and 1980s. For the second decade, we can get a gauge of such changes from forward estimates made with 1977 as a base, projecting up to 1995 (U.S. Department of Commerce 1980). These projections include corrections for anticipated changes in household size and composition, as these changes can be anticipated from ongoing sociodemographic trends. These corrections lead to a fall in the projected Me/Ave from .843 in 1977 to .833 in 1985 and 1990, and to .826 in 1995. Since then, actual data in the same statistical publication series show the Me/Ave falling from .843 in 1977 to .813 in 1985 and .800 in 1988. We can conclude that about one-fourth of the apparent fall in the inequality ratio reflects changes in household size and composition, while the bulk of the change must be real. For families, the changes are similar, but here the relevance is even weaker because families are a declining part of the population.

These changes are paralleled in data about persons. Here we get figures both in terms of full-time, year-round employment and actual employment, which includes the effects of part-time employment and seasonal unemployment. For male persons, the Me/Ave for full-time employment fell from .909 in 1967 to .890 in 1977 and to .851 in 1987. In data on actual employment, the changes are larger: from .917 in 1967 to .839 in 1977 and all the way down to .786 in 1988. There were more part-time workers among the men in the later than in the earlier years examined.

For female persons, the changes were different. Full-time–equivalent Me/Ave fell from .951 in 1967 to .924 in 1977 and .878 in 1987. Data on actual employment show the ratio moving from .725 in 1967 to .745 in 1977 and .721 in 1988. The larger difference (compared to the men) between changes in full-time and part-time employment reflects the greater occurrence of part-time employment among women than men. The lesser change in part-time inequality reflects a slight improvement in the relative wages of women: They now earn 70 percent of men's earnings on a full-time basis, and 50 percent in actual employment earnings.

The changes in inequality among male persons are much larger than those of households. The latter incorporate the composite effects of the changes in the wages of men and women. They also show only the welfare effects of changes in inequality—a change for the worse, in any event. The larger changes in wages, especially those of men, point instead to the effects on justice and incentive—decreased rewards and less prospects for improvement.

A study on how children fared under such income changes was done for the period 1973-1984 (Danziger and Gottschalk 1985a). Children were about evenly distributed among low-income, middle-income, and high-income families. It was found that during this period, children suffered declines in both the relative and absolute levels of income. The three lower quintiles (the lower 60 percent of the population) had these clearly negative effects; in the fourth quintile (61-80 percent) there was hardly any change either way, while the top quintile (81-100 percent) had some improvement in both absolute and relative incomes.

Already several years ago, in a study using data up to 1986, it was stated in no uncertain terms that recent changes have meant a shrinking of the middle class (Bradbury 1986). Families were investigated to establish the role of demographic change, which was found to be minor; the shrinkage of the middle class remains even after such scrutiny. Other analyses sometimes lose most of the change in inequality among the intricacies of statistical manipulation (for example, Blackburn and Bloom 1987, which used data up to 1985). Even these writers admit some widening of inequality in the early to mid-1980s.

The conclusion about the middle class is confirmed in still other studies. The median income (in dollar terms) is shown to have remained steady with little change since the 1960s even as the average income continued rising (Danziger and Gottschalk 1988-1989). Thus, the Me/Ave has been going down; the share of the bottom 40 percent of income recipients is also shown to have declined since the late 1960s.

Taken together, the evidence is solid. The rich and the very well-to-do now get a larger share of all personal income, and the poor receive a lesser share than before. In real terms, the lower half of the population—individuals with incomes below the median—now has less income than a decade earlier. Explanations have been sought in slower productivity gains, international competition, and the larger share of women in the work force (Thurow 1987). Increasing inequality of wages has also been under debate (Harrison, Tilly, and Bluestone 1986).

Taxpayer statistics underscore the shift toward more inequality, especially in the 1980s. From 1967 to 1977 there was little observable difference, but from 1977 to 1987 the Me/Ave of all tax returns fell from around .750 to .690. The downtrend was steady from year to year during the 1980s.

Analysis of tax data in terms of the Gini coefficient show little variation from 1952 to 1981 (Porter and Slottje 1985). This was true for both total income and wage and salary income. Inequality increased in the income categories rent and royalty, business, farm and professional, partnership, and estate and trust income, while inequality declined in pensions and annuities and in sales of capital assets.

Increasing inequality makes us expect changes in the factor shares: less going to labor and more to capital. The national accounts of the 1970s and 1980s show no such thing. "Compensation of employees" remains high, on the order of three-quarters of national income.

The contradiction is in appearance only if we consider the theory of rent as applying to high-paying positions, such as those in entertainment, sports, politics, and large-scale business leadership, plus some very highly paid technical occupations. The tax data show that salary and wage incomes have become increasingly concentrated in the higher income groups.

Comparing the tax data of 1987 with those of 1980, and applying a deflator of 35 percent to offset inflation in those seven years, we find that when total tax-return income rose by 28 percent, salary and wage income went up by 19 percent, and other income increased by 74 percent. The income of the highest 10 percent of tax returns had increased by 44.5 percent in total, by 41 percent in salary and wage income, and by 53 percent in other income.

Conversely, the lower 90 percent of the tax returns had an increase in total income of 20 percent, of which 11 percent was in salaries and wages and 83 percent in other income. The latter was a high percentage but not a very large amount; most of it consisted of pensions in an aging population. Most of the social security payments are, however, not included in taxable income. Of the entire increase in salary and wage incomes, 57 percent went to the upper 10 percent of the tax returns, where this component is relatively smaller than in the lower 90 percent.

These findings can be articulated in several ways. Looking at the median, we find that the lower half of the tax returns had an increase in real income of 15 percent in seven years, but only 7 percentage points of this was wage and salary income. Moving one step lower, to identify what happened to the lower 40 percent of the tax returns, we find that these had only a slight increase in total real income—on the order of 3 percent, which is hardly even certain, given the difficulties of index numbers. The wage and salary income going to these lower 40 percent of the tax returns had actually declined slightly, again assuming that the index numbers can be trusted in measuring small changes.

AFTER-TAX INCOME

The unmistakable trend toward more inequality, especially in the 1980s, was exacerbated by changes in federal income tax rates. The income after federal income tax is found by subtracting the amounts of federal income tax from the income amounts reported in the Internal Revenue Service (IRS) statistics, and by analyzing a large number of income size classes separately. We find that the upper 10 percent of the tax returns had improved their before-tax income share from the 35 percent tax level in 1980 to 39 percent in 1987, and had also increased their share in all after-tax income from 31.5 percent in 1980 to 34.5 percent in 1987. The 1987 after-tax share is nearly the same as the 1980 before-tax share.

The lower half of the tax returns, by contrast, lost ground. Their before-tax share was 16.5 percent in 1980 and 15 percent in 1987, and their after-tax share moved from 18.5 to 16.5 percent in the same seven years. The after-tax share of this lower half has not really been favored by the changes in federal income tax rates.

Before the mid-1970s, the distribution of income is sometimes shown to be less unequal after tax than before tax, largely because of government benefits, but this effect may have been reduced over the years (Reynolds and Smolensky, 1977).

The calculations of income inequality before and after federal income taxes are not the whole story, however. Already in the 1970s it was found that the total tax burden was virtually proportional for a large majority of taxpayers (in other words, there was practically very little progressiveness). Only under some extreme assumptions could it appear that the richest taxpayers pay a somewhat higher percentage of their income as taxes (Okner 1975). This was because state and local taxes are either proportional or regressive. Most state income taxes are not graduated (except by exemptions), and other state taxes, such as the sales taxes, are largely regressive. Home ownership also exposes the middle classes to a heavy burden of rigidly fixed real estate taxes, while those living in rented quarters usually have the landlord's real estate tax shifted onto them.

The tax changes of the 1980s had a dual effect. Not only were the federal income tax rates reduced for the rich and the well-to-do, so that the federal income tax became less progressive than before, but as the federal tax rates were changed and generally lowered, the other taxes, by states and local communities, went up. The total tax take (on all three levels) is on roughly the same magnitude as before, but the distribution is now different: the federal share has fallen from over 60 percent to about 55 percent, while the state and local share has risen from less than 40 percent to about 45 percent.

The net effect is that the lower income strata now carry a heavier burden of state and local taxes. Combined with what happened to the federal taxes, this means that the tax burden as a whole is now regressive. We can say with certainty that the lower 40 percent of all taxpayers now are worse off than a decade ago, and this probably extends to the full lower half of the population. Most of the middle classes have received no improvement in their net income. The bulk of the increase in the national product in the 1980s has come to those who already were very well off. Neither is the situation much modified by the taxation of estates or inheritance. In the United States, most large fortunes, and many lesser ones as well, have found means of avoiding these kinds of taxes (Cooper 1979).

RISING POVERTY

What were the effects of the tax changes on poverty? In previous decades, the rate of profit in business had remained steady, and wages could then also go up because of rising productivity (Wolff 1979). Before the 1970s, economic expansion, therefore, led to less poverty despite rather unchanging inequality in the distribution of income. But in the 1970s and 1980s, with productivity slowing down, rising inequality has led to increasing poverty despite some measure of continuing economic expansion (Danziger and Gottschalk 1986).

The Reagan budget deliberately reduced any concerns for the poor (Danziger and Haveman 1981), apparently on the theory that speedier economic growth would benefit everyone. The reasons why this did not come about will be discussed in Chapter 8, in the context of the entire contemporary economic problem.

5

Across the World

To know ourselves we must know others: Comparisons between countries and across the world are indispensable for judging economic performance. In trying to compare levels of income inequality, and trends in inequality, we cannot escape the problem of defining income, even beyond what was said about the subject in Chapter 3. Whatever it is that money buys, it is not the same everywhere. It is not even always the same within one country, and certainly not when the country is as large and as diverse as the United States.

After discussing the definition of income, we shall present some international findings that appear to shed light on the central problem—the origins and the roles of income inequality, and the whys and wherefores of its changes. This will have to be accomplished by examining groups of countries with somewhat similar economies and cultures, before we can begin attempting to gauge what may be going on in the whole world.

DEFINING INCOME

Income is usually defined in money terms. Real income often includes things that are not bought or sold, as is true of much housework and other services that people do without money transactions for themselves, for their families, or for other close communities. We alluded to this problem in Chapter 3.

International comparisons are nearly always made in terms of money income. International statistics on national product only admit one class of nonmarket goods, namely, the food that farmers consume directly out of their own production. Most countries have their own currencies. Dollars and yens cannot be compared directly. Therefore, we cannot, even in the most elementary sense, compare one country with another without using some common denominator. Currencies are made comparable by means of their international exchange values. In translating all currencies into a common one, such as U.S. dollars, we are, therefore, stuck with their official exchange rates. These exchange rates do not necessarily express how much the money is really worth. There is a lot of policy and other matters involved in the game of currency exchange rates. Until recently we had no common currency yardstick that was independent of national monetary policies. Devaluations and revaluations cause sudden apparent shifts in the relative incomes of countries, sometimes with results that are drastically misleading. In some recent years, for instance, it seemed as if West Germany had a higher per capita income than the United States. That was never really true; it only seemed that way when the exchange rates overvalued the German mark and undervalued the U.S. dollar in relation to each other, and in relation to many other currencies as well.

To remedy this problem, an international project was launched to explore the real purchasing power of money in different countries, so that we might get realistic comparisons of national product (Kravis, Heston, and Summers, 1978a; Summers and Heston, 1984, 1988). The resultant concept of Purchasing Power Parity (PPP) should give us an objective base for international comparisons. The ranking of countries as to relative per capita income would now change only when it did so in real terms. This should solve the problem of comparisons by making the valuations independent of monetary policy. The concept also brought in some new problems of meaning and interpretation, however. These are particularly vexing if we want to gauge income distribution across the entire world.

Assigning prices to important commodities and commodity groups to allow international comparisons of real income is relatively simple for comparing countries that are similar in economic structure and economic culture. Comparing the United States with Canada is easy. Comparing both of them with countries in Western Europe is only slightly less easy, even though important sectors such as housing and transportation raise difficult problems of comparing the quality of goods and services. For comparing the rich countries with the poor ones, the problem is of a greater magnitude.

In the simplest terms, the problem of comparing rich and poor countries is that their economic worlds are not closely comparable. In rich countries, goods are cheaper than they are in poor countries; for services, it is the other way around, because the prices of services are related to the level of income in each country. Applying international standard prices everywhere depresses the value of many commodities in the poor countries but also inflates the value of their services. The balance is far from even. Applying PPPs makes the poor countries seem less poor than they seem when national currencies are translated by conventional exchange rates.

The meaning of such calculations is not always clear at first. For instance, India has large numbers of service people who are low-skilled and low-paid. Is India better off than it appears to be because it has access to such an abundance of services? Applying the PPPs shows per capita income in India at nearly one-tenth of that in the United States (Summers and Heston 1988). Using the exchange rate of the rupee, we get an Indian per capita income which is only about 2 percent of that in the United States. Is the true figure one in ten or one in fifty? It makes for a very different comparison.

We have a puzzle: To what extent does the higher value of India's per capita income according to its PPP reflect the higher value placed on services—say, shoe shining? This is a country where most people cannot afford shoes, much less commercial shoe shine services. The higher value placed on manual services is certainly no substitute for adequate food or lodgings, nor does this numerical exercise do anything to change the extent of poverty in poor countries such as India.

The dilemma of measuring income in international terms is very much alive in any attempt at gauging income inequality across the whole world. For comparison of income inequality between individual countries, the problem has not even begun to be approached in these terms, and much less is there any solution for it on that level. The PPP alters the relative prices of many goods and services within a country, but how this might affect our understanding of the consumption of the rich and the poor in the same country has not even begun to be measured. Since the rich consume most of the services rendered by the poor, inequality of consumption might appear even larger if PPP weights were applied than it appears in conventional, national currency terms.

For the gauging of inequality separately within each country, we are simply stuck with conventional measurements in national economic statistics. These reflect, after all, economic power positions within each country in a way that no international comparison could. The problem of comparing currencies need not arise here at all. The measurement of inequality, whether by exponential functions, Gini index, or some other measure, is a matter of proportions, and not of levels of value. But the problems of establishing these proportions, and comparing them, are inevitably even more difficult between countries than within the same country.

COMPARISONS BETWEEN COUNTRIES

The literature on international comparisons of economic inequality whether by Gini index or some other yardstick, abounds in caveats on the difficulty of comparing countries (Berry 1985). From the U.S. material presented and discussed in Chapter 4 we saw how subtle changes in family life and household composition could cause apparent changes in income inequality that might not appear when demographic variables are held constant. For instance, the increase in income inequality of U.S. households in recent years was found to be real only to about three-fourths of its apparent extent—the remaining one-fourth reflected changes in the composition of households instead. How these latter differences might affect welfare in real terms is a more obscure problem that requires value judgments as part of the premises for a solution.

Such difficulties of meaning and interpretation are, of course, even larger between countries, because the very concepts of family and household are not the same everywhere, and neither are their changes over time necessarily analogous. This adds to the inevitable uncertainties stemming from differences in statistical concepts and accounting conventions generally—ranging from differences in the approach to unconventional or unrecorded income to differences in accuracy between national statistical services. When citing the degree of inequality set forth in several inquiries relating to one country or some group of countries, we can, therefore, take seriously only those differences that appear large enough that they must be real to some extent.

It is much more important here that we concentrate on findings about trends of change in inequality, provided they appear reasonably well established. Even more than focusing only on the United States, when looking at the world as a whole, we have to observe and interpret these changes and see how far they may relate to other economic changes.

CHOICE OF COUNTRIES AND REGIONS

The applied material is vast. To get some order to it, we will first present data by groups of countries, with the groups being tolerably homogenous as to level of development. Thereafter we will also present some of the research findings about inequality throughout the world. We will discuss data from Canada and Australia, from western and southern Europe, from the Pacific Rim (Japan and the "four tigers": Taiwan; South Korea; Hong Kong; and Singapore), from Latin America, from low-income regions of Asia and North Africa, and from Tropical Africa.

One group of countries that we will not analyze is the Soviet Union (USSR) and its former satellites in Eastern Europe, because in these countries there are unusually large discrepancies between the official statistical picture and unconventional, poorly recorded facts. On the face of it, these countries had less inequality than most others in the world. But the events of 1989 revealed that huge perquisite-type incomes were reaped by the political elites. We also now have more confirmation on the very large role of black-market trading both in the USSR and elsewhere, which of necessity modifies income distribution in ways that render the official statistics much less significant there than in any other part of the world.

CANADA AND AUSTRALIA

We begin with two countries that are economically very similar to the United States. Both ran through much the same gamut of development as the United States, but at a somewhat later time. At present, the differences in income level and economic structure are not large.

In Canada, recent data indicate a somewhat lesser degree of inequality than in the United States (Canadian Government 1989). From 1978 to 1988, the Me/Ave of family incomes fell from .914 to .893, while for unrelated individuals it rose from .762 to .766. For families plus unrelated individuals, it fell from .882 to .849, indicating demographic shifts as the main source of difference in trend. The Me/Ave for individuals remained unchanged at .788. Individuals as well as unrelated individuals increased faster than did families. Organization for Economic Cooperation and Development (OECD) data from the 1970s also indicated somewhat less inequality than in the United States (Sawyer 1976).

A study for the years 1947–1978, focusing on cyclical variation in Canada (Buse 1982), used the Gini index and fractiles (deciles and quintiles). Around 1950, the Gini index was going down, and then rose consistently (with cyclical variation) from around .36 to around .46 (corresponding to Me/Ave .875 and .780). Meanwhile, income of the first decile fell from over 3 percent of total income to about 1 percent. The income of the tenth decile first fell slightly around 1950 from 29.5 percent to 28 percent of total income, and then rose slowly, reaching 30 percent in 1978, at which time the Me/Ave was about .78. This is for taxpayers; inflation was found to be of little consequence for inequality. Unemployment had a greater effect, and the rate of participation in the labor force had even more impact.

A special inquiry into life-cycle earnings (Irvine 1980) showed the Gini index of family income for 1969 at .383 (Me/Ave .86). Net worth (wealth, not income) in 1970 had a Gini index of .724 (Me/Ave .39). Life-cycle earnings were found to be somewhat more unequally distributed than income from annuities. Yet another inquiry (Wolfson 1986) using whole quintiles confirmed the fact that income distribution in Canada has changed but little in recent times. Both inflation and unemployment were shown to have had little effect, and apparent changes were due to demographic variation.

For Australia, a study was conducted focusing on 1933 and 1980, with some data also for 1915, 1979, and 1981 (McLean and Richardson 1986). On the face of it, there were contrasting trends for the earnings of men and women. For males, the Gini index appeared to have fallen from around or over .5 (Me/Ave .69) in 1933 to .35–.37 (Me/Ave .82–.84) in 1979–1981. For females, the Gini index apparently rose from .4 to .5 (with the Me/Ave down from .84 to .69) during the same time span. For all persons, it is not clear whether the index really rose or fell.

The remarkably high inequality in 1933, with a Gini index .5 for males, is due in large part to unemployment and underemployment, which were very high for male workers in 1933. For female workers, increased labor force participation since then may have increased part-time employment, which would explain the contrasting trend. When employment factors are accounted for, the peak of the Gini index is not so high (only slightly higher than in 1915), and the subsequent lowering of the Gini index is also less extreme. Apparently, this reduction in inequality was accomplished by 1969, with very little change since then. The study also showed inter-quartile ratios, which fell from 5.35 in 1933 to 2.53 after adjustment—a shift from .61 to .83 in Me/Ave. For 1981, the same calculations show the Gini index at .29 (Me/Ave .92), and the inter-quartile ratio at 1.92 (Me/Ave .88). For families, the Gini index fell from .49 (or, when adjusted for unemployment, .41) to .31 in 1979, corresponding to a rise in the Me/Ave from .79 to .87. OECD statistics from the 1970s (Sawyer 1976) also showed the Gini index at .313 (pretax) and .312 (after tax), and thus showed considerably less inequality than in either the United States or Canada during the same period.

Tax incidence and other redistribution of income were the focus of an in-depth study with Australian data as the main exhibits (Kakwani 1986). Pretax, Gini coefficients and quintile shares showed income distribution in Australia as less unequal than in the United States, Japan, Ireland, and France, and on a level with the United Kingdom. Posttax, income distribution was less unequal than in West Germany, again on a level with the United Kingdom, and more unequal than in Sweden. Analysis of tax rates and government payments showed that the former had only a moderate effect on inequality of income distribution—the progressiveness of the income tax system is greater in principle than in practice. Government payments, by contrast, had several times the effect of income tax progressiveness.

WESTERN AND SOUTHERN EUROPE

An early compilation of data from the 1950s and 1960s (United Nations 1967) for West European countries showed moderate differences in income inequality. West Germany and France were the most unequal, with the Gini index near .50 (Me/Ave .69). Norway and Sweden were the least unequal, with the Gini index at or below .40 (Me/Ave .84). The United Kingdom came close to Norway and Sweden, while Denmark, Finland, and the Netherlands were intermediate. A comparison of income fractiles (deciles) showed Norway, Sweden, and the United Kingdom rather close to the detailed distribution that would be expected from the variant of the exponential function that corresponds to their Gini indexes. West Germany and France deviated clearly from what would be expected from the exponential function by having more income going both to the lowest decile (because of income transfers) and to the highest decile (because of large amounts of income from inherited wealth). The years under comparison were not the same in all countries, but roughly, the data compared some year in the 1950s with some year in the 1960s—sometimes a whole decade, and sometimes less. Over these years, inequality diminished in West Germany, the Netherlands, Denmark, and Norway; held steady in the United Kingdom; increased slightly in Sweden and France; and increased more sharply in Finland. Inferences from the exponential distributions are, on the whole, in good accord with those from the Gini indexes.

OECD statistics from around 1970 gave a similar picture, and included comparisons with the United States. The ranking of European countries (France, West Germany, the Netherlands, Norway, Sweden, and the United Kingdom, and in some tables also Italy and Spain) was about the same as in the U.N. data. Italy and Spain came close to the degree of inequality in France. In pretax income data, only France had a higher Gini index (and thus, was more unequal) than the United States, with the United Kingdom and Sweden close to the average for the group. In posttax income data, France and Italy had a somewhat higher inequality than the United States, with the United Kingdom, Sweden, and Norway below the average for the group, largely because of taxation.

Decile distributions both of total and per capita incomes again showed moderate differences between West European countries, with the United States consistently more unequal than the average for the group. This was evident also in the decile distributions of income, both aggregate and per capita: The United States was consistently below average in the lower deciles and above average in the higher ones. Again, Sweden, Norway and the United Kingdom were the least unequal, while France, Italy, and West Germany (in some measurements, although not in all) appeared closer to the United States.

A slightly later comparative study of some of the OECD countries (Schnitzer [1974] 1975) showed Sweden to have started in recent times with a similar degree of inequality as in the United States, but to have reduced its inequality since 1950, so that recently it has become one of the least unequal countries in the world. West Germany, again, was found to be somewhat more unequal than Sweden, with only a modest impact of the tax system. The United Kingdom also was shown to have a long-term trend toward less inequality of both income and wealth, with some effect from taxation.

Yet another comparison of the United States with Norway, Canada and Israel (Radner 1985) included several measures aimed at reweighting the data to fit the various countries; the comparisons came out essentially the same. A further comparative study of the United States and the OECD countries focused on the 1988 letter by the U.S. Catholic bishops (Buss, Peterson, and Nantz 1989). Several refinements on the statistics resulted in the conclusion that the OECD group in Europe showed less inequality than either the United States or Canada. Even the presence of large numbers of foreign workers in some European countries did not seem to have rendered the income distribution much more unequal. Among the countries studied, the incidence of poverty was, without doubt, highest in the United States.

Systematic studies of income inequality in the OECD group have been conducted under the Luxembourg Income Study (LIS). Microdata from the years around 1980 were treated statistically to render them as comparable as possible between countries. Further variations were studied based on the concept of needs (Buhmann et al., 1988).

The LIS has been used for intensive comparisons between countries (O'Higgins et al. 1989). The United Kingdom, West Germany, Sweden, and Norway were compared with the United States, Canada, and Israel. Comparison was by quintiles and deciles (of income received) and by Gini indexes. The data were regrouped in several ways, with various gross and net income concepts, and for families versus individuals. The results were essentially similar to the earlier ones published by Malcom Sawyer (1976). Sweden stood out as the least unequal of these countries, followed by Norway, and then the United Kingdom. The United States and Canada were much more unequal, with Israel an in-between case. In Scandinavia and the United Kingdom, the lesser inequality resulted largely from cash benefits stemming from public policy. The Gini index varied in Sweden from .33 (Me/Ave .86) for gross income of families to .21 (Me/Ave .96) for net income of individuals. In West Germany, the Gini index varied from .41 to .34 (Me/Ave .83 to .89), which was in some aspects less unequal than the United States, and in others more so; it was always more unequal than in Canada.

Another study based on LIS data analyzed the effect of family size (number of children) on income and poverty (Smeeding 1988-1989). In the United States, per capita incomes were highest among married couples with no children and lowest among couples with four or more children, followed closely by single-parent families with children. The poverty rate was highest in the latter category, and lowest among childless couples.

Comparisons were made with Australia, Canada, West Germany, Israel, the Netherlands, Norway, Sweden, Switzerland, and the United Kingdom. Concerning these countries, the conclusions were generally the same as on the United States as regards children versus affluence, but this was the least true in Norway, Sweden, and West Germany, followed by Canada, Australia, and Israel. The percent of affluent persons was lowest in Sweden and Norway, and highest in the United States, followed closely by Israel, the Netherlands, and Australia; the United Kingdom, Canada, West Germany, and Switzerland were intermediate in this respect.

Several studies have focused on the United Kingdom. A late-nineteenth-century study on the United States (Spahr [1896] 1970) that was cited in Chapter 4 and that found large inequality in the United States at the time also made the comparison with England, which for historical reasons had even more inequality. It is well known that inequality was wide in past centuries, but this has been profoundly changed since the tax laws of the 1920s which forced the breakup of entailed estates.

The history of inequality in England is of interest also because of the contrast with Ricardo's theory of rent, which actually matched conditions in North America better than those in England. In England, there had been political interference with land ownership, making it highly concentrated in the hands of the hereditary nobility and gentry. This began with the Tudor enclosures (1500s) and culminated with the parliamentary enclosures (late 1700s and early 1800s). The end result of the enclosures was the institutional exclusion of most of the rural population from any opportunity to own farms. The aristocratic land system rendered land more scarce by forcing the intensity of land use to be lower than might have been possible. Low-intensity uses ranged from extensive sheep pastures to the gentry's manorial gardens and hunting grounds. Such land uses rendered land for moderately intensive food production more scarce than it might have been otherwise. The access to low-cost food supplies from overseas countries would normally have rendered land in England less scarce, but the effect was blunted for about a century (mid-1700s to mid-1800s) by trade policies favoring domestic agriculture (the Corn Laws). During this whole period, before manufacturing really took over the economic scene in England, the politically leading classes in the country had a large part of their economic mainstay in land rents.

One inquiry into the inequality of wealth in England went back to the late 1600s (Lindert 1986). In 1670, the top 10 percent of estates held 58 percent of the wealth; in 1700, their share was 60 percent; in 1740, 58 percent; and in 1810 (after most of the parliamentary enclosures), 61 percent. In 1858 and 1875, the share of wealth of the top 10 percent of the estates had risen to 77 percent—in those years, the estates of titled gentlemen had begun to be exceeded by those of merchants and industrialists. For comparison the study noted that the share of real estate in total wealth went from 67 percent in 1670 to 47 percent in 1875 and to 24 percent in 1900, and then rose to 43 percent in 1973, reflecting the much larger share of buildings, which rose from one-third to nine-tenths of the value of real estate. The impact of death duties and the breakup of entailed estates in the 1920s was thus much less than if it had been done decades earlier.

Two recent in-depth studies were done in the 1970s (Atkinson 1975; Atkinson and Harrison 1978). A Georgeist perspective was provided by Phelps Brown (1983), emphasizing that income distribution is still influenced by the much more unequal distribution of wealth, but that more of the wealth is held by the middle classes.

One inquiry on British income distribution in recent times, and based on sample data (Nolan 1988–1989), found that the top 1 percent of income recipients had 11 percent of the pretax income in 1949, which fell gradually to 5.5 percent in the 1970s. The top 5 percent of income recipients meanwhile fell from one-third to slightly more than one-fourth; the top 20 percent fell from 47 to 43 percent of total income. The fourth quintile of income recipients rose from 21 to 25 percent of total income, while the bottom quintile showed little change, in the range of 5–6 percent of total pretax income. The Gini index fell from .41 (Me/Ave .79) in 1949 to .37 (Me/Ave .83) in 1975–1976. Unemployment was found to have a negative effect on the bottom quintile, but even the top 5 percent lost some income for this reason. Inflation has a somewhat favorable effect on the same group. Since the 1970s, inequality has again increased; the Gini index rose from .37 (Me/Ave .87) in 1978–1979 to .41 (Me/Ave .83) in 1984–1985. High incomes were rising, low incomes were stagnating, and middle incomes were falling.

An inquiry about the effect of inflation on inequality in the United Kingdom (Weil 1984) found this effect to be positive (advantageous) for the poor and slightly negative for the rich. Data from 1962 and 1978–1979 showed pretax inequality rather unchanged while posttax inequality increased somewhat.

A detailed study on Ireland, comparing it to the United Kingdom (O'Connell 1982) showed that for 1973 inequality in Ireland was somewhat greater than in the United Kingdom. The Gini index for direct income was .45 (Me/Ave .79) in Ireland versus .43 (Me/Ave .81) in the United Kingdom. In final income (adjusted for taxes and other modifying features), the index was .38 (Me/Ave .86) in Ireland versus .32 (Me/Ave .89) in the United Kingdom. Thus, there was substantial redistribution by fiscal and other economic policy means (cash and noncash benefits).

THE PACIFIC RIM: JAPAN AND THE "FOUR TIGERS"

The emergence of Japan as an economic world power would lead us to expect interesting parallels to the income distribution history of the United States and Europe. More recently, the rapid economic growth and development of four smaller countries in eastern Asia—Taiwan, South Korea, Hong Kong, and Singapore—gives further material to compare what happens to income distribution under rapid emergence from low-income antecedents to modern industrial society. To strengthen the parallels, Japan, Taiwan, and South Korea all had radical land reforms shortly after World War II, while the two city states had no case for that specific kind of change.

A comparative study of these five countries and some other Asian nations was aimed at verifying Kuznets' hypothesis of an inverted U-shaped curve for the development of income distributions (Mizoguchi 1985). For Japan, the material goes back to 1890 and shows steady increase in inequality up to the 1940s—the Gini index rose from .31 (Me/Ave .91) in 1890 to .42 in 1900, .45 in 1930, and .47 (Me/Ave .77) in 1940. Collapse of the economy at the end of the war brought the index back all the way to .31 in the 1950s, and thereafter it rose to .36 (Me/Ave .87) in 1962 and then varied between .33 in 1973 and .35 (Me/Ave .88) in 1982.

Data beginning in the 1940s shows Taiwan with a steadily falling inequality index. The Gini index was .56 in 1955, .44 in 1961, .31 in 1964, and .30 (Me/Ave .91) in 1981. South Korea, the "new economic giant" of the Far East, showed no clear trend—to generalize, however, inequality increased, as the Gini index went from .34 in 1978 to .36 in 1978 and .39 in 1981. This was a level close to that in Japan, and more inequality than in Taiwan in recent years.

Hong Kong and Singapore, city states with no agricultural sector to speak of, showed steady inequality with indexes higher than in Japan—.48–.49 (Hong Kong) and .46–.49 (Singapore). Large industrial and commercial fortunes contribute to the degree of inequality in both cases, as does also the sharper economic differentiation within large cities.

A thorough study of inequality in Japan used comparisons with Canada, the United States, and several countries in Western Europe (Ishizaki 1986). Inequality was shown to be greater than would appear from an official statistical series that reported mainly on wages and was incomplete in some of the income categories that are important in the higher income groups. Inequality was followed through four subperiods: 1945–1949, 1950–1962, 1962–1975, and after 1975. In the first subperiod, distribution was greatly equalized by the prevalence of minimum subsistence wages in the wake of World War II. In the second period, inequality increased because of increasing wage differentials according to the age of workers and size of firms. In the third period there was again some trend toward less inequality, but this was reversed again after 1977.

Overall, inequality of income in Japan was shown to be close to that in the United States, and greater than the average of the West European countries included in the comparison. The comparison was articulated by showing that wages were a lesser component of total income of the highest income groups than in North America and Western Europe, but a larger component in all the lower groups (deciles 1 through 8). Social security benefits were also a lesser component than in the major OECD countries (in all income groups), while property income was a larger component than in the OECD countries, both in the upper half of the income groups (deciles 6 through 10), and also in the lowest decile (decile 1). The latter feature may reflect the continued ownership of inherited farmland among Japanese urbanites who are reluctant to sell such property because they could never buy it back under the land reform law enacted just after World War II. Wage incomes, in the first analysis, included proprietors' incomes; when the latter are differentiated from wages, they are found to be a larger component of income in all ten decile groups than in the OECD countries, while wages, properly speaking, were less prominent in Japan, all the way from decile 4 to decile 10.

There were important differences in wages according to persons' ages, and between those paid by large and small firms. Wage differences by age were larger in Japan than in any of the countries included in the comparison; thus, the total income distribution varies more with the age distribution of the work force. There was also a much greater difference of wages in large and small firms—the latter offer much more uncertain and variable employment in Japan, and hence workers do not accumulate seniority as easily.

A detailed study of Taiwan (Kuo, Ranis, and Fei 1981) shows the Republic of China with an extraordinary record of economic growth and improved income distribution from 1952 through 1979. There was exceptionally rapid growth in the aggregate, leading to an unusually rapid rise in per capita incomes as well despite rather high rates of population growth—although these fell over time. The entire labor force became absorbed in gainful employment, making labor as scarce as other factors of production. There were also exceptionally rapid shifts in sector proportions: The agricultural sector employed 51 percent of the work force in 1952, but this figure had dropped to 21.5 percent in 1979, thus eliminating the principal ingredient that makes for increasing inequality in most low-income developing countries.

Reduction of inequality was substantial and real—and all this occurred in the period after the land reform, which must have made its contribution. How far foreign aid contributed to the high rate of growth was not spelled out. The Gini index stood at .56 (Me/Ave .64) in 1953, and then went to .44 (Me/Ave .77) in 1959 and to .33 (Me/Ave .90) in 1964. Income taxes were moderately progressive but had little influence on the Gini index, which fell even further to .29 (Me/Ave .92) in 1978.

Another study on Taiwan aimed at investigating how far inequality depended more on the family cycle versus the influence of social class (Greenhalgh 1985). This was an attempt at verifying the hypothesis set forth by A. V. Chayanov in Russia in the 1920s, who argued against the Communists' emphasis on social factors. As Chayanov believed, Susan Greenhalgh found that the family cycle had the greater influence. The effect of land reform was not included because this socieoeconomic change occurred before the period under study, which was also the case in Russia when Chayanov wrote.

LATIN AMERICA

The region started in modern times with wide economic inequalities, stemming from the Spanish and Portuguese colonial land systems. Most of these countries have had—and some still have—ample room for expanding agriculture onto unused land, but unlike in most of North America, this did not even initially lead to low land rent, as Ricardo's theory would make us expect. Instead, and in some analogy to the U.S. South, institutional constraints led to an artificial scarcity of land for the common people, which is the principal backdrop to high degrees of inequality. Contrary to standard economic theory, this high concentration of wealth and high incomes did not lead to particularly high rates of savings, capital formation, or economic growth.

Land reform has long been on the agenda in most of Latin America, but large-scale reforms have occurred only in Mexico and Bolivia, and to a lesser degree in Cuba. A move toward large-scale land reform in Guatemala was thwarted (in the 1950s) by a political coup assisted by the United States. In most Latin American countries, land reform has occurred only in token proportions. Even in Mexico and Bolivia, the effects have been less than hoped for, largely because of the continuing rapid population growth.

A comparative study of inequality in several Latin American countries stressed the low reliability and comparability of their economic statistics (Altimir 1987). Based on data mostly from around 1970, Gini indexes were shown to have been very high in Colombia with .618, Brazil with .605, and Peru with .568 (corresponding to Me/Ave in the range of .55 to .60). Mexico was less extreme, with Gini indexes around .500 (Me/Ave .69) in the period 1963–1977. Venezuela also appeared moderately unequal, with a Gini index of just under .50. Data on urban areas from Argentina and Uruguay showed such areas as less unequal than the national situations in the other countries.

With some exceptions, Latin America is economically better off than other low-income regions, largely as a result of large endowments of natural resources. Economic performance is in any event very uneven, both between countries and within the larger ones. Evidence of this can be found in the high rates of infant mortality, as well as glaring contrasts within some countries. A study comparing several countries (Psacharopoulos 1990) found the share of the lowest 20 percent of income recipients in total income to be the lowest in Brazil, Ecuador, Panama, and Peru, with about 2 percent; in Costa Rica, Mexico, Nicaragua and Venezuela, the same part of the population received about 3 percent of total income. Four percent went to the same group in Argentina, Chile, and Colombia; while these people got 5–6 percent in the Dominican Republic, El Salvador, Guatemala, Honduras, and Uruguay.

It is not easy to discern any connection between the degree of inequality and the general level of development. There have been many schemes of redistribution of income in order to help the poor, but the overall effects have been disappointing (Ascher 1984). The general remedy is thought to lie in economic growth, but the "trickling down" appears so slow that other measures may be needed to upgrade the status of the poor: Among the best are targeted programs for the poor such as food subsidies. There is a steady tendency for "leakage" of relief for the poor into the hands of better-off groups.

Two review articles covering several books each (Baer 1986; Berry 1987b) showed that Brazil and Mexico both have had very rapid industrialization but without the elimination of unemployment and without any decisive reduction in the relative role of the agricultural sector. If anything, income distribution has become more unequal. The poor did not necessarily become poorer, but the fruits of economic growth reached them only slowly.

In Argentina, most of the statistics are from "greater Buenos Aires" (Altimir 1986), where the Gini index was found to be around .40 (Me/Ave .84) through the years 1961–1980, with no trend that can be established very clearly. For the country as a whole, it was stated that Argentina in the early 1970s was among the Latin American countries with the least inequality, and that it had had no discernible change since the 1950s. In recent years there appears to have been some widening of inequality: The results cannot, however, be tested by any sensitivity analysis. In recent times there has been a sharp reduction in the share of wages in total income in Argentina (Orsatti 1983). Data were given from 1935 to 1982. The share of wages was over 40 percent in the early years, it rose to 50 percent in the 1950s, and then fell to about one-third in the most recent years in the study. Both wage earners and wage rates were reduced in their relative importance.

In Brazil, with rather wide inequality (Gini index .60, Me/Ave .61) it appears that inequality widened in the 1960s and 1970s (Pfeffermann and

Webb 1983). The numbers of both the poor and the rich increased as a percentage of the total population. The country has huge differences between regions and also between main sectors, all of which complicates any interpretation of what may be going on regarding income inequality (see Sahota and Rocca, 1985). Brazil has been characterized as "a piece of Japan within a piece of India." Such contrasts can only be expected to render distribution more unequal until more of the poor people are absorbed into the modern economy.

Brazil is still changing. There is evidence of increasing social and economic mobility as economic growth and development lead to the formation of a modern middle class. However, poverty still limits opportunity for most Brazilians, if less so than before (Pastore 1982). The relative increase in the price of food serves as an indicator of widening inequality (Yamane 1986).

In Mexico, the problems of inequality are complicated by several factors with opposing effects. One is the land reform, drawn out over several decades, which must have reduced inequality within the rural population. Another is the "green revolution" (the introduction of new high-productive crop varieties), which had some effect in increasing farm incomes in some regions but did not reach the poorest ones; hence, its impact on income distribution is uncertain (Tuckman 1976). State-directed industrialization may have had the opposite effect from that of the land reform, because it favored industrial concentration, and disadvantaged the small independent firms. Overriding all other problems was the continued very high rate of population growth (at least until very recently), which so increased the supply of labor that all other resources, both natural and man-made, continued to be scarce (Serrón 1980).

There have been some studies of the effect of public policy on income inequality (Aspe and Sigmund 1984). They include the distribution among deciles, which agrees with a Gini index near .50 (Me/Ave .70) in all three of the years 1963, 1968, and 1977 (Aspe and Sigmund 1984). Both the lowest and the highest deciles received somewhat more income than would be expected from the exponential function with Me/Ave around .70. However, both these deviations diminished from 1963 to 1977, so that the latter year came much closer to what would be expected from a Me/Ave of .70. Some trend toward a larger middle class was confirmed in another study (Gallardo 1983).

A peculiar trait in Mexico is that labor income has a low share in total income—less than half—while entrepreneurial and capital income are important also in the lowest income classes, where there are many small farmers and shopkeepers. Labor's share is largest in the middle-income groups.

Tax incidence is shown to be progressive, and hence it effects some reduction on inequality (Aspe and Sigmund, 1984). Taxes in Mexico also include the effects of inflation since this factor contributed to the incomes of the federal treasury; this peculiar type of tax was shown to be almost as progressive as the direct taxes. The indirect taxes are hardly progressive at all. Overall, it was shown that changing the income distribution through public policy has proved difficult (Aspe and Sigmund 1984, Introduction).

Financial subsidies have been shown to be important modifiers of income distribution in Mexico (Heroles 1988), especially because interest incomes are important and highly concentrated among the highest income groups.

ASIA AND NORTH AFRICA

By far the largest among these countries is India which, since independence, has attained a moderate rate of economic growth even as population increase has accelerated, hence, the change in per capita income has been slow (Sundrum 1987). In current terms, per capita income in recent times was shown as around 2 percent of that in the United States, while in PPP (Purchasing Power Parity) it approached 7 percent. Agriculture still employs 70 percent of the labor force while producing just over one-third of the national product. The agricultural population is still increasing slowly in absolute numbers while declining slowly as a percentage of the total population. Mining, manufacturing, and utilities supply about one-quarter of the national product, with the balance (39 percent) coming from services. Early planning did not distinguish between growth and development (Sundrum 1987). Basic conditions and trends can only be sketched in broad features, as the data will not always support precise conclusions.

The same author provided several inequality indicators in the form of Gini indexes (Sundrum 1987): These included figures for aggregate income of .42 (Me/Ave .82), of which .42 (Me/Ave .82) for the urban sector and .39 (Me/Ave .85) for the rural sector. For households 1975–1976, per capita income had a Gini of .38 (.42 urban, .34 rural). Inequality was thus moderate: The rich were not numerous enough to outweigh the relative equality dominated by rural incomes at the minimum subsistence level. In consumer expenditures, the Gini index varied from .30 in Punjab and Harayana (the irrigation states, and hub of the "green revolution" in India) but also in Uttar Pradesh, up to .47 (Me/Ave .77) in Rajahstan. In urban India, the Gini index varied from .30 in Rajahstan to .40 in Kerala (on the southwest coast). Poverty was least in Punjab and Harayana, but exceeded half the population in West Bengal, Tamil Nadu, Uttar Pradesh, Madhya Pradesh, and Bihar. Over time, the Gini coefficient showed only small variations in either direction from the 1950s to the late 1970s.

In India, inequality is perpetuated foremost by the system of education and human capital formation, followed by discrimination in labor markets (Tilak 1987, based on one district in the south Indian State of Andhra Pradesh). The returns to education are lower for the weaker sections of the population (women and backward castes); These same groups also have less access to education and suffer discrimination in the labor markets.

A somewhat earlier analysis of industrial wages (Horowitz 1974) showed them to have risen much faster than would follow from of all labor (which is actually abundant). This higher rate of rise was not so much the consequence of public policy or of union activity (which is weak in India), but rather of the marginal productivity of labor in the kinds of industries that were growing. In other words, labor is not a single factor of production but several, and the kind of labor needed in specific manufactures is often scarce in India.

In the Philippines, inequality is much wider than in India (Gini around .50, Me/Ave around .68). There was little change in inequality in the 1960s and some reduction in the early 1970s, followed by widening inequality in the late 1970s—a period of rapid growth (Mizoguchi 1985). Data for the period from 1956 through 1970-1971 also showed little change in inequality, but the Gini index was lower for consumption (.40-.45) than for incomes (.48-.51) (Berry 1985).

The effect of the economic slump in the 1980s was studied by an International Monetary Fund (IMF)-World Bank team (Blejer and Guerrero 1988). The highest 10 percent of the population received 44.6 percent of the income, and the lowest 30 percent got 6.3 percent. The poor were hurt by the slump because of the increase in underemployment, higher interest rates leading to less economic activity, and inflation (the upper income groups were better able to protect their real earnings). Even government spending had regressive effects in the Philippines because such expenditures mainly reached the upper income groups, whereas gains in labor productivity and external competitiveness would benefit the poor.

In Indonesia, inequality was widening in the rural population but was narrowing in the urban population (Yoneda 1985). In Malaysia, there were different trends according to regions and ethnic groups (Ikemoto 1985). Malays are more rural than average, as well as poorer and more unequal; the Chinese are more urban, richer, and less unequal; and the Indians are intermediate. In recent time, inequality appears to have widened in all three groups, in both their urban and rural subgroups. A special study on one rural area found differences in farm size largely offset by differences in land use (higher rice yields on smaller farms, and so forth), and by supplemental off-farm employment (Shand 1987).

In Thailand, poverty has been declining but inequality has been increasing, also according to regions and in the rural–urban comparison (Krongkaew 1985). There were special effects from agricultural growth, the rice premium, and the rice export tax—and the effects were found to be negative in both rural and urban areas. It is not clear how far the farmers' real income may have been distorted by the artificial rice price. An inquiry on oil price variation and its effect on income (Grais 1987) found no differences in the effect of alternative oil prices on the distribution of income.

A special study on Sri Lanka dealt with the period from 1969-1970 through 1980-1981, when the economy was liberalized (Glewwe 1986). Official survey data indicated increasing inequality, but based on consumption data it was concluded that inequality really decreased. Another study, with a much shorter time span (1978-1979 through 1981-1982) showed inequality increasing (Kakwani 1988), indicating the possibility that Kuznets' hypothesis may not always apply to this stage of development.

Turkey has been the object of in-depth studies (see Özbudun and Ulusan 1980). The country has developed rapidly in recent times, but due to continuing rapid population growth, the agricultural sector has continued to employ a large part of the labor force. Development has also been hampered by being based mainly on proceeds from agricultural exports. Inequality was found to be on the level of Gini index .5 (Me/Ave around .7), higher in agriculture, and lower in most urban occupations. However, the standard of living in the cities has been impaired by unsound overgrowth in five large cities (Istanbul, Ankara, Izmir, Adana, and Burga), where slum conditions are not factored into sector income. Between 1950 and 1975, cultivation increased rapidly, with a decline mainly in pastures, leading to a lessening of the equalizing influence on incomes from animal husbandry; hence, inequality within agriculture has increased somewhat. Overall, inequality has changed but little.

A set of intensive studies on Egypt (Abdel-Khalik and Tignor 1982) explained the coming of social activism in the 1930s and 1940s, dwelling on the land reforms beginning in 1952 and on subsequent economic development. Land reform has brought some reduction of inequality. Even so, inequality has remained substantial, if less so than in most low-income countries; in these studies, the Gini index was given as .40 (Me/Ave .84). Continued population pressure has rendered labor universally abundant, and inequality has increased somewhat. Economic growth rates have been high, with somewhat of a slowdown in the early 1970s and a renewed rapid rate in the late part of the decade, into the early 1980s, still without much reduction in the demographic trend. The urban-rural income disparity was close to 2:1. Rural electrification from the High Dam and land reclamation from the increased water supply also had some effects on distribution.

A special study focused on the agricultural sector in Egypt (Esfahani 1987). Labor's share in sector income was smaller than the sum of rents and profits. It increased where there was more investment in infrastructure, which also benefits rent. Thus, expansion of output leads to better labor income, improving the distribution of income within the agricultural sector. In rural Egypt, growth and reduced inequality may go hand in hand—but this refers only to one sector, not the whole economy.

TROPICAL AFRICA

This is the poorest of the regions, with low incomes, high poverty rates, slow growth per capita, and even retrogression in the agricultural sector in some countries because of dual economies (Bequele and van der Hoeven 1980). (This refers to the 1960s and early 1970s).

Traditionally, Africa was rather egalitarian, at least within the same tribe or village. To some extent the traditional land tenure system has been broken up, but more importantly, incipient industrialization has generated a modern sector with much higher incomes but also with large city slum areas. Varying endowment with "vent for surplus" in petroleum and other exportable minerals also has created substantial differences between countries. Unrecorded income—the collection of wildlife—is on the decline, hence, increases in conventional per capita incomes are exaggerated and the increasing inequality has been understated. Inequality in Africa has increased because of an economic strategy favoring the modern sectors (Gyimah-Brempong 1988). More emphasis on agricultural development, and on employment, would result in less inequality.

Africa falls into the general pattern of early development in the fact that incomes have risen much faster in the upper two-fifths than in the lower three-fifths of the population, resulting in widening inequality (Lecaillon, Germidis, and Kerneis 1977), even though all groups have rising incomes in absolute terms, at least as conventionally measured. The upper class includes some 1-2 percent of the population. The middle class is of variable scope, depending on the degree of development of each country. The rural masses can be grouped together with the small-scale operating craftsmen, petty traders, and the urban subproletariat. Even among farmers there are now large differences in income. Data were given for some of the francophone countries, among them Gini index for the Ivory Coast, Madagascar, and Senegal, varying from .48 (Me/Ave .76) to .56 (Me/Ave .64).

Nigeria has been the object of another in-depth study (Bienen and Diejomaoh 1981), paralleling the studies of Mexico, Turkey, and Egypt. The data showed a typical low-income development, accelerated and distorted by oil revenue in the 1970s. There was some widening of inequality in earlier years too, but the trend was much sharpened by the oil influence. Gini indexes in rural areas were around .30 (Me/Ave .92), and much higher in urban areas, around .70 (Me/Ave .43). Joint inequality for both sectors put the Gini index around .50–55 (Me/Ave .63–69).

THE WORLD COMMUNITY

Generalizing about inequality throughout the entire world is extremely difficult, as this would require answers to all the problems of comparing different economic systems and measuring their incomes in comparable terms.

Some heroic attempts have been made at measuring worldwide income inequality, and they deserve to be reported, if briefly. One such study (Berry, Bourgignon, and Morrisson 1983a) included China and other socialist countries, apparently without correction for their hidden, officially unrecognized sources of inequality (as mentioned earlier in this chapter). The study found some change toward less inequality in the 1950s due to conditions in China. Thereafter, inequality widened in the 1960s, both in the nonsocialist poor countries and in the world as a whole. The Big Leap Forward, and the Cultural Revolution, self-inflicted disasters in China, contributed to this result. Around 1970 all inequality measures were back at the same levels as around 1950, and the same level may still have prevailed around 1977. The Gini index was estimated at .67 (Me/Ave .47). In terms of consumption, the Gini index was found to be around .64 (Me/Ave .50).

When the socialist countries are not included, the Gini index for the world was around .56 (Me/Ave .64) for income, and in the range of .51–.53 (Me/Ave .67–.69) for consumption. Using PPP (Purchasing Power Parity) instead of conventional data still yielded essentially the same picture of worldwide inequality. (Berry, Bourgignon, and Morrisson 1983b). Rapid population growth and the consequent slow rise in per capita income in the poor countries has tended to increase inequality over time.

A somewhat more recent study (Grosh and Nafziger 1986) used income and population data for 1970. World inequality was found at Gini .67 (Me/Ave .48), based on PPP. The world as a whole was found to be somewhat more unequal than Honduras, which is one of the most unequal among individual countries.

6

Economic Growth and Development

We should make a distinction between economic growth and economic development. Growth means becoming bigger; development means becoming more productive, and usually also more advanced and more complex. Growth and development interact; more often than not, they are necessary for each other. Growth, in any event, is what interests most people, for it should mean more income—or so it seems.

Controversy about inequality and growth centers around the problem of savings and how they are affected by the degree of inequality. The simplistic argument has it that the rich save more of their income; hence there would be more savings and more investment in a more unequal society, and less in a less unequal one. Competing with, and often contradicting, this argument are many historical observations, but also arguments relating to economic structure, demography, class barriers and cultural constraints on both growth and development.

What inequality does to society as a whole, and thereby indirectly also to the economy, will be discussed in Chapter 7. For now, let us dwell on what is known (or is thought to be known) about the relations between inequality and economic growth. There are some general and special theory constructs, and there are a good deal of applied observations, some of which were set forth in the preceding chapter.

THE KUZNETS HYPOTHESIS

A general statement about the relation between inequality and growth (Kuznets 1955) says that it tends to increase in early stages of economic growth and development, and to decrease in later, more mature stages of development. This is often called the theory of the inverted U-shaped curve. There is a large literature expanding on or explaining the Kuznets curve, or attempting to refute it (for example, Cline 1975; Sahota 1978).

The recent turnaround in the United States toward more inequality on very high levels of average per capita income is not covered by the Kuznets hypothesis, and is in general not discussed in that connection either. We shall return to this subject in Chapter 8.

A tentative overview of income data from a sample of sixty countries—forty of them "developing," fourteen developed, and six socialist countries—used a statistical analysis of income data. The result was a confirmation of the Kuznets hypothesis of the inverted U-shaped curve—increasing inequality in early stages of development, and reduction of inequality in late stages (Ahluvalia 1976). The statistics were in terms of U.S. dollars 1965-1971, and showed the turning point (from increasing to decreasing inequality) varying from three to five hundred dollars of per capita income in those value terms. There was no support for the view that faster growth was associated with higher degrees of inequality. According to the evidence, the poor were not necessarily becoming poorer in early stages of development, they merely did not catch up as soon as the better-off income groups did. For a more articulate analysis, Ahluvalia pointed to inter-sectoral shifts in the economic structure and labor force and a reduction in the rate of population growth as things that affect the changes in inequality.

The result has not been left unchallenged. One study, using only fourteen countries for the analysis, came up with a refutation of the Kuznets hypothesis (Loehr 1980). A counter-analysis of the same material that Ahluvalia used endeavored to show that the inverted U-shape curve had been confirmed only because of statistical difficulties (Saith 1983). A subsequent analysis again claimed to have restored the initial result, again confirming the hypothesis (Campano and Salvatore 1988). Other researchers have found more negative consequences. A very elaborate statistical analysis of economic growth showed that in the early phases the poor actually become poorer—a "trickle-up" variant of the usual assumption (Adelman 1975).

There are many variations on the basic theme. An analysis of seventy-nine countries showed that inequality increased among the poor nations and decreased among the rich ones (Sarantides 1987), apparently without too strict a correlation. The observation has been made that any sample of countries is perforce heterogenous, but when low-income and high-income countries are held apart in the analysis, the inverted U-curve may be hard to distinguish among the former (Ram 1988).

Across a maze of arguments, Kuznets may in the end be shown to be basically right. We need, however, to distinguish a number of things that might cause the inverted U-shape of the inequality-change curve, and things that might distort or divert it. Among the former are sector proportions in the economic structure of each country (agriculture versus the rest), population growth and its changes, and rates of economic growth. Distorting or diverting traits might exist in inherited class barriers and cultural traits and peculiarities, and in the extreme concentration of industry or urban buildup. The problem of savings versus inequality seems at best elusive, and the question will be raised whether the U-curve is inevitable or just follows from some of the ways the world has happened to work.

SECTOR PROPORTIONS

Traditional agriculture is supposed to be a drag on economic growth and development. Emphasizing the word "traditional" in this connection is, however, unfair. Slow growth and development are often characteristic of agriculture, but not because of anything the farmers do or fail to do. Instead, the explanation is that agriculture labors with low demand elasticities for its products, which means that most of the time, agriculture must expand slower than the economy as a whole. How this plays out depends both on economic growth generally and on the rate of population growth. The faster it is, the later will be the phase when the agricultural sector ceases to support an increasing agricultural population. The relation between economic and population growth rates, as they affect the sector proportions (agriculture versus the rest) can be visualized by aid of a set of schematic charts (Figure 6.1).

The differences between these charts is sometimes dramatic. Some countries may achieve a radical transition in twenty years, whereas some others (with about the same growth rate in per capita incomes) will take more than fifty years to accomplish the same transition.

The matter would be even more realistic if instead of the agricultural sector versus all the rest, we could take all of the traditional, slow-moving sectors, including the city slums with their burgeoning population of low-paid service people, and place them in contrast to the modern, high-growth, high-income sector of a country in incipient modernization.

If the economy as a whole grows faster than the agricultural sector (or the traditional sectors), the slow-growing parts will become a lesser part of the whole. Their slower growth will affect the weighted average of the overall growth rate less and less. This will render possible an acceleration of growth as the economy rises into middle-income levels of per capita national product. It is then that the U-curve may begin to turn around, since the higher paid strata of society now begin to weigh more heavily in the whole economy.

Figure 6.1
Theoretical Examples of Sector Changes Covering a Fifty-Year Period

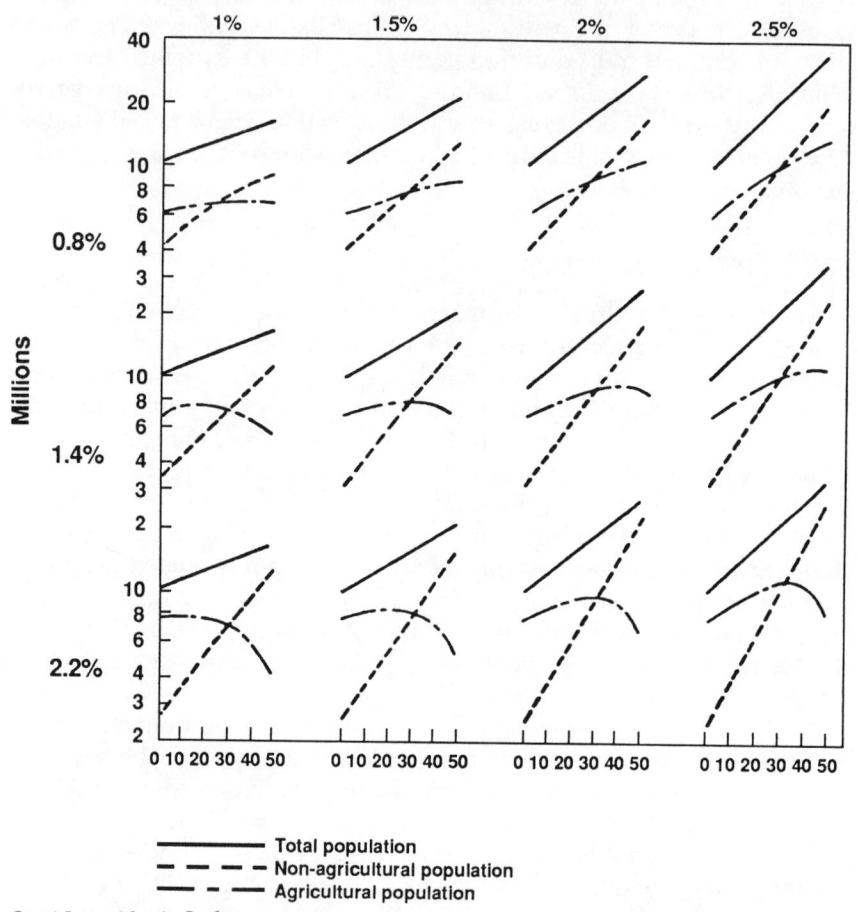

Total population
- - - - - Non-agricultural population
— - — Agricultural population

Semi-Logarithmic Scales:
The percentage figures along the vertical scale represent the differential growth of the nonagricultural population over the total population. The vertical scale on populations shows, in absolute numbers, millions from 2 to 10 in the two lower rounds (differential growth rates of 2.2 percent and 1.4 percent respectively), and from 2 million to 40 million in the upper round (differential growth rate of 0.8 percent).

On a theoretical level it has been shown that the rate of change in inequality, with economic growth, will depend to a large extent on how much of the added production stays with those who already have high incomes and how much comes down to those who had low incomes to begin with (Fields 1987).

How sector proportions have actually changed over long periods of time has been shown by statistical time series for a number of the present high-income countries (Dovring 1959). Several countries in Western Europe, which were among the very earliest industrializers, took many decades to effect the transition from a mainly agrarian to a mainly urban-industrial economy and society. This was the joint result of slow to moderate rates of population growth and as yet only modest rates of economic growth, measured by the yardsticks or expectations of the recent, more rapid, phase of world industrialization. Subsequently, some of the "runners-up," such as Sweden, Finland, the USSR, and Japan, changed their sector proportions more rapidly. This was the joint result of low to moderate rates of population growth combined with more rapid rates of economic growth, possible because technology was to a large extent imported ready-made from the front-runner countries. The United States, as a settler country, had the unusual feature that the agricultural population continued to grow in absolute size long after it had ceased to be the majority in the country (which happened in the 1870s). Despite this, the degree of income inequality turned from increase to decrease in the very early years of the 1900s. This contributed to the fact that the income disparity between farmers and city people was less in the new settlement areas of the West, as was noted in Chapter 4.

The problem with many of the low-income countries in recent times is that they often continue to have population growth rates that are higher than those in the present high-income countries at the corresponding levels of industrialization. As a consequence, sector shifts and a resulting reduction in the degree of inequality is slower to come. The pattern in Japan has been matched by Taiwan, and to a lesser degree also by Korea and Thailand. Most Asian countries continue with fairly high rates of population growth; hence, the sector proportions change more slowly. The matter came out most strikingly in Turkey and Egypt, but also in the Philippines, Sri Lanka, and elsewhere. In Latin America there is the appearance of more rapid sector shifts in some countries. But this is only because—in some analogy with England in the wake of the enclosures—some Latin American countries either expel people from agriculture or deny them entry to begin with, by reason of highly concentrated land ownership. This leads to expansion of the city slums, which should really be counted with the traditional low-income sector.

At the bottom of the scale are India and most of tropical Africa. India has moderately high rates of population increase but also only modest rates of economic growth, and therefore still has a very large agricultural sector. In tropical Africa, modern economic development has begun more recently than elsewhere, and major shifts in sector proportions are therefore also more remote. How far African demography will be influenced by the acquired immune deficiency syndrome (AIDS) epidemic does not appear clear at present.

Thus, the changing sector proportions that are so important in explaining how inequality changes or may change are the result of two sets of rates: those of population growth and of economic growth. The former can be discussed in a single framework, while economic growth rates must be attributed to several separate, if interacting, sets of forces.

POPULATION GROWTH RATES

An often repeated theory states that as the level of per capita income rises in a country, the rate of population growth should go down. This is also known as the principle of the demographic transition, and is well established from studies of Europe and North America.

The logic underlying the priciple of demographic transition is, briefly, that in rural society, and especially in traditional rural society, children are an asset; whereas in city life, they are a liability. Therefore, the gradual transition from mainly agrarian to mainly urban-industrial ways of life should be accompanied by a gradual lowering of the birth rates and the rates of population growth. The latter consequence would follow rather more slowly than the fall in birth rates, because the same transition also leads to lower infant mortality and higher life expectancies.

The demographic transition occurred in Western Europe and North America early in this century, and has been repeated in several countries in Eastern Europe more recently, and in the European parts of the USSR as well. As a general theory, the principle of demographic transition lets us expect that continued economic growth and development will generate the solution to any problem of rapid population growth from within, so to speak.

This may be an exaggerated extrapolation from the experience of Europeans and their offspring in new countries overseas. Other regions and cultures may in part have other motivations. It is characteristic that in Europe, before modern industry became established, it was common for wealthy families to have few children in order to avoid too much subdivision of wealth by inheritance. Various schemes of primogeniture endeavored to circumvent the problem, but the principle is clear: Material considerations were important to the birth rates. In eastern Asia, this was not the same. In Imperial China, one of the most important rewards for economic success was the opportunity to have a large family, often by aid of concubines, while the common peasantry often lived with the necessity of keeping to a minimum the number of children they could raise. This is also how premodern Japan came to have an almost static population that began to increase slowly at first, with the city sector in the lead for higher birth rates. Up to 1940, an accelerating population increase thus was the reverse of the European pattern, and the fall in birth rates after 1945 expressed a highly disciplined cultural frame of mind rather than strictly individual decisions by families.

There may be other variations to the theme of birth rates varying strictly with family economic considerations. In the Soviet Union, for instance, it is easy to see that the demographic transition is largely limited to the European populations, while the Muslims of central Asia still have much higher birth rates. This may extend to some other Muslim nations as well. In Latin America, birth rates have generally continued at a much higher rate than one would expect from the degrees of industrialization and urbanization, and it may be that the specific variety of family feeling in these countries may also delay any meaningful demographic transition.

There is no way to really predict the effect on population growth from economic growth rates or economic sector proportions. Cultural factors may also intervene. This does not prevent us from tracing some influences, intended or unintended, of policy on the demographic trends. France reached a demographic transition earlier in the 1800s than would have happened otherwise because the Civil Code (*Code Napoléon*) decreed the equal division of inheritance among all sons and daughters. This broke down previous de facto primogeniture, and so favored the prevalence of the two-children family in France, leading to the well-known demographic stagnation that was reversed only after 1945 when *allocations familiales* in essence paid people to have more children. A similar effect was had by the English "poor laws" at the time of Thomas Malthus, which inadvertently exacerbated some of the problems Malthus had addressed.

Population growth thus affects inequality, both by its effect on the demographic transition, influencing sector proportions, and by the direct effect on factor supplies and factor scarcities. It may also, in turn, be influenced by economic inequality; we shall return to this theme in the next chapter.

CAPITAL SCARCITY AND LABOR ABUNDANCE

This argument is related to the previous ones but must be discussed separately. It was anticipated in the exposition of rent in Chapter 2. Briefly, it runs as follows: In early stages of economic development, capital for investment is scarce almost by definition, at least in conventional economic accounting. Prevailing low per capita income levels leave only a thin margin that can be saved from an income level that is close to minimum subsistence and consists in large part of food consumption. Such consumption cannot be much reduced without debilitating the population, including the labor force. Hence, what savings can be marshalled for tangible investment in urban-industrial plant and equipment must be made to yield high rates of return, incorporating elements of monopoly rent. This is necessary if the urban sector is to grow at a rate much exceeding that of the economy as a whole—as it must if there are to be serious economic changes, reflected in a gradual sector-proportions shift, in the not-too-distant future. This argument is often flawed by overlooking the inner dynamics of the agricultural sector itself.

The high rates of population growth that prevail in most of the low-income countries, and the tendency for such population growth rates to accelerate as economic growth gets going leading to lower death rates, only render the initial scarcity of capital and abundance of labor even more striking and risks making it even more long-lasting.

The conventional statement usually overlooks how much of the gain in capital supply can be lost by inefficiency and luxury living among the leading classes, who may feel particularly secure in a society with a high degree of inequality.

As a complication, many countries have had their economic growth started through special export enterprises, more or less favored by the vent-for-surplus principle explained in Chapter 2. It is thus not uncommon for a modern sector to grow much faster than the traditional one, and with rather incomplete linkages to the older sector. The conflict of sector interests is often rendered worse by the modern sector's use of some of its newfound income for cheap food imports rather than for awarding larger economic opportunity to agriculture within the same country. The superficial economic gain in doing so may mask a net loss in comprehensive national account, which is rendered less visible because of the difficulty of factoring in increased unemployment among the agricultural population, which is low priced because of weak terms of trade.

The dualistic growth model inevitably leads to large economic inequalities in the early stages of economic development (Papanek and Kyn 1986). This may, in fact, be worsened if the growth of the agricultural sector is held back by cheap food imports. The large inequalities may then be mitigated only in a much later stage of growth, when the modern sector becomes large enough so that the capital needed for continued growth can be generated with less difficulty, leaving more of the economic product available as wages for labor.

Initially, this will mean principally the wages in the new industries and their attendant services. At the same time, as labor in the modern sector becomes more skilled and more of the available product can be used for wages, labor in the modern sector also tends to become more differentiated as to skill. Such differentiation of rising wages in the modern sector has been observed even in India (Sundrum 1987). Sometimes, scarce labor categories in a recently growing urban sector may overshoot their advantage, as happened with the longshoremen in Brazil, who caused some of the shift inland when marine coastal transportation lost some of its advantage.

SAVINGS, GROWTH AND INEQUALITY

According to received theory, which was frequently invoked in the United States in the 1980s, the need for savings and capital formation will be best served when there is not too much equality of income. Let the rich enjoy their riches, and they will save and invest, so conventional wisdom has ruled.

The statement has a superficial, simplistic appeal, but it is flawed in several directions. It overlooks the potentials for growth and development in traditional sectors such as low-income agriculture, it assumes too much about the propensity to save at various income levels, and it extrapolates to the future of affluent countries some of the experience from previous stages of development, which is not intuitively justified.

For the low-income countries, the discussion of savings and investment has tended to overlook the savings-in-kind that subsistence or semisubsistence peasant farmers often make as a way of rendering useful their surplus time. Land melioration and more intensive attention to the micro phases of both crop and animal production are avenues of increasing production without any visible access to conventional means of investment. The main requirements for this to take place are opportunity (no land-tenure constraints preventing it) and incentive in the ways that will serve the peasant farmers' self-interest, both in increased consumption by their own households and in increased sales to the growing urban sector. High inequality is often associated with the kind of land tenure that does not give the cultivators enough incentive, and with the tendency of the urban sectors to cover some of their demand for food through cheap imports rather than somewhat higher priced domestic farm production. Some of the contrasts are striking: Japan in the early stages developed rapidly, with high domestic food prices, while a policy of cheap food long tended to retard both growth and development in India. Urban-sector food imports, to the neglect of domestic agriculture, has perpetuated economic inequality between urban and rural areas (for example, in Peru), and may still do so in some countries of tropical Africa.

Second, do the rich really save more than anyone else? That is debatable. If it were true in the comparison between nations, we ought to expect the highest savings rate in the world to be in Latin America, which has the largest income inequalities anywhere. But the Latin Americans do not save more than other nations, and save less than some that have less inequality. It follows that the propensity to save is a separate function that cannot be derived directly from the level of income. If anything, it can be argued that extremely rich people, with large inherited wealth, may have less propensity to save than people of more modest means, for whom the reward for saving means a larger relative difference than it can ever mean for the super rich. One recent study of several countries using cross-sectional analysis showed the middle-income groups as the largest source of recorded savings (Venieris and Gupta 1986). This general objection to received theory as presented above cuts across all levels of national per capita income—it concerns the rich countries as well as the poor and the middle-income nations.

More specific to the higher income countries is a shift toward demand, rather than capital supply, as the main determinant of growth rates. The shift was present already in the capitalist dilemma of the 1920s and 1930s when there was, if anything, a buildup of excess capacity to produce. There was not enough effective consumer demand to buy all that industry could deliver. The size of the excess capacity showed itself, among other things, in the subsequent large ability of the industrial countries to step up production for war purposes during World War II. Hence, policies of reducing inequality would effectively lead to higher capacity utilization and higher growth rates in the short run, but also to higher rates of growth in the capacity to save and invest. The decrease of inequality in the United States since the 1930s fits this analysis, but the more recent widening of inequality appears to fly in the face of a demand-driven economy.

This last caveat against received theory is strengthened by the tendency for new, high-productive technology to need less industrial labor, leaving increasing numbers of workers with only low-paying service jobs (if any) to look forward to (Leontief 1983). This new perspective, which is very much present in the United States in the 1980s and 1990s, also calls in question the whole received theory of productivity, how it should be measured and understood, as well as how it relates to the welfare of society as a whole. The role of conventional net savings may not remain the same as before under high technology (Vatter 1982). Instead, the increasing tendency for high salaries in occupations with limited opportunity (the star effects) directs attention to the concept of human capital, especially the variants that are the most difficult to measure or explain.

Thus we find that inequality may remain either high or low whether there is economic growth and development or not. Therefore, we should discuss the morphology of development rather than the concept of development without further description (Gagliani 1987). In other words, for what purpose is the development, and for whose benefit? Increasing differences of skill among different categories of workers will at first increase wage differences, but because such changes also lead to increased mobility of labor, the same differences will thereafter (by way of human capital formation) lead to reduced wage differences (Morley 1988).

Neither Kuznets' hypothesis nor any of the theories addressing the causation of change in inequality do anything to explain the starting levels of inequality. This is important because much of the known record shows little effective change in inequality. The starting levels have a good deal of influence on the outcomes even after successful development and vigorous growth. The minimal influence of government policies on reducing inequality was documented in Latin America (see Chapter 5), and has been emphasized in comparative analyses (Gagliani 1987).

CULTURE, INSTITUTIONS, AND CLASS BARRIERS

The influence of culture on economic growth and development has been commented on many times (Henry Aujac, in Seligson, ed. 1984). Implicitly, this would also affect the ability to change inequality. The same is true of the variant of the culture argument that stresses the motivation to change (McClelland, in Seligson, ed. 1984). To cite Tunisian President Habib Bourguiba, each people has to proceed on the basis of its native genius, whatever that happens to be. Trying to be a culture they are not will not help; rather, the opposite is true. Neither is culture invariant, it has the ability to change, only we do not always know why or how.

The concept of culture as affecting both economic growth and economic inequality becomes somewhat more tangible when referring specifically to political culture. It has been shown, for instance, that countries with long-standing democratic regimes tend toward less inequality, and vice versa. Large inequality, as a starting point, tends to render newfound democracy unstable, and subject to reversal into undemocratic regimes (Muller 1988).

As a counter-hypothesis to the inverted U-shape of the Kuznets hypothesis (which is a variant of the divergence-convergence hypothesis of economic development), a consistent institutional perspective posits that institutions connected with wide inequality tend to continue to maintain or even generate wide economic inequality (Wright 1978). As a very persuasive case in point, Brazil is often cited for its large and still-growing economic inequality, despite vigorous economic growth and recently a rather high per capita income.

An institutional perspective is, in fact, the only framework that can explain the differences in starting levels of inequality—how much inequality there was at the beginning of modern economic development. The starting level is important because of the tendency for any changes in inequality to be small or moderate. This tends to leave initially very unequal societies still more unequal than others, no matter whether the changes reflect an inverted U-curve or not.

Starting levels of inequality can often be derived from colonial history and colonization history. A legacy of plantation economy has led to wide economic inequality as well as retarded economic development in large parts of Latin America and the Caribbean region (Beckford 1972). The U.S. South presents a clear parallel. Brazil also has large internal contrasts between regions, in part at least due to how far they were once dominated by the primitive plantation system of early, and aristocratic, colonization. The old plantation area of northeastern Brazil has been particularly hard-stricken with poverty and economic retardation as well as resource degradation—soil erosion and a depressed rural population.

Regions with widespread land ownership by independent family-scale farmers, where they occur in Latin America, contrast with the plantation areas (and other areas of concentrated land ownership) by more successful economic growth in recent times as well as by less economic inequality. Northwestern Argentina is one such region, and the Atlantic province of Colombia is another.

The plantation syndrome as a source of wide inequality and slow or unbalanced economic development, as well as political unrest, can be traced in other parts of the world as well. The Philippines and Malaysia have their share of both plantation and peasant agriculture. South Vietnam had a plantation economy as a legacy of colonialism (both French and North Vietnamese), while Cambodia and Thailand had predominant systems of independent peasant-farmer agriculture among their historical legacies.

The plantation system was sometimes maintained far into modern history, and sometimes evolved into systems of high-rent tenant farming. Either way, a high degree of economic inequality was usually maintained. Monoculture of commercial crops, for high landowner profits, was often combined with obstacles against self-sufficiency among the agricultural population. The Brazilian northeast is an extreme example, but there are many others in the plantation areas of both Asia and the Western hemisphere.

Once in place, a situation of large economic inequality in the agricultural sector or the rural areas tends to project itself also into the new economic sectors and the urban areas, where the dependency relations of the plantation economy come to dominate the entire economic scene. This was the case in the U.S. South (Dovring 1973), and more recently in Brazil. The remedy against the socioeconomic consequences of the plantation system, both in its immediate effect on incipient economic development and in its long-term aftermath, is land reform.

Contrary to opinions that still appear to be widespread among economists who are not familiar with agriculture, the family-scale farm is the most productive form into which agriculture can be organized. Evidence is plentiful, both from the United States (particularly the Midwest) and from many other countries in Europe, Asia, and elsewhere. The basic reason is that returns to size or scale in agriculture cease at rather small sizes of the firm—generally, the farm size that can absorb the labor of a farmer and his family. The contrary impression that large-scale operations are more productive comes from a confusion of the private profits of landowners with scale effects in agricultural production. The same intellectual mistake that still lingers among many advocates of large-scale capitalism today also runs through the whole history of communist agricultural collectivism, all the way back to Vladimir Lenin, who also confused profits with returns to scale in his analysis of various farm accounts.

Despite the demonstrably favorable effects of land reform on both economic and social development, such reforms are often thwarted by political forces reflecting the class interests of the large landowners and their allies. This will be explained in somewhat more detail in Chapter 7.

The positive effects of land reform have both been explained theoretically and demonstrated empirically from many applied cases, as in the Agency for International Development (AID) Review, Spring of 1970 (Dovring 1974). The literature on economic inequality gives further illustrations. Thus, a comparative analysis of South Korea, Iran, Malaysia, and the Philippines (Paukert, Skolka, and Maton 1981) found a clear relation between reduced inequality and rate of growth only in South Korea, where land reform in the early 1950s had been radical. Land reform was also far-reaching in Iran, but had occurred much more recently there, and hence less of the effect had been felt yet. Malaysia and the Philippines had seen much less in the way of land reform.

The postwar land reforms were clearly beneficial to economic growth and development in Japan and Taiwan as well. It was somewhat less so in Egypt, where the scope of land reform had been smaller (most of Egypt's agriculture was already in peasant farming).

In Latin America, important distributive reform occurred in Mexico, by installments, with the largest in the 1930s; and in Bolivia (in the 1950s). Other Latin American countries have had only piecemeal reform, or have had the process reversed (Guatemala in the 1950s, and Chile under the recent military regime). The Mexican reform led to a great surge in agricultural productivity, not only in the reform sector but also in the residual (and much reduced) private estates which now felt the need to compete for favorable attention in the country's policy-making. Halfway reform can have multiple effects. This reform did not do away with the class stratification in Mexico, which was further strengthened thereafter by continued, very rapid population growth.

Land reform also can contribute to stimulating the economy by the increased demand on the part of the peasantry for consumer goods. Some of the AID land reform reports of 1970 (see Dovring 1974) give examples of this. In Iran, some time after the reform, peasants were found to have acquired many more new clothes; this in turn benefited the Iranian textile industry, which at the time had a large excess capacity, and hence was able to expand its output merely by increasing variable costs. After land reform in Bolivia, peasant households were found to have many more household utensils, an increase in their standard of living that also should stimulate other parts of the economy. The Bolivian case also exemplifies the increase in economic opportunity that can follow from the breaking down of class barriers. Instead of the old landlords' local trade monopolies, the Bolivian countryside now had a new stratum of enterprising petty traders recruited from the ranks of the local peasantry.

URBANIZATION AND REGIONAL CONTRASTS

Does the inverted U-curve also apply separately to the development of the urban sector? A study of twenty-five countries, designed to answer this question, concluded that it did (Becker 1987). The hypothesis was confirmed, using urban per capita incomes as the measure of development.

However, there may be a special problem with very large cities. Many low-income countries have most of their urbanization concentrated in one principal city, or only a few. Egypt and Mexico are extreme examples of capital-city domination, but there are many others—for example, Turkey has been cited as having unsound urbanization due to concentration in only five large cities. Inequality within the urban sector has been found to be related to the degree of such concentration (Stewart and Lee 1986).

The causation is not hard to understand. Large cities exhibit wide ranges of location rents, as mentioned in Chapter 2. When the rent profile becomes steep, this may tend to affect the inequality of labor income as well, because high rents leave less to be distributed as wages. The attraction of major centers also tends to favor the accumulation of slum suburbs with large numbers of low-skilled and underemployed people.

Analogous contrasting conclusions also emerge from some of the regional studies of the United States. On the one hand, analysis at the state level has shown that continued economic growth and development contributed to reducing inequality in the decades from 1949 to 1969 (Grasso and Sharkansky 1980). Another study concluded, however, that rising income led to less inequality but only up to a point, after which a reversal tended to occur (Nelson 1984).

There is a similar contrast with regard to the effect of rising educational levels. There appears to be a correlation between higher per capita incomes and less inequality, which is strengthened when education levels are used as explanatory factors (Ruthenberg and Stano 1977), but the conclusion does not appear to hold at very high income levels.

We may add that the regional contrasts may have contributed to the recent reversal in the United States, in other words, the movement toward more inequality, particularly in the 1980s. The southeast region of the country has consistently had more inequality of income than the country as a whole, an apparent aftermath of the once-powerful plantation economy. Industry tended to follow the plantation type of organization (Young and Moreno 1965). The pattern has held in recent years as well, and the Southeast also has widening inequality. Since the region has received more than its share of the country's total economic growth, its wider inequality should have contributed to the widening tendency in the country as a whole. The reverse applies to the Northeast and Midwest (the Rust Belt), where inequality is less wide than in the United States as a whole, but where economic growth has also lagged somewhat behind the national trends. Only the West had (and continues to have) approximately the same level of inequality as the nation as a whole, so its more rapid growth would not of itself change the overall movement toward more inequality.

IS THE U-CURVE INEVITABLE?

The empirical material does, on the whole, support Kuznets' hypothesis of the inverted U-shaped curve in the changes of economic inequality with economic growth. Scholars differ in their interpretation even of the same facts, but on the whole, Kuznets' general hypothesis has stood the test of time as well as that of ongoing research. In general, inequality has tended to widen in early phases of economic growth and development, and then to turn around and become less wide in later phases. The turning point is somewhere in the region of low to middle incomes per capita.

This in itself does not explain the U-curve; nor did Kuznets try to explain it. In the above discussion we have looked at several of the factors that might lead to the kind of sequential changes that Kuznets sketched. Foremost are the sector proportions and their changes, prompted or delayed by economic growth and population growth. Unusually rapid economic growth can make the curve turn around earlier than would be expected, as in Taiwan. Continued rapid population growth can retard the turnaround, as in Turkey. Moving large parts of the poor population from the country to the cities, as in Latin America, can create a semblance of sector-proportions shift without a shift in the inequality curve. Several other specifics can be cited, as they were above, to show how and why a particular country differs from the regular path of inequality change.

However, such analyses explain what went on only because we accepted the national economies, as well as the world economy, as they actually existed. All this still does not explain why the U-shaped curve came about as it did, nor does it predict the future as we would want theory to do, or the trends that have already begun in the second U.S. turnaround toward increased inequality.

This dependence on actual experience, and consequent disregard of alternative possibilities, is evident in some recent writings about inequality in this country. The question has been raised about the degree of inequality that could be regarded as desirable, and as to whether the United States (in the 1970s) had not come far enough (Browning 1976). Education benefits and in-kind transfers raised the bottom quintile from 8.1

percent (1952) to 11.7 percent (1972), an improvement of 44 percent in the relative position of low-income families. A warning has been voiced against taxing the higher incomes too much. It was even stated that greater equality could increase inequality, because when teachers, for instance, get the same level of direct pay as business employees, they get the same amount of money plus more satisfaction at doing what they like most.

Such reflections appear to regard distribution as a limited good. The possibility of obtaining economic growth of a kind that might benefit the poor more than the rich has not even been approached. A little of that may be found in a study of public-sector employment in the United States (Durden and Schwarz-Miller 1982), which was found to have contributed to reducing inequality.

Some clues could come from the habitual directions of international economic relations. This aspect has received relatively little attention. One ambitious study used a cross-section of 120 different polities. (Ward 1978). The use of cross-sectional data from so many countries precluded the simultaneous use of time series from them all—there just were not sufficient data. The results pointed to some interesting connections between trade and inequality, but as yet only tentative answers, and not enough to contradict any alternative interpretations.

More light appears to be shed by an intensive comparative study of a limited number of countries with substantial time series of statistics. One OECD study focused on six countries—Costa Rica, Malaysia, Malawi, Morocco, Peru, and Taiwan (Bourgignon and Morrisson 1989). Their conclusion was that there may not be anything inevitable about the inverted U-curve. Economic policy may change that course of events under certain circumstances.

The main key lies in labor intensity. In particular, if export industries are labor-intensive (for example, small-scale agriculture), then growth with decreasing inequality may be possible, and even logical, at any stage of economic development. Small-scale industries will, of course, also fit this model. Large-scale export production may have the opposite effect. This is especially evident with plantation-type agriculture, but often appears also with large-scale manufacturing. Tourism may appear ambivalent—for example, hotels are sometimes capital-intensive.

These observations fit well with the general theory set forth in Chapter 2 as a whole. Increasing labor intensity will render common labor less abundant, and hence will increase the likelihood of its capturing as rent some of the general surplus value in the economy. Capital intensity, by contrast, not only holds down the employment opportunities of the low-income masses, but also attracts monopoly rents because of the scarcity of capital.

These observations will serve us well in the analysis of recent trends in the United States, to be discussed in Chapter 8. Before that, we shall have to turn to the general and specific consequences for society of maintaining a degree of income inequality higher than the requirements of competition between people renders necessary, to be examined in Chapter 7.

7

Consequences for Society

Differences in income and wealth influence much more than the rates of economic growth and development. They also determine the class stratification of society and the distribution of power. In our time, economic power is the main source of political power, by way of the power to control the means of public communication, among other things.

The degree of economic injustice in the distribution of income goes a long way in deciding what kind of society we will live in—and live with. Wealth and poverty greatly influence the development of people as both human beings and members of society, and their integration or isolation in relation to each other. Social classes can be defined by just income and wealth, but they are rendered more exclusive and more definitive when there are differences in background culture, national origin, or physical appearance. The class distinction between women and men—which nearly everywhere is the most pervasive discriminant both in income and in access to the things that money can buy—is the largest of all.

Many of the social or class groupings also have effects on the rates of economic growth and development, and so we shall have several occasions to refer back to Chapter 6. In extreme cases, class or group interests, narrowly understood, can be detrimental not only to society as a whole, but may also hurt even those who reap the immediate and apparent benefit from the pursuit of such limited interests. The Mafia is not the only such case. Development of the human potential, by way of education in the wide sense, and by way of access to all the society's culture, has many facets, and interacts in many ways with economic development and growth.

CLASS SOCIETY

"Two societies," mused Benjamin Disraeli, reflecting on the degree of social alienation in his England, which he wanted to improve upon by constructive conservatism. "Two societies," echoed after him Lenin, as he wandered from the elegance around the British Museum into some of the deeply degraded working-class regions of metropolitan London. Little did Lenin imagine that his own egalitarian revolution would necessitate the creation of a new upper class in party and police-state structure.

The consequences for society of wide inequalities of income and wealth are foremost in the formation and maintenance of more or less distinctive classes, with all the effects flowing from the lopsided power of the private purses. Such effects run the gamut from conspicuous consumption through manifold applications of economic and political power, which eventually threaten to replace democracy by plutocracy—government by the rich and for the rich.

The literature on class society is vast. A useful anthology of both classical and recent writings is the thick volume edited by Reinhard Bendix and Seymour Lipset ([1953] 1966). Among recent monographs focusing specifically on the United States are those by Gabriel Kolko (1962), Robin Barlow, Harvey Brazer, and James Morgan (1966), and Lee Rainwater (1974).

Wealth and poverty translate into luxury and penury in most of the world; witness many of the urban landscapes of the United States. In remote times, penury of the masses was simply the general human condition, from which the luxury of the ruling class was an exception possible only for a small minority. In the industrial age, the problem is different, since enough is produced that no one really needs to live in penury.

CONSPICUOUS CONSUMPTION

The term conspicuous consumption has been with us since Thorstein Veblen put forth his theory of the leisure class (1899). He explained that the conspicuous consumption of the rich was by no means intended only to satisfy genuine demand for luxuries among those who had the means and really appreciated the particular luxuries they consumed. To a large extent, such consumption instead has the purpose of solidifying the social position of that class. This is still evident in much of what goes on in elegant society. Riches also have the function of articulating a hierarchy, with the preeminence of the upper classes (Dugger 1987). Helping others by way of charity is sometimes also a form of conspicuous consumption, depending on how well advertised it is. The injunction of the gospel, to do good in secret, is seldom followed.

Conspicuous consumption for the sake of display is a form of social waste. It is a misdirection of resources as well, because those who need it most are those members of the ruling classes who cannot maintain their positions by natural authority—those who least deserve to be leaders. The economic effects are twofold: the neglect of some of the potential of industry, and the promotion of the production of goods that only the idle rich can appreciate.

The first of these effects comes about when the income share of the upper classes is so large that all that industry can produce cannot be consumed for lack of effective demand. To this extent, upper class luxury consumption may act as a drag on economic growth and development. There will then be less manufacturing and more personal services—direct or indirect—than would occur under a less unequal distribution of the power to consume.

The counterpart, in the penury of the masses, is in part the consequence of the direction the luxury consumption of the rich may take. One example is the recent shortage of affordable housing for low-income people because gentrification of older urban areas has caused the wrecking of some of the buildings the poor had called home, and the rate of profit in building for the rich may have left the construction industry without the means of building for the poor. A high-interest, high-rent economy would logically lead to the same result.

This example also points to the second distorting effect of conspicuous consumption: More of society's resources are directed away from the general welfare and channeled into producing things we could well do without. For example, facelifts for those who wish to continue appearing young take up resources in the medical establishment while many poor people cannot afford any health care.

The preference for upper class luxury consumption over general welfare is even more pronounced in Latin America, as we would expect from the wide economic inequalities and the moderate rates of saving in that region. Imported luxury articles often use up foreign exchange that is needed to import investment goods.

In the United States, there is relatively more inequality in *capital services*, that is, housing and consumer durables (Slesnick 1989). This falls in line with our discussion of conspicuous consumption, and helps explain why policies of income distribution have had relatively modest results.

TECHNOLOGY CHOICE FOR INVESTMENT

A high-rent, high-profit economy prefers capital-intensive investment to labor-intensive forms. Only under full employment may this kind of investment be without strong objection. Even then there may be alternatives that favor a less centralized economic structure. A preference for capital-intensive investment is at the core of the general industry bias that has done much to distort the development of low-income countries in recent decades. The case is illustrated by both the export industry and the import substitution industry (Ranis 1981).

A favorable effect of labor-intensive export industry has been noted where industry has taken that path, which does not generally occur. The prime case is Taiwan, followed by South Korea. Taiwan moved rapidly toward less economic inequality, and South Korea at least escaped the usual path of sharply widening inequality in the early phases of economic development.

The opposite case is best illustrated by import substitution industries in low-income countries, which have, for the most part, favored concentration of production. This means concentration also of high incomes and economic power, as well as high capital intensity. This is well known in Latin America, but also occurs elsewhere in the low-income countries, where government (usually controlled by the economically powerful) has often used currency management and import licensing as indirect subsidies to the importation of equipment for capital-intensive industries. This sometimes also extends to agricultural machinery being imported before it is really needed in labor-surplus agricultural systems.

The effect of such a technology choice is to strengthen the position of the rich and delay any narrowing of the general income inequality. This comes about in two interconnected ways. On the one hand, capital intensity in situations where capital is still scarce contributes to capital remaining more scarce than would be the case under a more labor-intensive production system. This maintenance of capital scarcity helps to maintain a high rate of return on what capital there is. It also, at the same time, contributes to limiting the amount of new employment, and thus to the continuation of a large surplus of low-wage labor, which logically leads to wages remaining low. A direct result of capital bias is to maintain the power positions of the rich classes.

This capital-intensive bias, pursued in the narrow interest of the rich classes, has a curious parallel in the Soviet economic system, which has been characterized by industry bias and capital bias since its early years, even in agriculture. The centralization inherent in large-scale, capital-intensive operations has facilitated the Soviet authorities' pursuit of centralized power. This has extended to agriculture, where the emphasis on heavy machines served just that purpose. It also created a cleavage between favored "mechanizator cadres" and "auxiliary hand labor." The latter group, containing more women than men, remained partly redundant, and hence low-paid and subservient.

There are parallels also in capitalist countries, and not least the United States. This is very evident in the ongoing debate about the energy sector, where oil companies and power companies join forces to play down the perspectives of less capital-intensive and less centralized energy developments in solar and biomass sources. We shall return to that topic in Chapter 9.

Nowhere has a capital bias been more harmful to the general interest of society than in low-income agriculture. The peasant farmers of the world are, in fact, by far the largest part—and maybe the majority—of all poor people in the world (Schultz 1980). Their poverty is a large part of the explanation for the very wide income inequality in the world as a whole.

To upgrade all these poor peasant people, it is not enough to industrialize each country as quickly as possible. Developing the peasants themselves is equally important, and that requires both some measure of general education and better economic opportunities (Schultz 1980). A preference for large-scale agriculture is clearly hostile to the real needs of these peasant masses who live in poverty. Land reform, giving more general direct access to land and to entrepreneurial opportunity, should be high on the agenda for agricultural development (Adelman 1975), as should *appropriate technology*, a concept that has only recently gained general attention as a main key to achieving development without deepening misery. The land reform issue has been, and still is, a central case in the antisocial use of economic power on the part of the entrenched rich classes.

PREVENTING LAND REFORM

When the ownership of land is concentrated as a static fact supported by the laws of inheritance, this economic inequality has great power to perpetuate itself unless something is done to break such oligopoly of ownership. The idea of land reform, no matter how obvious its claim to promote social justice and economic efficiency, is almost always resisted by the entrenched interests of concentrated ownership.

In many countries, the historical origin of concentrated ownership is nothing better than robbery, sanctioned by the power of the powerful. In the United States, a country of recent settlement, the problem has some extra facets because of the way the various parts of the country were turned from wilderness into a settled environment. Most of it happened in the course of the 1800s. There were two distinctive and opposing systems for transfer of the public domain into private ownership. In most of the North, and especially in the Midwest, federal domain land was turned into private property in ways that favored the creation of a system of family-scale farms; land reform ex ante, if you will. In the South, the slave-owning plantation interests succeeded in expanding their system westward all the way to Louisiana. The result was a perfect example of two societies.

After the liberation of the slaves through the Civil War, there were some departures toward creating communities of small-scale farms on the ruins of some plantations. These beginnings were wiped out after the 1870s compromise, and the South continued as a region with much wider economic inequality than the rest of the country, even in the urban sectors. From this starting point, southern politicians have used their influence to prevent land reform, both at home and abroad. They prevented reform at home in order to shore up their privileged position, and abroad to avoid embarrassing suggestions as to what might be done domestically.

In the rural United States, redistributive land reform could have done much good, both economically and socially, in two regions. One is the region of plantations inherited from the antebellum years in the Deep South. The other area is made up of the regions of irrigated agriculture in the California valleys, where large-scale agriculture has also become the norm through the illegal manipulation of access to federally subsidized irrigation water.

In the southern plantation areas, politicians have succeeded, through committee chairs in Congress, to have federal agricultural policy tailored in ways that would favor the economy of the plantation owners. Of themselves, the plantations are not particularly efficient, but the landowner incomes can be high because the ownership units are large. For instance, food stamps in recent time have been allowed to plantation workers in the winter months but were discontinued when the farming season was to begin in the spring. This amounted to a wage subsidy to the large farm holdings, which was not really to the net benefit of the workers. In this and similar ways, the large landholdings of the South have been awarded a degree of economic success that they would not have had under completely free competition with family-scale agriculture.

In the California valleys, the use of federally subsidized irrigation water is limited by law (of 1902) to 160 acres per person (or 320 acres per family). This law has been systematically disobeyed by large-scale producers, who have found ingenious ways to block enforcement, advancing arguments about the purported superiority of large-scale farming that have never been substantiated. The optimum holding size would, in fact, be much smaller than many of the present farm holdings.

The result of this dominance of large-scale farming is not only minimal economic benefit (except to the large-scale operators themselves), but also deplorable social conditions in which poverty and squalor among the people who do most of the work on these large-scale holdings contrast to the opulent life-style of the holdings' owners, who derive part of their income from federal subsidies for irrigation water (Geisler and Popper, eds. 1984).

In both these cases, self-professed conservatives usually side with the large landowners, without regard for the long-term consequences. There is an interesting parallel in the Junker estates in Prussia before 1914. The owners of these estates manipulated policy to prevent land reform, and chose to hire labor at the lowest possible wages, which increasingly meant Polish workers. Thus, their short-sighted class policy laid the groundwork for a nationality change in their homeland.

The influence on land reform abroad is another matter. In the immediate wake of World War II, the United States was instrumental in promoting redistributive land reforms in Japan, Taiwan, and South Korea. The results are generally recognized as having been highly beneficial to these countries, socially as well as economically. The recent agricultural problems in Japan are no counter-argument, for they are now the problems of an affluent country that can easily afford to solve them. Poor countries cannot as easily afford the problems stemming from a lack of land reform.

Early in the 1950s there was an abrupt change in U.S. policy toward land reform. Along with the general political, reactionary trend of McCarthyism, land reform was denounced as a red herring, which might even be suspected to be a forerunner of communist revolution, when in fact it would have been the best possible antidote against communist propaganda, as the South Korean example shows. The man who masterminded the land reforms in eastern Asia, Wolf Ladejinsky, found himself in political limbo for the rest of the decade.

The policy of the 1950s was to some extent reversed in the 1960s, but haltingly—the momentum had been lost from the land reform drives, and the resistance of large landowner interests in the United States did not soon fade away. It took almost two decades for an official turnaround to be articulated. In the Agency for International Development's Spring Review of 1970, one of the top-level administrators of the AID stated that "in the past the U.S. has been notably reluctant to become involved in any aspect of land reform and its attitude has sometimes actually prevented progress." Now, however, AID hoped to move "from apathetic neglect to benign interest and a willingness to share in the effort" (see Dovring 1974).

This retrospect statement is extremely low-key. In 1954, a legally elected government in Guatemala was overthrown, and a legally enacted land reform was kept from implementation. These political changes were actively aided by the United States, and would not have been likely to succeed without such foreign intervention. What the United States did was not only illegal under the United Nations charter, it was also shortsighted. Helping shore up the land holdings of United Fruit (one of the U.S. motivations) should never have been a major policy objective, and the company's successor not long afterward began selling out landholdings in Central America anyway, for purely economic reasons. Above all, successful land reform in Central America in the 1950s would have spared us much of the costly and demeaning policy intervention in that region in the 1980s.

U.S. attitudes had their effects elsewhere in the world, too. The Philippines, for instance, came out of World War II as a foster child of the United States, and it would not have been difficult for the latter country to have used its influence to help enact a sweeping land reform. This would, no doubt, have taken the wind out of the smoldering communist insurrection in the Philippines which to this day continues to sap the strength and to call into question the future of Philippine society.

The worst case of missing the land reform opportunity occurred in South Vietnam. The country was established as a separate polity by the Geneva truce accords of 1954. The United States was not formally a party to these accords, but became, in fact, the main sponsor of the new republic. With foreign economic aid and military advice, it would have been logical also to promote land reform—the country needed it. If there had been a radical redistributive land reform in South Vietnam in the 1950s, it stands to reason that there would never have been a Viet Cong movement in the South. No grass-roots insurgence would have been possible, and South Vietnam would now still be an independent, noncommunist country. In the 1960s, when land reform again could be discussed in the United States, the proposals were too little and too late. The aftermath of the red herring propaganda of the McCarthy years was the mistaken notion that full-scale land reform must be preceded by pilot reform and a complete cadastre—none of which was done in the early East Asian cases. These were delaying tactics, conducted because outright refusal was no longer possible. Thus the war in Vietnam was lost, with many lives snuffed out or shattered, and tremendous resources of arms and goodwill squandered, for no purpose that ordinary people could see.

All told, the large landowner interests in this country have much to answer for. The "southern syndrome" in U.S. politics is a strong case for showing that shortsighted class interests can be a destructive force of immense consequence.

EFFECTS ON POPULATION INCREASE

The old adage is that the rich get richer and the poor get children. Poverty has often been associated with large families, and *demographic transition* should be among the consequences of economic progress. How far that transition also requires social progress is a question on which opinions differ widely.

Back in the 1700s, before Malthus, most of the thinking about population in Europe concerned ways in which rulers could increase the number of subjects. More people would provide a larger and cheaper work force for the expansion of manufactures.

Preference for rapid population increase may be logical, within limits, for the maintenance of economic privileges for the few. Historically, an abundance of labor meant shortages of land and capital, and hence, high rates of rent for both. Even in our time, one may be justified in suspecting that behind some of the moralistic preaching against birth control lies a lingering preference for the case in which the children of the poor are too numerous to pose any threat to the class privileges of those with inherited wealth.

Redistribution of income, and of landed wealth, can have some effect on population increase. Just what the effect may be in the short run depends on the background culture—what the experience of the poor was just before the redistribution took place. This is why some recent research came out with ambivalent conclusions as to whether redistribution of wealth and income would decrease or increase the rate of population growth (Winegarden 1984). Redistribution seemed to lead to somewhat higher population growth rates in very poor countries, and the opposite in the richer ones. Economic growth might have a greater immediate effect on the demographic trends than redistribution.

Both conclusions may be logical. Under extreme poverty, the immediate reaction to some degree of economic relief may well be to have larger families. This also depends, of course, on how the relief is handed out. The Poor Laws in England (in the time of Malthus) paid a certain amount per head in a family, and thus encouraged large families (an unintended effect), as did the Aid to Dependent Children program in the United States in recent times. In France, the *allocations familiales* implemented after World War II were intended for (and led to) the analogous effect, relieving what had been perceived as a problem of declining population.

At a somewhat less penurious level than the Poor Laws, the supplying of modest wealth to many people might bring out a tendency not to have too large families, either because the land can only feed so many mouths (as in premodern China and Japan) or because of social competition for a display of wealth, as happened in earlier times in some areas of Europe. In between such situations, systems of limited inheritance (primogeniture, and so forth) would tend to maintain a stable population, with a reserve of unmarried people to fill the losses from such things as war and pestilence. The French *Code Civil* ruptured such a balance and set off the tendency (in the nineteenth century) to limit families to only two children.

Because of such experiences, the long-term expectancies from land reform and other economic redistribution include the possibility that they will encourage habits and life-styles leading to smaller families. The positive effect of the same kinds of reform on further economic growth should help in the same direction. By contrast, resistance against land reform also fits in with a motive to maintain high birthrates among the poor, and hence to perpetuate poverty and secure a large supply of cheap labor.

POWER TO MAINTAIN POVERTY

In order to continue paying low wages for valuable productive work, many employer classes have been known to resort to tactics that would directly prevent their workers from advancing toward more affluence and leisure.

A well-known case is from the plantation areas of the U.S. South. Landowners, in concerted action to protect their perceived class interests, would exercise their local or regional monopoly on some kinds of employment by holding their workers to purchasing life's necessities—on credit—only in stores owned or controlled by the employers. Credit practices and rates of interest on unpaid debt balances prevented many of these workers from ever getting any economic independence, no matter how thrifty their life-style. The moral weight of permanent debt could be heavy, as expressed in the statement, "I owe my soul to the company store."

Parallels range from the Prussian Junkers (in the late 1800s and early 1900s) to Brazilian plantation owners in more recent times, as well as other plantation systems in the Third World (Beckford 1972). Keeping workers on small household plots would mean they had something too valuable to abandon but too small to live on, and hence were prey to the employers' dictates.

Even in quite recent time, industrialists in the United States have been quite happy when unemployment rose to substantial enough levels to form a counterpoise against the workers' wage expectations. The effect differed according to the level of skill, however. Not surprisingly, rising unemployment has been found, in economic analysis, to lead to wider inequality of income in the United States (Blinder and Esaki 1978).

TRADE AND LABOR MOVEMENTS

The main complication of the unrestricted freedom of international trade is in the differing mobility of factors across political boundaries. Land (including mines) is immobile; only in the economic sense can it move through trade in its products. Capital is mobile without limits, but the mobility of labor is restricted by immigration laws in nearly all countries. These range from zero immigration, as in Japan and India, for instance, to a willingness to accept whatever the domestic economy can carry in the way of more people and more workers. The unspoken limitation, in all countries, is that no sovereignty will permit itself to be colonized by foreign people to the extent that the nation is no longer master of its homeland. This will inevitably hold most of the world's disadvantaged population in place, and prevent the flooding of the affluent countries with poverty-stricken millions. It is, of course, arguable that completely free international migration would mean a premium on high birthrates and a penalty on low ones.

This general background is often not mentioned when the effect of international labor movements is discussed. Much depends on how many foreign workers are admitted. In the European Community, in its days of most rapid economic growth, foreign workers were admitted precisely to the extent that this was perceived as being in the interest of the European economies. In the United States, the surreptitious toleration of illegal immigrants has, in some ill-defined way, answered the same criteria.

Economists' opinions have differed as to the effect of immigrant labor on the national economies. It seems clear, in any event, that the immigration of low-wage labor does contribute to holding down wages of domestic labor, foremost in low-skilled and semiskilled labor categories (Rivera-Batiz 1983). This, in turn, must mean higher profits to employers. To the extent that it also contributes to real economic growth, the side effects on environment and exhaustible resources are usually overlooked or disregarded in short-term analysis, either because these effects are difficult to compute or because it is considered impolite (not to say impolitic) to mention them. In a culture dominated by the economically strong, what is good for them is too often assumed to be good for the country.

Would large international population movements reduce international income inequality, even as it increases the inequality in the high-income countries? The proposition is doubtful. Relieving population pressure in the countries where it is at its highest might simply lead to higher birthrates or higher survival rates, and so leave the poor countries without any real relief.

For the high-income countries, the effects would be (and to some extent already are) more complex. A more far-reaching breakup of the existing income distribution system would also mean disruptions in the way such economies function. We shall return to this problem as it concerns the United States in Chapter 8.

EDUCATION AND OPPORTUNITY

A class society typically leads to unequal starting opportunities for individuals, which are projected into life-long inequalities. There are always some exceptions, but they do not add up to any solution of the societal problem that stems from an unequal basis. This basis, in turn, is complicated and usually magnified by unequal education reflecting the differences in economic resources available to the different economic classes in society.

An extreme and classic example is found in the British gentlemen's schools at Eton and Harrow, which used to mold the life-style of the highest elite in a sharply divided class society. In modern Britain, which has much less economic inequality, it is reported that the level of schooling accounts for only a minor part of observed income inequality (Layard and Zabalza 1979).

In the United States, social classes are supposed to be somewhat less apparent than in most of the Old World. This may be true with regard to white males, but the large lower income classifications of nonwhite males and females of all colorings, have, until recently, been every bit as distinctive as any social classes elsewhere in the world, and the problem has not disappeared.

Education and opportunity make up one of the large areas of disagreement in today's United States. The whole study of human capital formation, which attempted to show the rate of return to education, ran into the difficulty of correcting for the influence of social class on the distribution of education. Which was the more important factor for career success—the level of education received, or the family background that set the stage for the receipt of education?

There has also been a debate over the cost of public education and the inequality of schooling that follows from the family's residence in a rich or poor school district (Jencks et al. 1972). Equalization of school taxes became a constitutional problem that is, as yet, far from being solved. It appears that people who attended school in poor districts did in fact have less economic success in their lives than those from rich school districts, but the differences were believed to stem from family background as such more than from the level of school expenditures. Only project Head Start appeared to make a real difference.

Differences concerning elementary and secondary education between rich and poor school districts were not found to be very large (Jencks et al. 1972), as far as anyone could measure. However, recent news has focused on very low educational results in many schools, especially in urban slum districts. High schools graduating students who cannot even read their mother tongue do not present much of an educational advantage.

Whatever the problems of the lower schools, when it comes to attending college, inequalities caused by the families' economic situation are much larger. A large part of the youth, even in the United States, never attends college, and this is clearly related to income classes. This is important, for the payoff on a college education, over time, far exceeds its cost (Bryan and Linke, 1988). Theoretically, there should be no problem, because poor students, calculating these future payoffs, could always finance their studies by borrowing. However, conservative economists who advance this argument are overgeneralizing rather than considering individuals and their natural risk aversion.

It is a different matter to argue that some creative geniuses never had much formal schooling. This may point to some paradoxes in the workings of the formal education system, but such cases offer no solution to the general problem of economic classes as they limit opportunity.

The conclusion is that formal education has only a limited force in breaking class barriers. This is a serious problem, for it has been shown how social rigidities can have negative effects on economic dynamism (Young and Moreno 1965, with data from the U.S. states). It is not enough to establish, as some researchers have done, that income derived from inherited property represents only a minor portion of all income. This does not limit the influence of inherited property, for it often also leads to access to higher "earned" incomes, as when the heir to a firm succeeds to a position with high salary within the firm, education or no education. The heir's salary in a directorial position is labor income rather than income from inherited property, but such a classification is thoroughly misleading.

The problem is by no means limited to the United States. Even in Sweden, the quintessential welfare state of our time, it has been reported that the higher income classes have found means to close their ranks and secure a surprisingly large part of all advanced opportunities for their offspring. The emergence of an additional elite recruited from the leadership of the dominant political party in the country only renders the situation even more difficult for those not belonging to either elite, the old one or the new.

If starting income inequalities are to blame for their own perpetuation despite educational opportunities, then society may have to do something about the initial inequality if it is to derive the full benefit from its entire talent pool and its educational system. This leads us directly into racism and women's rights.

RACISM

Wage discrimination against nonwhite workers is of long standing in the United States, and far from having been overcome yet, as shown in Chapter 4. Historically, it derives from the aftermath of slavery, specifically as this was shaped by the 1870s compromise.

The relation of race to social class in the United States is complex. There may be a primary element of aversion against people who appear different, but this works out differently in countries with different cultures and socioeconomic histories. Such primary aversion will not last unless it is nurtured by other social forces, among which is class egoism.

In the South of the United States, there has, among other things, been an element of hostility against blacks on the part of the poor whites, because of the perceived favored position of black servants employed in rich white households. In the antebellum North, there was a parallel aversion to the slaves because they were suspected of reducing economic opportunities for common people among the free population. This was not without reason; white farmers in the South were, in fact, disadvantaged by the policy of public land disposal, which favored the plantations. The paradox came out in a phrase sometimes used to characterize the southern effort in the Civil War as "a poor man's fight in a rich man's war."

All these events took place a long time ago, however, and with civic equality on the books, standard economic theory would have us expect that wage differences should have disappeared by now because employers would see the advantage in hiring people according to their ability as workers. For this to happen, however, individuals need equal opportunities to develop their talents. The continuing depressing effects of a disadvantaged childhood environment prevents this (Wallace and LaMond 1977). Racial income differences thus continue to persist because of a continuing social disadvantage. The source of this disadvantage is not hard to find. For generations, a large part of the black population continued to be tied to the plantation economy of the South, with its power to perpetuate poverty.

This might not explain continuing wage differentials in other parts of the country, far from the plantation milieu, although it is true that even in the North, the black population continued to receive numerous inmigrants from the South. This was especially striking as the cotton estates began to mechanize the harvest (mainly in the 1950s), which reduced the plantations' demand for labor.

Nonetheless, wage discrimination in the North—and in the recently expanding manufactures in the South—calls for some additional explanation. It appears plausible that employers have utilized the wage discrimination as a means of reducing any incipient solidarity among their workers, and thus to hold down the entire wage level. Discrimination not only held the wages of black workers at a lower level than would have been reached in an entirely free and competitive labor market, it also held down the wages of white workers. Most white workers also received somewhat lower wages than they would have obtained without wage discrimination (Reich 1981). The opposing opinion, that white workers, and not employers, earn rent from discrimination (Cloutier 1987), appears weakly founded. The only winners have been upper income whites.

Continuing wage discrimination has also been responsible for making the black population more vulnerable to the vagaries of an entrepreneurial economy that finds it logical to abandon unprofitable plant sites without regard for the losses that the "ghost town" syndrome inflicts on people who are unable to move and take their assets with them. This erosion of private wealth does not enter the balance sheets of firms that move away, which is one of the chief objections against the claim of capitalist enterprise that it always acts in the interest of the whole economy because of equilibrium conditions. The resulting slum formation does more than ruin the value of some physical capital, however. It also ruins the many lives of those who cannot move away, and who find themselves trapped in a locality with no economic mainstay. This was found, for good reason, to be the main explanation for the occurrence of a permanent underclass, mainly of black people, in many U.S. city areas (*Chicago Tribune* staff 1986).

Lower wages for black people also have had the consequence that rich and well-to-do whites could more easily afford personal servants in their homes.

Class interest is without any doubt a major factor in maintaining black–white wage differentials in the United States.

WOMEN'S RIGHTS

The economic oppression of women by men is an old story. Its projection into the economy of the modern world has many features of anachronism. In part, the continuance of sex discrimination follows the same dynamic as that of racial discrimination.

The primary dependence of women on men has varied a good deal over both time and cultural geography. Under Islam (as in Egypt around 1950), a man could divorce a wife with a simple oral declaration in the presence of witnesses. Under Catholic Christianity, a man could not really divorce his wife at all. Either way, much depended on how property was acquired, held, and administered. English law used to hold women in particularly strict dependence because of property laws, as in John Galsworthy's novel, *The Man of Property*. In some areas, such as Sweden and northern Portugal, lengthy habitual absences of men in war or overseas ventures could convey a measure of authority to married women as acting heads of households.

Economic substance sometimes led to a degree of individual freedom. Hugo Grotius (1620s) related how, in the Netherlands, a housewife who could sell a whole ovenload of bread would acquire individual property right to the proceeds of such a sale. In Sweden of the 1700s, a few women (mainly widows) actually had the right to vote in elections for Parliament (the House of Burgesses) if they were heads of a handicraft shop, a trading house, or an inn.

The present status of women's rights is varied and complicated, and almost everywhere women have little economic equality with men (*Women, A World Report* 1985). The sometimes limited reach of law is illustrated by the Soviet Union, where two-thirds of a century under the same civil code has not eliminated the traditional differences in women's position in the Muslim versus the European areas.

In a country such as the United States, the degree of wage discrimination against women is complicated by the fact that much of it takes place by way of maintaining separate occupations that are treated as women's work. In the traditional domain of household work, the low wage expectation of women follows directly from the theory of rent, as explained in Chapter 2. When women were barred from most other occupations, their place in the market for household chores was that of labor in excess supply. Wives and female relatives were interchangeable, in a market sense, with hired labor, of which there was a surplus.

This general situation forms the backdrop to the eventual formation of special female occupations. Take the case of the telephone switchboard operators. This was a new occupation in the late 1800s, and the telephone companies soon realized they could get labor more cheaply by recruiting women. These women were so disadvantaged, generally, that they could be hired at wages well below those of male clerks. This, of course, also helped the early expansion of the telephone system. Its service could be offered somewhat more cheaply in this way, to the extent the companies felt sufficiently pressured by competition to pass on the cost savings to customers. Some of the gain, no doubt, became higher profits to capital invested in the telephone system. Society as a whole profited, but this profit was not evenly distributed. In a way similar to racial wage discrimination, the invention of special female careers also split the solidarity of workers and served the class interests of the established upper classes.

Thus it continued, from school teachers to secretaries to restaurant help. Wage scales for women were routinely set lower than those for men, and thus the same principle was long maintained also in occupations where women work alongside male workers, doing the same work for lower pay. So entrenched is this aftermath of age-old injustices that many male workers react strongly against any proposals that their wages be lowered as part of the cost of wage equalization—as if they were to be deprived of their birthright.

Recently, some chemical industries have taken the need to protect a pregnant women's fetus from chemical damage as a reason to exclude all women of child-bearing age from employment. Protecting men from genetic damage would, of course, require better worker protection, the obvious solution for women as well.

All this is not merely a matter of injustice directed against roughly half the human population and work force. At the risk of repeating ourselves, we must insist once more that discrimination because of sex or race hurts society as a whole because it deprives it of the full use of the entire potential talent pool of the population. As is often the case, the victims of discrimination are not only the obvious ones. The apparent winners in this game are also victimized, even though most of the time they are not aware of it.

The problem of domestic violence has also been discussed in this connection. Inequality of men's and women's wages may not appear to be a primary cause, but there is less violence when the family's income level is higher, so the lower incomes of women do contribute, if indirectly (Weede 1981).

PLUTOCRACY

The economy as a system of power has been studied from many viewpoints (Tool and Samuels [1980] 1989; cf. Kolko 1962). Against the public power of the purse, there is sometimes enough power within some individual (private) purse to make it an element in the system of government.

There is first of all the sheer weight of concentrated incomes and wealth, known already under conditions we now think of as rather primitive. As industrial society grew forth, monopolies and oligopolies began to be seen as threats to the whole community. More recently, we have witnessed how money influences elections, more and more openly favoring class interests through the political process. Where may all this lead us, if it is not checked in time?

Primitive power accumulation through concentrated wealth is known from many ages and countries, at least since the late Roman latifundia and right into the vast estates of many Latin American landowners in our own time. The expression "he who owns the land, owns all" is very aptly phrased. On some Brazilian estates, the landowners may own so much land that they literally own their whole local community. They have power to hire and to fire anyone, including the priest and the police force. They can prevent anyone whom they dislike from residing in their community. They really control everything.

Of course, we no longer have that kind of community in the United States. In the past, many plantations and some cattle kingdoms could wield power far in excess of what the laws of the land intended. Lingering traces, where the group influence of a handful of local landowners can throw its weight around with impunity, are not entirely reassuring merely by their small share in the total social milieu. These landowners may still ally themselves with some of the newer tendencies toward private political power because of concentrated income and wealth.

Corporate power may appear to be a separate issue; which will be discussed in Chapter 8. The matter is complicated by the fact that the corporation as such is created by law. It can be changed and disciplined by the same legislative powers that once created it. The trouble is that the corporation was, in fact, created to serve the same interests that find expression in the existing corporate structure. As money power influencing politics, the large corporations are more likely than ever to have any problems concerning their effect on society as a whole solved in their own favor. The multinational corporations are the ultimate result of this trend toward private economic power to be sovereign, and no longer subject to the discipline of democratically elected legislatures.

This brings us to the buying of elections. The phrase about "the best legislators that money can buy" is not merely a joke in bad taste. There is, unfortunately, more to it than we can comfortably accept. In case after case, elections—and especially nomination campaigns—are being won by the candidates with the largest election treasuries.

Ironically, some of the advanced thinking about government power focuses on public institutions. A true utopia would mean a minimal state (Nozick 1974). This seems to skirt the question of government through concentrated, private money power. Long before we even approach a utopia, we must ask what any degree of inequality does to society, not only by the way it acts on many of society's members, but also by the way it acts on the political process.

The drift toward plutocracy as replacing democracy has come some way in this country, now that the members of Congress belong among the 1 percent of highest income recipients. The advice of the late Senator Paul Douglas (an economist of some repute) that those who govern should not be too far removed from the conditions of those they govern is seldom repeated nowadays. Majorities in Congress have thought so little of revising the federal income tax laws that the total tax burden is now regressive: The richest people in the country pay a lesser share of their income as taxes than do the middle classes.

The fate of democracy in the world may well hinge on the outcome of the wealth–power conflict in this country. Despite a relative decline, the economy of the United States is still so large and impressive that the examples it sets carry enormous weight. The other economic leaders—Japan, Germany, and Italy—all have only a rather recent experience of democracy. In Latin America, democracy rests even more uneasily on high concentrations of wealth and economic power in only a few hands. The rest of the low-income world is even less likely to withstand a shift in the political winds.

The last chapters will focus on the inequality problem in the United States, and where it may carry us unless something is done to reverse recent trends.

8
What Is New in the United States?

The recent trend toward more inequality of income in the United States is new and is not covered by any prior experience from the history of economic development. Contrary to conservative ideological assumptions, this trend is not connected with any general improvement of the economic system; rather, it is associated with many negative tendencies in economy and society. The relations between the economy of the 1970s and 1980s and the new trend in inequality must be discussed. Moreover, means must be sought to reverse this trend, as well as many of the concomitant signs of deterioration in the social fabric.

The policy syndrome of the 1980s was based on the extreme belief in the blessings of free markets conducted without government interference. This was supposed to lead to high prosperity, the flourishing of culture, and a general rebirth of national confidence and related traditional virtues. Low taxation was assumed to lead to an increase in savings and investment.

The realities are sluggish economic growth under heavy deficit financing at the federal level, accompanied by large international trade deficits as well as large and growing informal deficits in environmental overheads. The overgrowth of speculative business was followed by large breakdowns in savings-and-loan associations, insider trading on securities markets, and junk bond financing, not to mention a dramatic increase in televised religious programs. Attempts at advancing this social Darwinism are accompanied by general confusion about values both ethical and cultural.

Some of these problems had forerunners in the 1970s or even earlier. Overuse of energy had made the economy vulnerable to oil shocks, which were worsened by locked-in positions of transportation and housing. Cultural and ethical downtrends were also under way well before 1980. The failure of the presidential administrations of the 1980s was in not recognizing the true nature of the problems. Seen at close range, much of what passes for conservatism in the United States is little more than wishful thinking. This concentration of economic power has been interpreted as harboring the danger of "friendly fascism" (Gross 1980). We are not experiencing this yet, but we could if current trends are not reversed.

The case calls for renewed analysis to uncover some of the mechanisms underlying these disquieting trends. The alternatives, both of the right and the left, may not be adequate to the problems of today and tomorrow. The question is not of regulation versus nonregulation, but of the best mix of both.

ECONOMIC GROWTH IN THE 1980s

Debate about economic growth in the last ten years has been obscured by unrealistic claims of success on the part of the incumbent presidential administrations. The claims were repeated in the campaign speeches at the Republican national convention of 1988, and are well summarized in statements originating in the Hoover Institution. The United States, we are told, saw "the greatest economic expansion in history" (Anderson 1988, p. 175), a claim variously restated in related writings (for example, Duignan and Rabusha 1988). Building further on the same kind of analysis, some recent writers have been extremely optimistic in forecasting a veritable economic boom in the 1990s (Morris 1990; Naisbitt and Aburdene 1990), even as the opening of this decade witnesses a weakening of the economy even in comparison with the 1980s. In contrast, some forecasters see economic breakdown ahead (Batra [1985] 1987), even if no such thing has yet happened.

Reality has not been one of rapid sustained economic growth. There have been bursts of more rapid growth, lasting less than a year each, but the compound rate of economic growth in the 1980s has been well below the historical record for the United States, specifically for the period since World War II. Even so, this historical record of the United States is by no means the highest in the world. For the period 1950-1985, for which we have comparable data, the world economy grew by a compound rate higher than that of the United States, even per capita, despite higher population growth rates in the world as a whole than in this country. Europe, the Middle East, and eastern Asia had rates higher than those of the United States. Latin America and even Africa had higher rates than the United States in the aggregate but not per capita, because of very high population growth rates in those regions.

This discouraging rate of growth in the United States in the 1980s took place under heavy deficit financing. Not only did the federal budget deficit grow at rates higher than ever before during peace time, the country has also begun (since the mid-1980s) to accumulate large deficits in international trade. The long-standing deficits in environmental overhead capital have been neglected to such an extent that this vaguely defined burden of debt must now be larger than ever. In net terms it is uncertain whether the country as a whole has made any progress at all during the 1980s (Dovring 1987a). Rising real income for the rich and the well-to-do has been obtained at the expense of falling real income for the lower income members of the population, who often have to live with most of the environmental degradation as well.

DEFICIT FINANCING AND GROWTH

It is elementary that one expects some growth under deficit financing. That is what happened during both world wars when the U.S. economy was propelled by large orders from the command economy of the war effort. These waves of economic expansion also meant less inequality of incomes because these periods of expansion tended to have full employment of factors, both labor and capital.

The 1980s also were marked by deficit financing of the federal budget, to a degree unparalleled in peacetime in the United States. The buildup of military strength (such as it was—there are divided opinions as to the adequacy of the effort), also led to large orders under a command economy system, but these orders were on the whole very capital-intensive, and did not lead to as much new employment as during the world wars. The all-volunteer armed forces also do not withdraw as many people from the civilian labor force as did the conscription of the two large wars. Some orders were also placed abroad, adding to the trade deficit.

Some defenders of government debt policy have contended that the deficit is not unparalleled; rather, it was proportionately even higher in the 1950s. That was in the wake of World War II, however, and was not a result of excess borrowing during peacetime. The difference compared to the 1950s is due not only to the rapid buildup of federal debt in the 1980s, but also to its combination with high real rates of interest; in the 1950s, the real rate of interest was negative (in other words, the current rate of interest was below that of inflation). Now, the high real rate of interest means that the deficit feeds on itself through the continuing high costs of debt servicing.

The trade deficit means, first of all, that some of the consumption (and the capital formation, both military and civilian) was paid for in paper money. This meant an increase in the national debt (as distinct from the federal budget debt). Such an increase in national debt in part materializes as foreign takeovers of capital assets in the United States. Another part of this dollar debt continues to float on capital markets, leading to more volatile currency markets. In both cases, the consumer economy of the United States behaves like a family that would mortgage its home in order to pay for grocery bills they could not otherwise afford. It may go on for a time, but not for any length of time.

The deficit in environmental overhead capital is more difficult to define, but it is no less significant for that sake. When these bills come due, either in higher cleanup costs later on or in debilitated resources for production, health protection, and so forth, this deficit may well turn out to be the most important of the three. Ironically, some of the bills do come due in the form of what appears as new production and additions to the standard of living. An example is bottled drinking water, replacing natural wells that have become unsuitable. The bottled water is counted as an addition to national product, but no subtraction is made for the natural water that was lost. The same illusion of increased well-being extends to many other areas, such as health care: The expenses to heal what a poisoned environment made sick are counted as income, without adjustment for the negative income represented by the poisons in soil, water, and air.

THE FREE-MARKET IDEOLOGY

The official ideology of the 1980s praises the merits of free enterprise and market forces, as standing in simple contrast to the economic failures of socialism in the Soviet Union and Eastern Europe. In its extreme form, this version of free-market ideology disregards one of the basic principles of economics: the principle of marginality, which is based on the law of variable proportions.

This law, which underlies the whole theory of economic margins, says briefly, that as factors of production are combined, there is at each juncture—in each specific situation of technology mix and factor prices—one combination of factors that is more productive than any other combination. If the combination of factors that is actually adopted in a given case differs from the most productive combination by using too much of one factor and too little of another one, the deviating combination will be less productive, no matter if the factor of which too much was used is one that in other circumstances appears the most productive. That improper amounts spoil the balance is what margin theory says in lay terms.

This actually applies not only to factors of production as they are understood in conventional economic production theory. It applies just as much to the combination of externalities that bear on the economic process. This includes the way in which the polity combines freedom and institutional order to develop an environment in which the system of economic activities may operate. Contrary to what some free-market ideologues may believe, there has never been any completely free market in the relations between people. The only perfect market that ever existed was and is that of the jungle, the wilderness void of human interference. All else is or has been modified by culture. All human societies, even the most primitive, have always been arranged in some way by ruling systems and rulers, whether theocratic, military, bureaucratic, technocratic, or plutocratic. Never has competition been completely unhampered, and neither could there ever have been any economic relations between people without some institutional rules telling them how these relations are to be handled.

The ideal of complete freedom from societal interference is, therefore, an unreal construct—a myth. Without any institutional framework, an economic system could not function at all, let alone function efficiently. Any meaningful debate about societal control versus economic freedom must, therefore, be about the factor mix of public arrangements versus individual freedoms—it cannot be about an either-or situation. It is from such a perspective that one can discuss the economic policies of the 1980s.

While it may have been found that a surfeit of public interference in the economy of the socialist countries has been bad for them, it does not follow that the best level of public interference in the economy is the least amount possible. The optimum mix is a matter of empirical observation, not of abstract theory.

Calling recent policy conservative is, at any event, misleading, for a reversion to a supposed past will not safeguard the future. Such a conservative standpoint is sometimes associated with the doctrine of social Darwinism, a theory according to which the survival of the fittest in the economic field of endeavor will improve the population of economic leaders that survives. Whatever one thinks of social Darwinism, the least its adherents could do would be to call for a removal of the more glaring of the market distortions that at present allow the economic survival of some unfit actors on the economic scene. The right of inheritance to very large fortunes certainly causes one such distortion. Discrimination by sex and race are also institutional barriers preventing natural selection at the level of economic activity and economic leadership.

Improper amounts spoil any balance also as regards economic inequality. There must be some degree of inequality that is maximally productive for the system. That this means less inequality than we usually have should be clear from the analyses in Chapter 7. Wages below the true replacement cost of labor will not maintain the social fabric. The theory that rising prosperity of the upper income classes would tend to trickle down to the poorer strata of the population has been exposed as a myth

(Arndt 1983; Treas 1983). The increase in inequality in the United States in the 1980s certainly violates the rules of economic efficiency.

TAXES AND SAVINGS

An assumption underlying the tax changes in the 1980s was that lower income taxes would bring about more savings and more investment (for example, see Regan, 1988). This result did not come about. The rate of private savings in the United States did not change much, and is still among the lowest in the world.

The 1980s tax changes were so large that the total tax burden is now regressive. The progressiveness of the federal income tax was reduced so radically that it is now more than outweighed by the regressive character of many other taxes, especially on the state and local levels. The taxes on estates and inheritance were also made lighter, even though they had long been voluntary, practically speaking (Cooper 1979).

Taxes have, in fact, never been much of a motive for rich people to work either more or less. The incentive effect is somewhat stronger on the middle class (Barlow et al., 1966). The propensity to save has been shown not to be closely related to the absolute level of income; rather, both consumption and savings are related to what is expected of people in their social context (Duesenberry 1967). There is striking evidence that the savings ratios have been different among blacks living in areas where they lack strong social interaction with whites—higher, in fact, in relation to absolute income levels. There is sometimes a "Veblen effect"; for example, in Latin America, it appears that the middle classes consume more and save less to the extent that they try to emulate the life-styles of the very rich.

The bulk of the savings are, in any case, produced by the middle classes (Venieris and Gupta 1986). It even seems that higher taxes on the rich can lead to an increase in savings.

The question of work incentives among very-high-income people is complicated. As an example, let us discuss the anecdotal instance of "Reagan's fifth movie." To support the idea that the graduated income tax stymies production, the fortieth president was quoted as making a statement to the effect that when he was a movie actor he was deterred by the tax system from making more than four movies in a year; with less taxes, he might have made more. We do not have to insist on the authenticity of this statement, or its precise wording. It is, in any event, typical of the kind of arguments that were advanced in the tax debates of the 1980s.

As stated, the proposition is in fact an excellent argument in favor of the graduated income tax, with high marginal tax rates on high incomes. The country and the world did not need five or more Reagan movies in a year, four were quite enough. Instead, after satiating its appetite for Reagan movies, the public would need movies of some other style and content: more variation in the sphere of cinematic culture. This would also have meant more of a chance for other talent, besides what was already sufficiently recognized, to make its contribution to the cultural marketplace. This would also have meant somewhat more real competition to offset the weight of the star effect of those already in the limelight. There is no reason why this would have led to the production of fewer movies, or to a lower quality in those produced.

If, on the other hand, individuals acting in several movies in a year were to go ahead and make more, taxes or no taxes, then the progressively graduated income tax would have taken away from them no more than some of the monopoly rent coming to them because of the limited room on the public stage, as explained in Chapter 2. However, it may be that those in star positions are not as tax-sensitive as the theory of the 1980s would have us believe.

From a different vantage point, an analyst connected with the International Monetary Fund found that tax policy has rather little effect on private savings (Bovenberg 1989). In conclusion, public savings would be a more dependable way of raising the savings rate in a country such as the United States. This could be accomplished through higher taxes.

INVESTMENT AND PRODUCTIVITY

The decline in private savings is not limited to the United States, it is a worldwide phenomenon. Its relation to economic growth and productivity is by no means clear. When we are told that productivity went down (or, more accurately, slowed its progress) in the United States in the 1970s and 1980s while rising (at least initially) in other industrial countries, the meaning of this statement is also not clear. A country that was a leader in new technology, with the burden of paying for innovative research and development, could hardly be expected to advance in productivity as rapidly as those countries that took advantage of technology that had already been developed by the leaders. This, however, does not account for the continued discrepancy in U.S. technological leadership and productivity in the 1980s. At that time many other countries had moved to the forefront of innovation. Apparently, the policy prevailing in the United States in the 1980s did not have the intended effect. Some reasons will be discussed in the following. It is necessary, in any event, to point out that productivity is often an ambiguous concept (Dovring 1987b). The trends about which we hear are not the only trends that could be chosen to describe what occurs in the economy. With a different conceptualization, the statistics could yield trends that are quite different from the conventional ones. Striking cases are the exclusion from conventional statistics of deteriorating overheads in physical environment and social fabric (such as illiteracy, poor health, and homelessness).

To concentrate on the economy as conventionally understood, it is certainly true that most modern industry depends somewhat less than before on conventional investments in plant and equipment and more on highly qualified labor—a form of human capital (Vatter 1982). This leads to the same conclusion that was set forth in Chapter 4: When it appears that the share of labor in the proceeds of the economy has not changed much, this masks a differentiation between very-high-paid labor (reaping some amount of monopoly rent) and the lower paid categories that now are paid even less than before, in real terms.

To judge productivity trends in a way that has meaning for the social fabric and its possible changes, we would need instead to measure productivity separately for classes of final outputs—which goods serve the rich only (or mainly), and which are serving the population at large? In other words, the productivity trends should not be read or understood independently of who benefits from them the most.

In addition, we should also watch the modifications in real productivity that follow from environment degradation. Declining environmental quality, whether reversible or not, reflects costs of production for goods and services that were not paid in full at the time these were produced and consumed—it represents real costs postponed to the future, a real deficit if there ever was one.

SOCIAL WASTE

The question of productivity—for what, and for whom?—makes necessary a presentation on the general subject of social waste, which is a large and pervasive problem in the U.S. economy, and more so than in most other countries. It is larger in the United States than elsewhere because of attitudes and trends that were established and became entrenched in not very distant times, when natural resources in North America seemed boundless (Dovring 1984b).

The matter came to public awareness through the oil price crises of 1973-1974 and 1979-1980, which both originated in events outside the United States. The phenomenon of stagflation, that is, a combination of inflation and economic stagnation, which came in the wake of both crises, was new and apparently puzzled many economists. It should not have, for the explanation is simple enough. Unlike wage-push inflation, where the inflationary force immediately translates into increased demand for ordinary consumer goods and services, oil price inflation transferred large amounts of purchasing power into rather few hands, to a large extent abroad. This led, at best, to a weak and indirect increase in the demand for what is produced in this country. In the United States the matter was made worse both by the unusually high level of energy consumption and the manner in which this part of domestic demand was tied up in a multiple lock-in system encompassing transportation and urban design, especially in widely sprawling residential areas. Tax subsidies have long favored the building of more one-family dwellings, often on large lots. Urban sprawl boosted the market for automobiles, and often for more than one per family. This, in turn, caused mass transportation to dwindle away, and it could not be easily restored when the need arose.

This lock-in system rendered a direct response to the oil price changes difficult, especially in the short run—which is what market forces usually look to, expecting the longer run to be cared for by public policy, which in this case turned out halting and indecisive. There have been gains in energy efficiency in engine performance and household operation, but the vast fixed investments in housing inventory and urban overhead fixtures have not changed much. We are still stuck with the transportation concepts that were laid down when domestic oil was plentiful and cheap, and mass transit is as inadequate as ever.

The built-in social waste in transportation and housing has parallels in many other parts of the U.S. economy—from the food complex, with its emphasis on white bread and "beef as food for real people"; to the education systems, with their overemphasis on classroom sitting and spoon-feeding of boring materials; and the health system, which excels in advanced technology that turns out to be too expensive for most people; and there are many other instances as well. At the extreme, the drug enforcement system keeps emphasizing police action and building more prisons even though this does not reduce the problem, and instead strengthens the hand of organized crime (Sterling 1990).

Through all the cases of systemic social waste in the United States runs a common thread that leads us to a very disturbing conclusion: Waste is good for profit because it increases scarcity. Thrift and careful economizing lead to less demand, and hence, depressed business conditions. This is the real skeleton in the closet of capitalism, especially in the United States. It goes a long way to explain the seeming difficulty of writing a complete economic theory of capitalist production and growth, a difficulty that has been acknowledged repeatedly by economists from C. A. Pigou, John Maynard Keynes, and Joseph Schumpeter to rather recent analysts (Harris 1978).

This also goes some way to explain the recent trend toward more inequality in the United States: High profits through social waste are best realized in capital-intensive and expertise-intensive activities with opportunities for oligopolistic restrictions on competition. Characteristic has been the reaction from within the energy industries to the prospect of solar energy: "Nobody owns the sun." No excess profits are to be expected there, there is only rent based on the land where solar-derived energy is to be produced. This kind of energy industry promises to be more small-scale and decentralized, and thus not to convey the kind of economic power associated with the petroleum complex or the conventional or nuclear power stations.

OVEREMPHASIS ON MONEY RETURNS

One of the striking tendencies of the 1980s has been a stepping up of business mergers, often through hostile takeovers. It may be true that the root cause of this disturbance in the business world was in an accumulation of inefficiencies in many of the firms that were taken over or went under (Segal 1989). Nonetheless, it is acknowledged that many takeovers have been destructive because of their extreme emphasis on high returns to capital at the expense of other stakeholders, namely the personnel and the community (Bennett 1990). Other analysts have pointed to the lack of personal loyalty: the recent absence or destruction of so-called corporate culture in most large business firms (Miller 1989; cf. Heller 1989). Followers of the new "lean and mean" business style simply got rid of whomever was no longer needed to maximize profits—the employees might go on to meager pensions or welfare, even as departing chief executives were rewarded for their inefficiency with generous "golden parachutes."

Emphasis on money income was not always as extreme as in the 1980s. There were also in the United States built-in moral reserves of people who wanted to do a good job to justify themselves. This basic fiber becomes weaker when net return, the bottom line, is all that counts. A disturbing symptom of the same trend is in the rising tide of gambling industries, from greyhound racing and television contests to the misnamed Taj Mahal complex in Atlantic City.

All this manipulation of money makes little of what it really means to hold a job. Time was when toiling in a sweatshop or on an assembly line was an affliction to wish oneself rid of, and such conditions still exist in a few places. Generally, however, in today's industrial and business world it is different. A job of forty hours (or less) per week means more than just a paycheck. It also entails human dignity, social context, and entertainment. Forced early retirement cuts out more than money, and easily leads to demoralization.

The power of money over purpose can be illustrated in many corners of society. A strong instance appears to be the medical research establishment with its obvious emphasis on the most expensive research techniques. The "cancer industry" continues to consume hugh amounts of resources with little to show for it (Moss 1989). Preventive medicine does not seem to gain as much attention as spectacular cures that few can afford.

Writers on the problems of U.S. industry point to firms that are "in search of excellence" (Peters and Waterman 1982), but these seem to be exceptions; most firms appear passive (Waterman 1987). The tendency in most corporations, even in the 1980s, seems to be to value both machines and depreciation of capital more highly than people (Bennett 1990). The lack of corporate culture is deplored repeatedly in the literature. The takeovers, hostile or otherwise, have increasingly been accomplished by people who have never produced any real goods or services—their whole life lies in manipulating assets created by others. The management experts often conclude that a move toward smaller firms would be healthy in many cases.

INDUSTRIAL POLICY AND PROTECTIONISM

Among the tenets of U.S. official policy in the 1980s has been the dictum that the public powers should stay away from any positive industrial policy. What to produce in the country is supposed to sort itself out in the course of international competition under theoretically free world trade.

This proposition concerning industrial policy is just as theoretical as its premise in free world trade. In the world as it now exists, international trade is far from being free. Nations look after their separate interests as they see them. There is a welter of specific trade measures adding up to a considerable degree of protectionism. Even the United States engages in some protectionism—for example, domestically made broom-corn brooms are protected against competition with brooms made in Mexico.

On a much larger scale, many nations engage in positive industrial policy, either to build up infant industries or to achieve superior competitiveness in one line of production or another. This struggle for international markets has been characterized as a "silent war" (Magaziner and Patinkin 1989). The contest is waged by a variety of means: taking advantage of lower labor costs (Singapore as "Silicon Island," Chapter 2), by more sophisticated machines (West Germany, Chapter 4), by new and more humane forms of industrial organization leading to less recall of defective products (Sweden's Volvo, Chapter 5), or by new energy development (Japan is in the forefront in developing solar electricity, Chapter 7). A few U.S. examples can be cited as pointing in similar directions (Chapter 3, 6, and 9), but they are admittedly exceptions in this country.

A major theme in international competition is comparative costs. Low wages in low-income countries are sometimes decisive in firms moving production abroad to where the cheap labor is, or in employing foreign labor in the United States; witness the uncertain policy in regard to illegal aliens. To some extent, such foreign competition leads to (and recently has led to) lower wages in U.S. industry. There are limits to this, however. Take the much debated case of automobiles being assembled in Korea. Why cannot U.S. workers work for the kind of wages the Koreans receive? The answer is that then they could not afford the house and the car that are now so much a standard part of life in the United States because of the lock-in of transportation and city layout. In the absence of paying workers wages sufficient to buy and hold these expensive amenities, both auto manufacturing and housing construction would find themselves in a slump. Thus, the very structure of U.S. society militates against full equalization of wages across international boundaries.

In a wide sense, economic protection, whether directly by tariffs and quotas or indirectly by positive industrial policy, is a question of which countries' workers are admitted to employment, in what activities and at what wages. The ultimate consequence of free world trade would be to allow free movement of labor between countries. But this is not national policy in any country. Some countries have frankly zero immigration quotas (for example, Japan and India). Others are more or less restrictive, depending on what they perceive to be their needs. The large influx of foreign workers in western Europe in the 1960s was not free movement of labor; it was allowed strictly according to the need for extra labor at the time. Many of these foreigners have since been repatriated. The European experience with foreign labor includes the observation that having more than 10 percent foreigners in a locality or area tends to be disruptive to community life.

The United States also has immigration quotas, which are frequently violated by illegal entrants. Many of the illegal residents are employed at wages lower than anyone else in this country would accept. Under extreme business freedom, many employers might prefer to have more foreign workers. This could increase profits at the same time as income inequality became wider, and there would be downward pressure on wages. Some economists even would encourage more importation of low-wage labor, on the grounds that these workers by their presence and their low-wage work contribute to the national product. This is, of course, only the national product as conventionally understood and measured. No allowance is then made for damage to the environment (a deficit in informal capital account), nor for the fact that labor would be used without paying the full cost of producing and maintaining it (health, schooling, and so forth).

If borders were really open, a country such as the United States would be flooded with low-income workers. Income inequality in this country could then widen to something close to the inequality in the world as a whole (see Chapter 5). The entire world would not become measurably less unequal for that sake, as low-income countries would lose some of their recent motivation for trying to control the birthrate and the rate of population increase.

UNEMPLOYMENT AND UNDEREMPLOYMENT

The nearly full employment during the two world wars was, without doubt, important in reducing income inequality. It is plausible, according to the general rent theory set out in Chapter 2, that nearly full employment would in general have some equalizing effect, even in peacetime.

In the 1980s, we have become accustomed to regard 5-6 percent unemployment (of the registered labor force) as full employment. This evidently sets our sights low and accepts the fact that there should be less scarcity rent to labor. Sometimes the 5-6 percent level is defended on the grounds that many families have more than one member in the labor force, and hence, unemployment of one family member does not mean a total absence of earned income. This focuses on welfare only, in the narrow sense of income for the days' immediate needs. It does not regard the effects on the unemployed, nor does it regard the effects on society.

The figure of 5-6 percent unemployment is misleading, however, for several reasons. One important fact is that partial employment—or partial unemployment, as we might well call it—is now much more frequent than before. This means that in full-time worker equivalents, employment is substantially less than the 5-6 percent figure suggests. Further, there are the "discouraged workers" who no longer are included in the labor force (which is the total from which 5-6 percent are reported as unemployed). Discouraged workers typically are more numerous when official unemployment is high. If they were included in the labor force, unemployment would be higher for this reason also. Finally, it is doubtful whether we really should count as fully employed those who work for wages that are below what is needed to produce, maintain, and reproduce the same kind of workers. Those working at substandard wages should be counted as underemployed.

We must conclude that the U.S. economy now has a serious problem of chronic unemployment and underemployment. This is linked to the deterioration of health care and schooling for the same people who are disadvantaged in the workplace. This points to the danger of increasing class cleavages in U.S. society.

CLASS SOCIETY

Class in the United States has long been under scrutiny (Schumpeter 1951). In this country, class is relative, depending on money, job, education, social identity, and life-style (Coleman and Rainwater 1978). There have in general been no castes, yet ethnicity has a role that sometimes approaches that of caste status. Although blacks have made progress toward less inequality, both economic growth and federal subsidies have proven inadequate to close the gap anytime soon (Thurow 1970). The differences caused by color discrimination are acknowledged also by writers who emphasize the social fluidity in the United States (Duncan et al. 1984, ch. 5).

Now, however, the differences are widening, not only in money income but in many other respects, too. The number of homeless people is under dispute, but it is undeniable that their number has increased in recent time and increasingly includes families with small children. As much as a third of the population has been estimated to have substandard literacy, which often continues through the generations (Kozol 1985). Somewhere in the range of 30 to 40 million Americans can not afford regular medical care, at the same time as luxury care (such as face-lifts) takes up an increasing part of all medical capacity in the country.

Some writers have singled out labor unions in the United States as sources of a class cleavage within the ranks of wage workers (Pettengill 1980). Others have even concluded that unions make the country poorer than it would be without them (Reynolds 1987). In both cases, the unions are studied simply within the context of U.S. society as it currently functions, including the fact that labor unions are now a minor, and a declining, factor in the country's life. Experience from countries (for example, in Europe) where unions are more important than in the United States would lead to more positive conclusions. Business analysts searching for answers to more general questions of industrial decay and renovation sometimes also show a more positive attitude toward labor unions, as long as they contribute to strengthening the community context of business (Waterman 1987).

CULTURAL CRISIS

The most obvious sign of a cultural crisis in the United States is the disarray in education. Early in the 1980s, the President declared that because of this problem, the United States was "a nation at risk." Nothing has happened since then to indicate that the country is any less at risk in 1991. Not only are total illiterates proportionately more numerous in this country than in other advanced countries, the people who are not fully literate are even more numerous, as mentioned above. Grade inflation in the schools and many colleges tends to gloss over some of the problem. When some high school graduates cannot even read their own diplomas, this attracts media attention. When it is routine that college undergraduates cannot spell their own mother tongue, however, this is taken in stride.

Neither is there much in sight that could let us expect any improvement in the near future. Most of the debate turns around school budgets: If there were more money, the schools could provide programs in some additional subject. There is very little attention to the problem of whether the entire school system may be on the wrong track by trying to enforce standard curricula rather than fostering a will to learn. Curiosity, that original wellspring of active minds, is being dulled by a surfeit of obtrusive information over television and other public media, which leads logically to a closing of minds. If there is any serious attempt at innovation in education (other than "unschooling" at home), not much of it is being heard over the din of the superactive marketplace.

A retreat from too much teaching to allow more learning is not in the interest of the teaching establishment. There can be more economic success in pushing for higher salaries when it appears that teachers are a scarce factor in the economy.

With this basic cultural problem, it comes as a surprise to find some of the more extreme advocates of the 1980s economic policies declaring that modern capitalism is highly creative also in the arts and other forms of high culture (Anderson 1988). This cannot refer to scientific research that is mainly funded by the public powers, both federal and state. We have also been told recently that one of the "megatrends" in the United States for the 1990s will be a cultural renaissance (Naisbitt and Aburdene 1990).

Concerning the creative arts, we have the word of former president Reagan that he found the quality of television fare deplorably low. No one contemplating the soap operas and all the other garbage offered as entertainment sandwiched between bouts of advertising that fill most of the television broadcasts could possibly detect much creative influence from capitalism as it functions here and now. In the case of the authors writing about megatrends, there is a confusion of medium and message, and of quantity with quality. What they refer to as cultural renaissance is really mass merchandising of media, including videocassette recorders and other advanced paraphernalia for "home entertainment centers." For content, there is widespread scavenging of museums, archives, and classical literature for motives that the present cultural scene appears unable to produce by itself. There may be a hunger for art, but not much new to satisfy it.

To the contrary, the "lean and mean" marketplace of the 1980s has not been very kind to cultural institutions. A clear instance is the defeat of the United Press International, which now holds only a fraction of its once important position (Gordon and Cohen 1990), while the Associated Press continues to thrive because it is a cooperative, with no budget problems because the member newspapers always fill any deficit. In the same vein, competition for the music market does not appear to emphasize cultural quality, but rather something quite different (Eliot 1989).

ENVIRONMENT

We have insisted on this fact already: The physical environment must be included in any realistic balance sheet of economic change. It is quite plausible that the poisoning of air, water, and soil has increased to a degree that outweighs any progress made per capita in conventional terms during the last decade. The record of cleaning up toxic waste dumps (both legal and illegal) has been miserable. Even the more conventional "war on waste," that is, the everyday garbage problem, is far from having any guaranteed long-term solution (Blumberg and Gottlieb 1989). Replacing landfills with incineration seems to replace one problem with another. Making peace with the planet is no small task for the future (Commoner [1975], 1990). One complication is that the poisons and the misery of pollution often weigh more heavily on the low-income part of the population. The rich have many opportunities to escape the same things—Palm Springs (California) always enjoys clean air, and there are no toxic dumps anywhere near it. For this reason, the degree of inequality is in real terms wider than the statistics admit, and the trend toward more inequality is also understated.

Environment is more than ambient chemistry, however. Quality of life in slum tenements is lower than the rental price would have us assume. The unceasing assault of technology and the ever-present media also becomes more oppressive on those with the least access to expensive escape routes.

Environment also includes the direct impact of technology on innocent lives, often before the danger has had time to be acknowledged. Technological progress is in fact two-faced: Technology wounds many people. This includes a great deal of illness caused by poisonous articles of consumption as well as by medicines released without sufficient foresight (Glendinning 1990). Looking for statistics on this problem, Chellis Glendinning found few; apparently, there is not much will to know. Some quantity indications were supplied by associations of victims, such as the victims of asbestos, radiation, and the Dalkon shield intrauterine device. Even in these cases, industry and government alike resisted investigation and publicity as long as they could. These delaying tactics actually increased the incidence of specific dangers and suffering. Again, national product is overestimated: The harmful products were additions to national product in their time, and the costs of belated remedies are also added to gross national product (GNP) as benefits rather than being subtracted as costs. Ironically, the expenses to be met by industry and government were reduced by these delays, because many of the victims died before they could receive any compensation.

Albert Einstein is cited as having said, long ago, that technological progress is like an axe in the hands of a pathological criminal. It should be time for us to sober up and appraise each step of alleged progress in its wider context rather than just cashing in on the immediate apparent benefits.

The economic theory of the "invisible hand" does not apply here, for the sellers of dangerous goods do not have enough will to apply adequate restraint, and buyers are often far from having the very considerable expertise to judge for themselves. The case of hexachlorophene comes to mind: In the early 1960s, some manufacturer bragged about including this supposedly beneficial ingredient in its product. After a few years' silence, however, another manufacturer began praising itself for *not* including this harmful ingredient. How many consumers would know enough chemistry to appraise hexachlorophene for what it may be worth? Adam Smith never faced this kind of problem. Nonetheless, both black lung and brown lung were rampant during his time if not yet widely acknowledged.

Above all this hangs the vague and widespread problem of technology fatigue: How much stagnation depends on the limits of human beings, and how much change can individuals survive in one lifetime? Some of the cultural crisis may depend on this aspect of the human factor in production.

This again puts population growth into more serious perspective (Ehrlich and Ehrlich 1990). Feeding the poor of the world is not sufficient if in so doing we must use methods of production that place the whole planet at risk and expose people to more stress than they can take. Accepting more immigrants, or agreeing to place more of the production abroad, we would merely substitute short-term solutions for the long-term ones which, finally, we cannot escape.

9

To Turn the Trends

The detailing of national problems in the previous chapter is long. The reason for presenting all of them here is that they all converge into the same syndrome that causes economic inequality to worsen. Not only are the rich getting richer, but the poor are actually getting poorer in any realistic sense, and so will the United States if recent trends cannot be reversed.

Looking for remedies, we are often countered by conventional estimates that purport to show that little can be done; for instance, that we might not be able to afford much more equality than was at hand in the 1970s (Browning 1976), or that there is some inescapable tradeoff between equality and efficiency (Okun 1975). Attempts at fighting poverty in the past have been found to backfire: The poor may even have lost ground (Murray 1984). Such criticism may have merit, but only if we accept that the economic system is essentially as it ought to be. If that is the premise, then the system will, of course, continue to produce the same consequences it has already produced so abundantly.

SYSTEMIC SOLUTIONS

This goes to show that if we want important changes, the problems must be approached in some systemic way, and not just piecemeal. Correcting what is wrong looks simple on paper (John Silber 1989). However, it cannot really be done by going back to where we were some time ago, when the problems seemed less pressing. Doing this, we would just start the same decay process over again.

Recognizing that the United States is suffering from a surfeit of free enterprise and not enough community care, we can first state the problem in terms of margin theory: improper amounts spoil the balance. In some way, the United States needs a fresh start, which the political parties do not yet seem prepared to formulate. Some analysts have called for an economic Bill of Rights (Carnoy, Shearer, and Rumbecker 1983). Public policy needs to focus on the common good (Daly and Cobb, 1989). This new emphasis must be attentive to the means, and not only the goals (Harrington 1989), and here we find an apparent dilemma.

The dilemma is this: We need to find means of controlling the excesses of private enterprise and the snowballing of private economic power, but we must also face some new realities which include the tendency for industrial technology and marketing techniques to become so complex that public interference with the details of business is in many ways hopeless (Drucker 1989). This, no doubt, has contributed to the defeat of state socialism in the communist countries. Both technology and industrial organization were so much simpler in Stalin's time that a semblance of rationality could be maintained, and the absurdities of centralized control had not yet become as apparent as they are now. When that happens to the as-yet relatively backward countries now emerging from the East Bloc, then a fortiori, any attempt at detailed regulation of business in the advanced countries must become even more absurd.

The dilemma is only apparent. It is true that the solution already attempted in some kinds of enterprise, to privatize public functions, is a mixed success at best (Donahue 1989). More important is a caveat also voiced by the analyst of new realities: Environmental overheads and multinational firms pose problems not solved by the free enterprise system (Drucker 1989). There is, however, another approach to overall problems, which is seemingly more remote from any direct interference but potentially more effective.

REMOTE CONTROLS

To use a medical analogy, we need less surgery in the economy and more of the kinds of treatments that promote general health. We need to apply the analogy of hormones rather than scalpels, inducements more than prohibitions.

The economic prototype of this kind of control is the Federal Reserve System. By fine-tuning interest rates and the money supply, the "Fed" sends pervasive signals through the entire economic system. The "Fed" makes itself obeyed without looking into the balance sheet of any one firm, and without arresting any single culprit. Markets continue to function within the parameters set by monetary policy. On this level, the economy of the United States is more thoroughly controlled than could be done by any other means.

Other means of the same general type are in tax policy, in active industrial policy, and on the part of the Federal government taking on the role as employer of last resort and educator of last resort. In their several ways, these kinds of policy can set other parameters—of money left as private power, of opportunities to enter the market place and remain there, and of the supply of workers at various levels of competence and wage expectations.

TAX POLICY

Taxation has been touched upon repeatedly in the previous chapters. There is no doubt that the inequality of spendable income, and of income as a source of power, could be reduced by the progressive income tax (Moyes 1988; Theil 1988). A tax-based incomes policy could be used to considerable effect (Alexander 1989). Even a value-added tax could be used to increase distributive justice as well as allocative efficiency, as shown by the experience of West Germany (Kaiser and Spahn 1989).

There is also a strong case for increasing the inheritance taxes (see Brittain 1978; Tomes 1981; Ioannides 1986). The usual counter argument that there are too many loopholes is just an excuse, and not a serious policy argument.

It has also been argued that only about 10 percent of the incomes of rich people are derived from inherited wealth. This is viewing the situation too narrowly. Apart from the income derived from inherited wealth directly, such wealth also conveys the possibility of the continued large accumulation of new wealth from this kind of income, and even more from high-income employment in owned firms, which is easily within the grasp of heirs to large wealth, whether they are highly competent or not. In total, incomes of rich people depend on inherited wealth much more than it would appear on the surface.

There would probably have to be some considerable tax-free amount on the magnitude of what is normally invested in a family-scale firm, such as a substantial farm without a large number of hired workers. The real target of a greatly increased inheritance tax should be accumulations of wealth that are so large that the heirs tend to become permanently removed from the conditions of people in general.

A study of the ultra rich (Packard 1989) showed such heirs to be, on the whole, rather unhappy people, because they never had a chance to test what they would be worth in honest competition. Rich parents have so many other ways of helping their offspring to an unfairly good start in life that continuing such class support indefinitely is not in anyone's real interest. A greatly increased tax on very large inheritances would no doubt increase donations for cultural and humanitarian purposes, and this would be all to the good provided there could be safeguards against using such donations as a disguise for political action committees or family welfare trusts. Breaking the tendency toward unsound concentration of private economic power is more important here than the amounts of tax revenues to be secured in this manner.

POSITIVE INDUSTRIAL POLICY

Such policies have worked well in other advanced countries and are likely to continue to do so. No policy favoring international free trade is likely to change the situation. For instance, the German "economic miracle" of the 1950s and 1960s was not a case of pure, unfettered capitalist free enterprise. It was, explicitly, "guided market economy" (*gelenkte Marktwirtschaft*) according to Ludwig Erhard, the economics minister in West Germany in those years.

For the United States, positive industrial policy could reap large benefits, and indirectly could also benefit the world by the more positive influence that the U.S. economy could then exercise. The purpose should be, in general, to foster growth of production in directions deemed desirable for reasons of economic as well as environmental health. These activities would be on or ahead of the competitive frontiers of the world. In promoting economic growth generally, this would also draw more completely on the country's total resources, including labor that is now unemployed, underemployed, or discouraged. Specifically, positive industrial policy is more likely than desultory competition to remove some of the unfair advantages now taken by many foreign firms. Positive industrial policy is also likely to be the best means of tackling the two general problems to which Peter Drucker pointed as not well suited for the ordinary competition between firms, namely, the problem of overhead environment damage and the economic anarchy represented by multinational corporations.

Let us take the simple instance of substitution for a product we do not want to import. A number of years ago, when the sperm whale was declared an endangered species, the U.S. government placed an import ban on sperm whale products. The automobile industry objected that sperm whale oil was indispensable as an engine lubricant. Then, the U.S. Department of Agriculture (USDA) came up with not one but three substitutes from plants growing and thriving in this country. If the U.S. government had sided with the whalers instead of the whales, it could have told the USDA to keep quiet about the findings. That would have been shortsighted, and would have only postponed the matter. In this case, foresight had the upper hand, "Moby Dick's" species continues to live, and some U.S. farmers got a modest addition to their incomes.

The example is telling: Circumvention of the law by black-market trading was avoided by sound new substitutes. Substitutes do not have to be fully competitive. As long as the price difference is minor, legal trade will prevail. Black-market merchants have to charge higher prices to cover their higher costs of transaction, including the higher risk they incur.

There will be many analogies in cases where foreign suppliers violate environmental protection to undersell their competition. Prohibitions and tariffs are imperfect tools; substitute products are much better tools of enforcement. The same applies when foreign manufacturers are competitive only by extreme disregard of the welfare of the workers. In such cases we may also well seek remedy by fostering substitute products. Once in place through positive industrial policy, such products may very well become competitive in a few years. This may sound like protectionism, and in a way it is: protection of the environment at home directly, and in the world at large indirectly.

Neither would this kind of policy have to mean any serious violation of the economics of comparative advantage. We must understand that in classical theory, comparative advantage dealt a great deal with natural resources, or with climate-bound products, while technology was slow-moving and difficult to transfer across cultural boundaries. Now the situation is quite different. Most comparative advantage now is in manufacturing and based on superior technology. Such advantage is much less durable than advantages based on geography. Industrial technologies are, on the whole, site-neutral and easily transferred. In most modern lines of manufacturing, existing comparative advantages can be overcome by research and development in five to ten years—and, by simple technology transfer, even faster.

Industrial policy in a country such as the United States will, therefore, mean very little in the way of taking advantage of other countries. Overwhelmingly it will mean that the country will resume its leadership role in the world. Not only will the nation itself become richer for such a policy, its ability to help others will also be greater. U.S. foreign aid in recent years has been nothing to brag about, while the countries that do use positive industrial policy have had much more to contribute to the world.

In the way discussed above, industrial policy will also make it easier to protect and improve the incomes of the poor in this country. There will be more real income to share, and with less unemployment, labor will again be able to claim a larger share of the rent in the economy.

Such a policy could also be used to favor and protect small-scale business whenever such business is, in fact, more efficient than the large corporations with their superior economic muscle (which does not have to mean superior economic efficiency). This refers particularly to agriculture. We may not have to go to direct land reform—expropriation of large estates may not even be needed to steer more of the production into family-scale enterprise. It would be sufficient to remove the unfair competitive advantage now conferred upon some "green giants" by federally subsidized irrigation water, or on the remaining southern plantations by manipulating subsidies, for example, by giving out food stamps in the off season only. Another case of desirable small-scale or moderate-scale production may be in the energy industries of the future, contrasting with the extreme concentration of the oil complex at present. A biomass-based methanol industry to replace petroleum fuels in moving vehicles would be likely to be spread out in numerous small plants scattered all over the rural United States (Dovring 1988). Obtaining new energy sources within the country would, of course, also be part of the answer to the "Persian Gulf syndrome" so much in evidence in late 1990 and early 1991. Military costs, and associated stresses on the economy, are not included in the price of gasoline in this country, so the cost advantage of petroleum is not as great as it seems, and it is certain to dwindle in years to come. Energy should be a prime case for positive industrial policy in the United States.

Positive industrial policy can be important also for changing the product mix in the economy, thus making it more beneficial for the whole population. A good example is in the medical complex. It is logical that the national government should have a say in the direction of medical research, for the research funds come from the federal government to a large extent. The experts—the researchers—are experts only on means, but not on ends. They must be for the political powers to decide. For the direct users of funds, the temptation is too great to use them in a way that entails social waste, for that, as we have seen, is what leads to the largest paychecks, especially on high levels of decision making and income.

FULL EMPLOYMENT, FULL EDUCATION

The problem of chronic poverty is being attacked with more vigor in many other countries than in the United States. Several of the low-income countries have made significant gains in reducing poverty, among other things, by making the poor productive through unconventional means, using techniques that evade the usual traps of conventional market mechanisms (*Finance and Development*, September 1990). There is no reason why the richest country in the world could not be even more effective in cleaning up its chronic problems of permanent underclass, widespread underemployment, and illiteracy.

The federal government could do much to improve the nation's socio-economic health by taking on a policy of nearly full employment and by acting as employer of last resort, and educator of last resort.

Public works, which could employ many of the unemployed, are urgently needed to upgrade decaying parts of the infrastructure network, and especially the transportation system. Road beds, rail beds, bridges, and many other objects of overhead capital must be improved before we have a general crisis in their performance. Recent military requirements should have brought that point home, if nothing else has.

Another, and potentially an even larger area, of public works employment is in restoring the quality of the physical environment. In particular, the many toxic dumpsites and the increasingly difficult problems of garbage disposal, call for large efforts, some of which are likely to be labor-intensive. By degrading the environment, we have for many years enjoyed goods for which the real cost of production and distribution was not paid in full at the time of purchase. Paying off this deficit in environmental overhead capital is clearly a task that the national government must take in hand, since no one else appears able and willing to do so.

The country needs a Department of Environmental Defense, which is now no less necessary than the military Department of Defense. There is a great deal to be done before the accumulating deficit in environmental overhead capital has been paid off. The record of the 1980s in clearing up the toxic dumps has been miserable—by all accounts, the problem is now larger than it was in 1980, in part because some of the wastes were only shifted from one site to another one. The incipient habit of shipping out toxic sludge to foreign countries must, of course, be stopped short once and for all—in this regard, the planet is indivisible.

These public works should be able to absorb the surplus labor of the unemployed, part employed, underemployed, and discouraged workers. This is not to say whether such works should be handled directly by federal agencies or "farmed out" through privatization. The main thing is that the federal government initiate the actions, underwrite their net costs (there will be some income by recovering squandered scarce materials), and supervise that the work is done as intended so that funds are not misused. It is entirely appropriate that funds for such purposes be generated by higher income taxes on very high incomes and higher taxes on very large inheritances.

To counter the risk of competing too directly with the regular labor market of private business, and to secure competent workers from the ranks of the unemployed (in the wide sense), many of the workers will need remedial education, both primary and secondary. Here the federal government (again, perhaps, through a Department of Environmental Defense) should act as the educator of last resort, giving the unemployed, where needed, the skills they must have in these public works jobs. This again would be analogous to the Department of Defense (DoD), which often hires as recruits men and women who are not yet educated enough to receive the appropriate military training. The DoD acts as a remedial educator. Unfortunately, it appears that the General Accounting Office (GAO) insists that the recruits receive only training in the narrow technical sense, and not basic education. This is unfortunate, because these men and women will not remain soldiers forever. Sooner or later they will return to civilian life and, lacking basic civilian schooling, they will not be fully equipped as citizens in a democracy. The GAO policy in regard to military recruits should certainly be reversed. For the purpose of employing undereducated individuals in public works programs, it is equally necessary that they receive basic schooling, and not merely the kind of training needed on the specific jobs. The purpose is to prepare them to become members of the regular work force, and not permanent public works employees. The task of such remedial education is large, and apparently no one in the country is prepared to undertake it, except for various piecemeal efforts. Such piecemeal efforts, where they occur, should not be duplicated, but rather supplemented.

TOWARD LESS INEQUALITY

Full employment and vigorous industrial expansion should of themselves lead to less inequality. We have the lessons from Kuznets' inverted U-curve, which promised less inequality as an industrial economy matures (see chapters 5 and 6). Rising employment and an increasing abundance of ordinary consumer goods and services should render the rent profile less steep and thus allow more of the surplus product of society to become wages for the lower income classes. That this logic of economic development was reversed in the United States in recent times can only be read as a sign of decay in an aging economic system. The proposals set forth in this chapter—or some sensible analogy—should again set us on the path that is the logical outcome of economic development, toward less inequality.

To visualize what we are talking about, the reader may want to refer back to the tables in Chapter 3, especially Table 3.2. Recently, earned income of individuals (the incentive aspect of inequality) in this country has fallen to where the ratio of median to average is close to .70:1.00. At that level of inequality, the upper half of the population gets five-sixths of all the income, while the upper one-tenth of the population receives about sixty times as much as the lowest one-tenth. Between households (the welfare aspect of inequality), inequality is somewhat less; the median/average ratio is close to .80:1.00, and the upper half of the population gets only four-fifths of the income, while the highest one-tenth of the households receives between twenty-five and thirty times the income of the lowest one-tenth of the households.

This is much more inequality than was the case twenty years ago. To get back to the level of the late 1960s or early 1970s is hardly satisfactory, however. Even then, the United States was more unequal than many other countries, especially the highly developed nations. The inequality of the years around 1970 did set the stage for the following downslide, so we should aim at something better. As an example of what may be possible, look at the case in which the earned income of individuals has a median/average ratio of about .85:1.00, and that of households about .90:1.00. For individuals, the upper half of the population will still get three-quarters of the income, and the upper one-tenth will have between fifteen and twenty times that of the lowest one-tenth. For households, the proportions would again be somewhat closer: The upper half would get over two-thirds of the income, and the upper one-tenth about ten times the income of the lowest one-tenth of the households.

Would such proportions not provide sufficient incentive for gifted and energetic individuals to exert themselves? Most people have to be content with such prospects—in a high-income society, they are indeed quite good. We will even argue that getting away from the kind of lottery jackpot mentality that underlies much of the star performance in arts and sports would be a good thing. The economy cannot at length live and thrive on high records. A quality job well done has many rewards of its own, and the economic rewards, therefore, need only be substantial; they do not need any astronomical prospects of star incomes.

Where does that leave the cultural crisis? The quality of culture is not in the province of economics, and we therefore will not match the promises sometimes made by conservative economists who represent capitalism as culturally productive. However, it is arguable that the truly creative minds, which are now too often drowned out in the din of cash registers and bottom lines, will find society's climate somewhat more hospitable when the pressure of money has been reduced. The pressure will be reduced, but not eliminated. Within new parameters of competition, the role of the market mechanisms—as distinct from market forces—will continue to be the same.

Appendix I

Population and Distributed Good: The Problem of a Companion Function

In the literature of economic distributions, in general there is not enough attention given to the fact that we should be looking at two interrelated functions—the distribution of the population and the distribution of the good that is distributed among the population. Whether the distribution is of income, wealth, size of business firm, size of farm, or some other factor, it is always true that any function portraying the distribution of population numbers (of income recipients, farms, and so forth) must have a companion function portraying the distribution of the good being distributed (aggregate income, total farmland, and similar elements). The distribution of the good cannot be described in arbitrary numbers, but rather must bear a distinct relation to the distribution of the population.

Distribution of the good has a place in economic analysis for its own sake, as discussed in several of the chapters in this book. The viewpoint is then focused on economic power rather than welfare or distributive justice. The companion function can, however, also be used as an important indicator as to whether the population function, as written in mathematical terms, can exist in the real world.

This point must be discussed because, among other things, the distribution of the good is far from always evident from the published statistics of income by size groups, farms by size groups, and so on. Sometimes it is not published at all, and we are left with income size groups without any data on how the income itself is distributed. Often we are left with too little information because of the size intervals given in the statistics; sometimes they are too wide to reveal what is going on. In many cases, the highest, open-ended size group is too large to allow any intuitive guess as to the share of the good that belongs to this group, or how it may be distributed within this group. Estimating it by subtraction may not be accurate enough.

When the distribution of population numbers by size groups is given in some detail, the distribution of the good can be inferred, if approximately, from that of the numbers. In a given population function there can be only one possible distribution of the good. Given the slope of the main function, each size interval must have an average size (within the interval) that is consistent with the slope of the function at that part of the curve. Obviously, the interval average defines the interval's share of the good. The sum of all the interval shares of the good must add up to 100 percent of the good being distributed. If some other total is reached, then the population function as written cannot be accepted as a portrait of any real economic distribution. Sometimes this kind of analysis can be used to unmask very bad statistics. It can be used also to weed out theoretical distributive functions that cannot exist in the real world.

The following discussion will examine this problem, starting with a class of distributive functions that, until recently, has received only limited attention, namely, the negative exponential function and its transformed versions (Dovring 1973). Writers dealing with other distributive functions have seldom approached this problem. Let us first discuss the case of the linear (untransformed) exponential function.

The untransformed exponential function comes close to portraying many economic distributions in which the median/average ratio (Me/Ave) is close to .693 (the natural logarithm for .5, the median point). For decumulative presentation, let y be the percentage of the population remaining above size limit x, with the size limits expressed as fractions or multiples of average size. Then

$$y = e \exp -x \tag{1}$$

which is linear in semi-logarithmic scale—see Figure A.1. To match other values of Me/Ave, the function can be transformed in ways that will be described in Appendix 2.

For the untransformed exponential function, the companion function that portrays the distribution of the good can be established with simplicity. Let z denote the percentage of the good remaining above size limit x (expressed as above); then, the distribution of the good is obtained in decumulative presentation by the expression

$$z = y(1+x) \tag{2}$$

Note that this companion function is not linear (see Figure A.1). Distribution of the good could hardly ever be linear in economic distributions.

Proof of the validity of equation (2) is obtained by tabulating some of its results, as shown in Table A.1. The table shows two different levels of interval span. In each part of the table it is evident that the interval averages represent a constant proportion to the interval midpoints. Interval averages are a different fraction of interval midpoints in the two parts of the table. The interval spans in the two parts of the table are in the proportion of one-to-ten; the interval averages relate to the midpoint in a way that comes close to the tenth power (or root, depending

Figure A.1
Negative Exponential Function and Companion Function for Distribution of the Good (as shown in Table A.1)

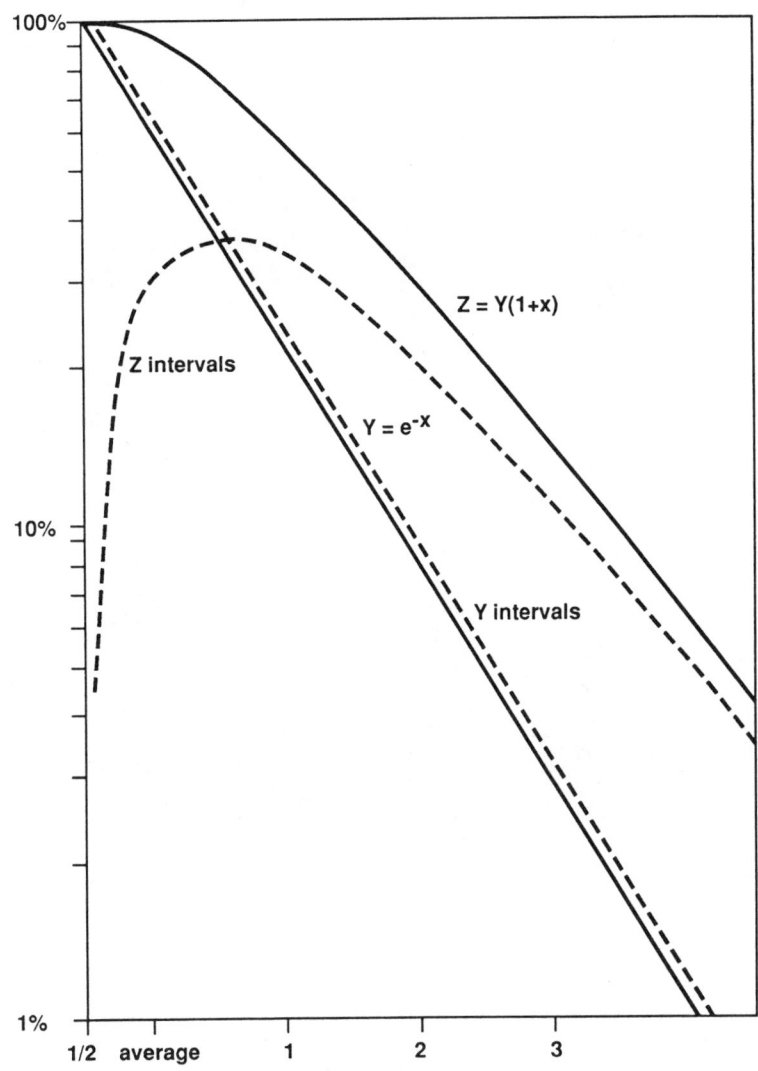

Semi-Logarithmic Scales:
Vertical scale: Percent above each size limit in decumulative representation or in interval, respectively. Horizontal scale: Size limits as multiples and fractions of average size. Full-drawn lines: Decumulative representation of functions. Broken lines: Interval percentage (density function) at intervals such as 0-1, 1-2, and so forth, plotted at interval midpoints.

Table A.1
Negative Exponential Function and Companion Function

x	Decumulative Frequencies		Interval Frequencies		Interval Averages
	$Y = e \exp -x$	$Z = Y(1+x)$	Y	Z	Z/Y

For Intervals of 1/10 Average Size

x	Y	Z	Y	Z	Z/Y
0	1.000000	1.000000			
.1	.904838	.995322	.095162	.004678	.0492
.2	.818732	.982478	.086106	.012844	.1492
.3	.740818	.963063	.077914	.019415	.2492
.4	.670320	.938448	.070498	.024615	.3492
.5	.606531	.909797	.063789	.028651	.4492
.6	.548812	.878099	.057719	.031698	.5492
.7	.496585	.844195	.052227	.033904	.6492
.8	.449329	.808792	.047256	.035403	.7492
.9	.406570	.772483	.042759	.036309	.8492
1.0	.367879	.735758	.038691	.036725	.9492

For Intervals of Average Size

x	Y	Z	Y	Z	Z/Y
0	1.000000	1.000000			
1	.367879	.735758	.632121	.264242	.418
2	.135335	.406005	.232544	.329753	1.418
3	.049787	.199148	.085548	.206857	2.418
4	.018316	.091580	.031471	.107568	3.418
5	.006738	.040428	.011578	.051152	4.418
6	.0024788	.0173516	.004259	.023076	5.418
7	.0009119	.0072952	.0015669	.0100564	6.418
8	.0003355	.0030195	.0005764	.0042757	7.418
9	.0001234	.0012340	.0002121	.0017855	8.418
10	.0000454	.0004994	.0000780	.0007346	9.418

on which way we calculate it) of each other, or as closely as the approximation in the table allows.

This linear property of the proportions between interval midpoint and interval average proves that the formulation we used is correct, and is, in fact, the only formulation that is possible (or at least, the simplest one). If the interval distribution had no slope at all (and all intervals had equal frequency), the curve would have no slope, and each interval average would equal the interval's midpoint. Now, it is evident that the untransformed exponential function has a consistent (constant or monotonous) negative slope, giving higher size intervals lower and lower frequencies the higher they are. The interval frequencies (of equal interval spans) on the numbers side (the y side), when plotted on a semi-logarithmic chart, will also form a straight line, parallel with the decumulative exponential function and with the same slope (see Figure A.1). All interval averages must then be below the interval midpoints. Since the function is linear in semi-logarithmic terms, it is clear that the proportions between interval average and interval midpoint must be the same in all intervals of equal span. This condition is met by our tabulated results. It is thus clear that the interval averages shown in the two parts of the table are the only ones (for those interval spans) that can match the untransformed exponential function of numbers (or population). This follows because in equation (2) we are distributing z, which always must total 100 percent. If, for instance, the first interval in the table had an average larger or smaller than .492, then the z in that interval would be different too, leaving a different residual for the following intervals to share, and then they would have interval averages that were a different proportion to their interval midpoints but deviating in the opposite direction from the change introduced in the first interval. This would violate the linear property of the y function.

Not only is equation (2) the only possible companion function for the negative exponential function, the negative exponential function is also the only linear semi-logarithmic function that has a companion function to portray the distribution of the good. Other logarithmic curves (those with a base other than e) have their uses, but portraying economic distributions is not among them, for they lack the property of having a viable companion function.

Proof of this can be found by computing negative logarithmics for bases other than e and investigating what interval averages they may have. Two examples, with logarithmic bases 10 and 2, are shown in Figure A.2, and have been elaborated in analogy with Table A.1 (Dovring 1979). In both cases, size intervals of one-tenth average (0-.1, .1-.2, and so on) were assigned interval averages equal to their midpoints. The true averages would be hard to compute, and they would, in any event, not differ much from the midpoints. The results showed that these averages could not in fact exist because these distributions could not exist—they could never portray economic distributions. The choice of midpoint for the average in the small groups would lead to a slight understatement of the results for log-base 10 and a slight overstatement for log-base 2. The larger size intervals (0-1, 1-2, and so on) were assigned interval averages with the same relation to interval midpoint as resulted from the specification of the small intervals.

There is no possibility whatsoever of fitting a companion function to either of the two logarithmics chosen. For log base 10 (where Me/Ave would be close to .3), the small units are so numerous and the large ones so few that between them they only absorb about 44 percent of the good. The rest remains undistributed, which is absurd. The proportions show that in a case where the small units are relatively so numerous, the large ones ought to be proportionately more numerous, which is what regularly happens in the real world. Thus, a function with a Me/Ave at .3 must be curvilinear, and in fact extremely so.

The same is equally evident for the high curve, the logarithmic based on 2. Here the Me/Ave would be 1.0, which is unlikely, to say the least; the distribution would have to be normal, which economic distributions never are and this one is evidently not. Here the small units are so few and the large ones so numerous that the

Figure A.2
Negative Exponential Functions for Three Logarithmic Bases (2, *e*, and 10, in decumulative representation of functions)

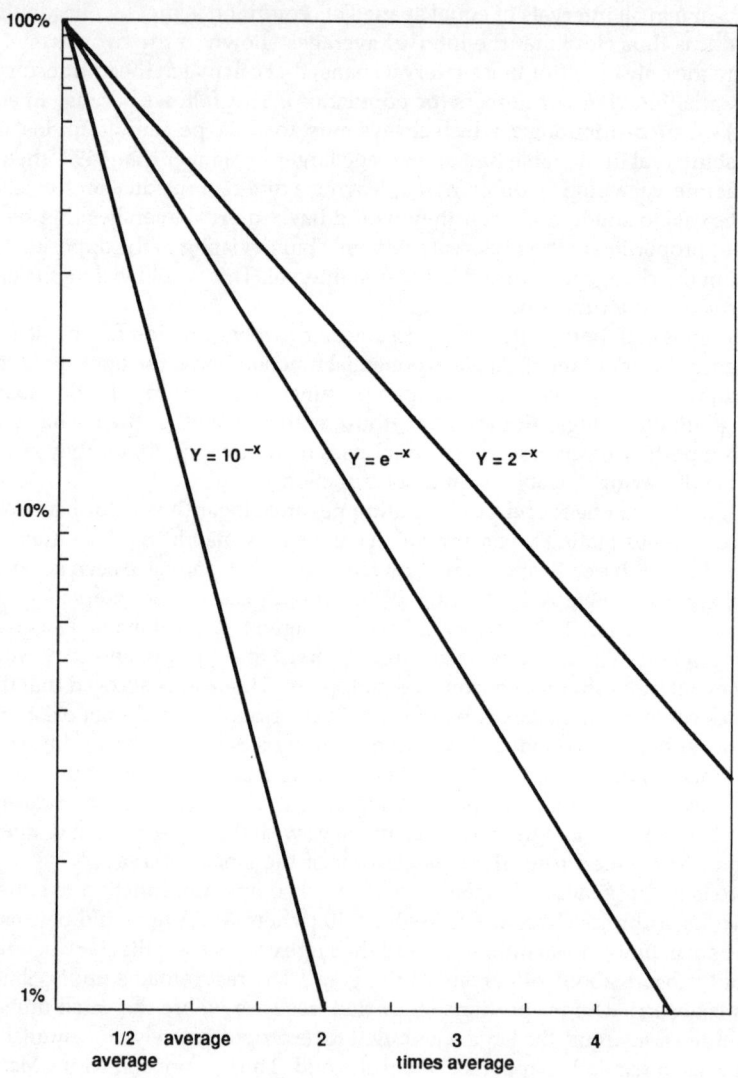

Semi-Logarithmic Scales:
Vertical scale: Percentage; Horizontal scale: Size limits, as multiples or fractions of average size.

good cannot satisfy all claimants. There would be a shortfall of about 43 percent of the good, which proves that such a distribution cannot exist.

There is no way in which the difficulty could be overcome by accepting interval averages much higher or lower than those used in the tables. Such modified interval averages, to distribute all the good or to absorb it all, would violate the relation to slope (as illustrated by the interval averages shown for the large intervals and derived from those of the small ones). Interval averages that would allow the distribution of the good to break even would sometimes have to exceed the upper or lower limits of the intervals themselves, which is conceptually excluded. Such absurd results are ruled out also because when size intervals are made very small, all interval averages must be very close to midpoint, and intervals in the larger groups then could reflect nothing but slope.

The two chosen examples are extreme but typical. If we choose log bases closer to e, the surplus or shortfall of the good becomes smaller but does not disappear. At log base 3 (with Me/Ave .63) and at log base 2.5 (with Me/Ave .76), surplus and shortfall are about 8 percent in both cases. It is still impossible to reconcile the numbers to the exacting conditions of slope combined with a specification of narrow size intervals. With log bases differing only slightly from e, the absurdities would be more difficult to detect, but this can not obscure the conclusion that ($e \exp -x$) is the only logarithmic—the only linear semi-logarithmic function—that can be used to portray economic distributions.

This is, in fact, the only completely linear function that is possible. In logarithmic terms (on both axes), the whole distribution can never be linear, as has often been observed in connection with the Pareto function, which is linear only in the upper tail, and never in the lower or even the middle part. In natural terms, a linear decumulative function implies that all size intervals have the same frequency, a condition that is never met in real life and conceptually at variance with the scarcity principle in economics. Lognormal functions, finally, can be made linear on log-probability graphs, but the insufficiency of lognormal distributions to portray economic phenomena is now well established. It follows, then, that all economic distributions in which Me/Ave differs significantly from .69 must be curvilinear, as experience shows them to be.

This exercise has served two purposes. It has shown that accounting for the companion function—distribution of the good—can help us discard certain functional forms that might seem plausible in isolation but that reveal themselves as absurd because they have no viable companion function. It has also shown the negative exponential function to be unique as the only linear function that can be used to portray economic distributions.

Without any transformation, this linear function can be used only where the Me/Ave is .69 or close to that value. For all other Me/Ave values, the distribution must be curvilinear if it has at all anything approaching a functional form and is not just (exceptionally) a set of random numbers creating the semblance of linearity.

Any attempt at treating curvilinear functions as if they were linear will inevitably lead to serious errors, which will increase the more the Me/Ave of the function at hand differs from .69. Linear regressions, and various statistical tests assuming linearity, will produce the illusion of a linear function with large random variation. In reality, however, much of the variation is systemic, reflecting the curvature of the distribution. Recognizing the curvilinear characteristic of most distributive functions will reduce the apparent amount of random variation and will make it easier to trace such variations, where they exist, to their causes.

For a comprehensive analysis of economic distributions, we must find a class of transformed exponential functions that will meet the exacting condition of having a viable companion function, as discussed above. The closest to such a class of functions discovered to date was published in 1973 (Dovring 1973). A set of formulas that meet the criteria even more closely is set forth in Appendix II.

The significance of such a class of functions is that, as functions developed in each case from a single parameter of inequality or skewness, the exponential functions will allow us to see what this distribution would be, in the absence of random influences, when a stated degree of inequality is taken as given. The single parameter used in exponential function analysis has been found to be closely correlated with the Gini coefficient, so the meaning of a single inequality expression should not be hard to grasp (Dovring et al. 1974). Assuming that one single, overriding factor decides most of the distribution, one can then identify various specific deviations from the main function and trace them to the material influences that caused them.

Appendix II

The Exponential Functions

Before explaining the transformation of the exponential function and its companion function, let us first reiterate the two basic formulas shown in Appendix I:

$$y = e \exp -x \qquad (1)$$

where y is the percentage of the population left above size limit x, and

$$z = y(1+x) \qquad (2)$$

where z is the percentage of the good left above size limit x, and where x in both formulas is expressed as a fraction or a multiple of average size in the population.

To reiterate, these formulas are valid when the median/average ratio (Me/Ave) is .693 (the natural logarithm of .5, the median point). Where the Me/Ave differs from .693, we need transformed versions of both formulas.

In developing the following formulas to transform the basic functions, close attention was paid to the requirement that each y formula must have a matching z function (the companion function). Previous formulations of the y functions (Dovring 1973) came close but not sufficiently so.

To expand equation (1), we first write

$$y = e \exp -f(x), \qquad (3)$$

substituting a function of x for x itself.

The parameter $f(x)$ is found by computing

$$f(x) = (ax \exp (b \exp c))/a \qquad (4)$$

The a parameter is the reciprocal of the relative size at which the curve at hand intersects the untransformed exponential function.

APPENDIX II

In specifying the parameters, we make a distinction between high curves (those where Me/Ave is larger than .693) and low curves (where Me/Ave is lower than .693). The former intersect the untransformed function from above (on a diagram), and the low curves intersect it from below.

The b parameter is a constant for each value of a, while c varies, covarying with $x/.693$.

The b parameter can be formulated as follows:

$$b = (1-.693)/(1-a) \tag{5}$$

for high curves, and

$$b = (a/.693) \tag{6}$$

for low curves. Note that under both formulations, when $a = .693$, $b = 1$.

The c parameters are also different for high and low curves. For high curves, we use

$$c = (1/(1+(1-x/.693)^2)\exp(1/1+a^2) \tag{7}$$

for x values under .693, and

$$c = (1/(1+(1-.693/x)^2 \exp(1+a^2) \tag{8}$$

for x values over .693.

For low curves, we use the following:

$$c = 1/(1+(1-x/.693)^2) \exp(1-a^2) \tag{9}$$

for x values under .693, and

$$c = (1+(1-.693/x)^2) \exp(1-a^2) \tag{10}$$

for x values over .693.

In all four formulas, at $x = .693$, $c = 1$.

Let us now turn to the z function as it will apply to the transformed versions of the y function. Expanding on equation (2), we first write

$$z = y((1+f(x) \exp(b_1 \exp c_1)) \tag{11}$$

Again, the parameters b_1 and c_1 are different for high and low curves. For high curves, b_1 can be written

$$b_1 = (1/\sqrt{b}) \exp(a/.847) \tag{12}$$

with .847 being the halfway point between .693 and 1.00. For low curves, we write instead

$$b_1 = (1/\sqrt{b}) \exp((1/.693) \exp(1-a)) \tag{13}$$

The parameter c_1 turns out to be more complicated. The following will serve for high curves:

$$c_1 = (ax \exp \sqrt{e}) \exp(k \exp(1/1-ax)) \tag{14}$$

for ax values under 1, and

APPENDIX II

$$c_1 = (1/ax \exp 1/\sqrt{e}) \exp (k \exp (1/1-(1/ax))) \tag{15}$$

for x values over 1. In both formulas,

$$k = ((a-.693)/.307) \exp ((a/.847) \exp 2\ e) \tag{16}$$

For low curves, c_1 is found by

$$c_1 = x \exp (k \exp (1+(1-x)^2)) \tag{17}$$

for x values under 1, and

$$c_1 = x \exp (k \exp (1+ (1-1/x)^2)) \tag{18}$$

for x values over 1. In both formulas,

$$k = a \exp ((a/.347) \exp e)) \tag{19}$$

These various formulas may be very slightly off the mark. It is possible that formulations could be found that would satisfy the criteria of a matching companion function even more closely. However, for the purposes of this book, these formulations are sufficiently close to the requirements. Selected results from the calculations based on these formulas are shown in tabulated form in Chapter 3.

References

Abdel-Khalek, Gouda, and Tignor, Robert, eds. 1982. *The Political Economy of Income Distribution in Egypt.* New York and London: Holmes and Meier.

Abercrombie, K. C. 1967. "Incomes and Their Distribution in Agriculture in Relation to the Rest of the Economy," *FAO Monthly Bulletin of Agricultural Economics and Statistics* 16, no. 6 (June), pp. 1-8.

Adelman, Irma. 1975. "Development Economics—A Reassessment of Goals," *American Economic Review* 65, no. 2 (May), pp. 302-9.

Ahluvalia, Montek. 1976. "Inequality, Poverty, and Development," *Journal of Development Economics* 3, no. 4, pp. 307-42.

Aigner, D. J., and Goldberger, A. S. 1970. "Estimation of Pareto's Law from Grouped Observations," *Journal of the American Statistical Association* 65, pp. 712-23.

Aigner, D. J., and Heins, A. J. 1967. "On the Determinants of Income Inequality," *American Economic Review* 57, no. 1, (March), pp. 175-84.

Aitchison, T., and Brown, A. C. 1957. *The Log-Normal Distribution.* Cambridge: Cambridge University Press.

Alexander, J. Davidson. 1989. "The Political Economy of Tax-Based Incomes Policy: Wealth Effects of Post Keynesian TIP," *Journal of Economic Issues* 33, no. 1 (March), pp. 135-46.

Al-Samarrie, Ahmad, and Miller, Herman P. 1967. "State Differentials in Income Concentration," *American Economic Review* 57, no. 1 (March), pp. 59-72.

Altimir, Oscar. 1986. "Estimaciones de la distribución del ingreso en la Argentina, 1953-1980," *Desarrollo Economico* 25, no. 100 (January-March), pp. 521-66.

———. 1987. "Income Distribution Statistics in Latin America and Their Reliability," *The Review of Income and Wealth* 33, no. 2 (June), pp. 111-56.

Anderson, Martin. 1988. *Revolution*. San Diego, New York, and London: Harcourt Brace Jovanovich.

Arndt, H. W. 1983. "The Trickle-Down Myth," *Economic Development and Cultural Change* 32, no. 1 (October), pp. 1-10.

Ascher, William. 1984. *Scheming for the Poor: The Politics of Redistribution in Latin America*. Cambridge, MA, and London: Harvard University Press.

Aspe, Pedro, and Sigmund, Paul E., editors. 1984. *The Political Economy of Income Distribution in Mexico*. New York and London: Holmes and Meier.

Atkinson, Anthony B. 1970. "On the measurement of inequality," *Journal of Economic Theory* 2, no. 3. (September), pp. 244-63.

———. 1975. *The Economics of Inequality*. Oxford: Clarendon Press.

Atkinson, Anthony B., and Harrison, A. J. 1978. *Distribution of Personal Wealth in Britain*. Cambridge: Cambridge University Press.

Baer, Werner. 1986. "Growth with Inequality: The Cases of Brazil and Mexico" (review essay on seven books, 1980-1982), *Latin American Research Review* 21, no. 2. pp. 197-214.

Barlow, Robin, Brazer, Harvey E., and Morgan, James N. 1966. *Economic Behavior of the Affluent*. Washington, DC: Brookings Institution.

Batra, Ravi. [1985] 1987. *The Great Depression of 1990*. Foreword by Lester Thurow. New York: Simon and Schuster.

Becker, Charles M. 1987. "Urban Sector Income Distribution and Economic Development," *Journal of Urban Economics* 21, pp. 127-45.

Beckford, George L. 1972. *Persistent Poverty: Underdevelopment in Plantation Economies of the Third World*. New York, London, and Toronto: Oxford University Press.

Bendix, Reinhard, and Lipset, Seymour Martin, eds. [1953] 1966. *Class, Status, and Power: Social Stratification in Comparative Perspective*. 2d ed. New York and London: Free Press.

Bennett, Amanda. 1990. *The Death of the Organization Man*. New York: Morrow.

Bequele, Assefa, and van der Hoeven, Rolf. 1980. "Poverty and Inequality in Sub-Saharan Africa," *International Labour Review* 119, no. 3 (May-June), pp. 381-92.

Berrebi, Z. M., and Silber, Jacques. 1987. "Dispersion, Symmetry and the Gini Index of Inequality," *International Economic Review* 28, no. 2, pp. 331-38.

Berry, Albert. 1985. "On Trends in the Gap between Rich and Poor in Less Developed Countries: Why Do We Know So Little?" *The Review of Income and Wealth*, 31, no. 4 (December), pp. 337-54.

———. 1987a. "Evidence of Relationships among Alternative Measures of Concentration: A Tool for Analysis of LDC Inequality," *The Review of Income and Wealth*, 33, no. 4. (December), pp. 417-30.

———. 1987b. "Poverty and Inequality in Latin America," (review essay of six books, 1980-1984), *Latin American Research Review* 22, no. 2, pp. 202-14.

Berry, Albert, Bourguignon, François, and Morrisson, Christian. 1983a. "Changes in the World Distribution of Income between 1950 and 1977," *The Economic Journal* 93 (June), pp. 331-350.

———. 1983b. "The Level of World Inequality: How Much Can One Say?" *The Review of Income and Wealth* 29, no. 3 (September), pp. 217-41.

Betz, D. Michael. 1972. "The City as a System Generating Income Inequality," *Social Forces* 51 (December), pp. 192-98.

Bhatt, V. V. 1988. "Growth and Income Distribution in India," *World Development* 16, no. 5, pp. 641-47.

Bienen, Henry, and Diejomaoh, V. P., eds. 1981. *Inequality and Development in Nigeria*. New York and London: Holmes and Meier.

Blackburn, McKinley L., and Bloom, David L. 1987. "Earnings and Income Inequality in the United States," *Population and Development Review* 13, no. 4 (December), pp. 575-609.

Blejer, Mario, and Guerrero, Isabel. 1988. "Stabilization Policies and Income Distribution in the Philippines," *Finance and Development*, 25, no. 4 (December), pp. 6-8.

Blinder, Alan S. 1974. *Toward an Economic Theory of Income Distribution*. Cambridge, MA, and London: MIT Press.

Blinder, Alan S., and Esaki, Howard Y. 1978. "Macroeconomic Activity and Income Distribution in the Postwar United States," *The Review of Economics and Statistics* 60, no. 4, pp. 604-9.

Blumberg, Louis, and Gottlieb, Robert. 1989. *War on Waste: Can America Win Its Battle with Garbage?* Foreword by Jim Hightower. Washington, DC, and Covalo, CA: Island Press.

Bourgignon, François, and Morrisson, Christian. 1989. *External Trade and Income Distribution*. Paris: OECD Development Centre.

Bovenberg, A. Lans. 1989. "Tax Policy and National Saving in the United States," *National Tax Journal* 42, no. 2, pp. 123-38.

Bradbury, Katharine L. 1986. "The Shrinking Middle Class," *New England Economic Review* (September-October), pp. 41-55.

Braun, Denny. 1988. "Multiple Measurements of U.S. Income Inequality," *Review of Economics and Statistics* 70, no. 3 (August), pp. 393-405.

Brittain, John A. 1978. *Inheritance and the Inequality of Material Wealth*. Washington, DC: The Brookings Institution.

Bronfenbrenner, Martin. 1986. "Income Distribution and 'Economic Justice,'" *Journal of Economic Education* 17, no. 1, (Summer), pp. 35-51.

Brown, Henry Phelps. 1983. "Egalitarianism and the Distribution of Wealth and Income," *Industrial Relations* (University of California) 22, no. 2 (Spring), pp. 186-202.

Browning, Edgar K. 1976. "How Much More Equality Can We Afford?" *Public Interest* 43, pp. 90-110.

Bryan, William R., and Linke, Charles M. 1988. "Value of a College Education," *Illinois Business Review* 45, no. 5 (October), pp. 3-7.

Budd, Edward C. 1970. "Postwar Changes in the Size Distribution of Income in the U.S.," *American Economic Review* 60, no. 2, (May), pp. 247-60.

Buhmann, Brigitte, Rainwater, Lee, Schmaus, Guenther, and Smeeding, Timothy M. 1988. "Equivalence Scales, Well-Being, Inequality, and Poverty: Sensitivity Estimates across Ten Countries Using the Luxembourg Income Study (LIS) Database," *The Review of Income and Wealth* 34, no. 2, (June), pp. 115-42.

Buse, Adolf. 1982. "The Cyclical Behavior of the Size Distribution of Income in Canada: 1947-78," *Canadian Journal of Economics* 15, no. 2, (May), pp. 189-204.

Buss, James A., Peterson, G. Paul, and Nantz, Kathryn A. 1989., "A Comparison of Distributive Justice in OECD Countries," *Review of Social Economy* 47, no. 1 (Spring), pp. 1-14.
Cain, G. 1976. "The Challenge of Segmented Labor Market Theories to Orthodox Theory: A Survey," *Journal of Economic Literature* 14, no. 4 (December), pp. 1215-57.
Campano, Fred, and Salvatore, Dominick. 1988. "Economic Development, Income Inequality and Kuznets' U-Shaped Hypothesis," *Journal of Policy Modeling* 10, no. 2, pp. 265-80.
Canadian Government. Household Survey Division. Annual. *Income Distributions by Size in Canada*. [Also pub. in French; data for each year published the subsequent year].
Canadian Government. Minister of Supply and Services. 1989. "Income Distribution by Size in Canada 1988," *Statistics Canada 1989*. Ottawa: Minister of Supply and Services.
Carnoy, Martin, Shearer, Derek, and Rumbecker, Russell. 1983. *A New Social Contract: The Economy and Government after Reagan*. New York: Harper and Row.
Chakravarty, Satya R. 1988. "Extended Gini Indices of Inequality," *International Economic Review* 29, no. 1, pp. 147-56.
Champernowne, David B. 1973. *The Distribution of Income between Persons*. Cambridge: Cambridge University Press.
———. 1974. "A Comparison of Measures of Inequality of Income Distributions," *Economic Journal* 84 (December), pp. 787-816.
Chenery, Hollis, Ahluvalia, Montek S., Bell, C. L. G., Duloy, John H., and Jolly, Richard. 1974. *Redistribution with Growth: Policies to Improve Income Distribution in Developing Countries in the Context of Economic Growth*. London: Oxford University Press for the World Bank and the Institute of Development Studies, University of Sussex.
Chicago Tribune Staff. 1986. *The American Millstone: An Examination of the Nation's Permanent Underclass*. Chicago: Contemporary Books.
Cline, W. R., 1975. "Distribution and Development (A Survey of Literature)," *Journal of Development Economics* 1, no. 4, pp. 359-402.
Cloutier, Norman R. 1987. "Who Gains from Racism? The Impact of Racial Inequality on White Income Distribution," *Review of Social Economy* 45, no. 2, pp. 152-62.
Coleman, Richard P., and Rainwater, Lee, with Kent A. McClelland. 1978. *Social Standing in America. New Dimensions of Class*. New York: Basic Books.
Commoner, Barry. [1975] 1990. *Making Peace with the Planet*. New York: Pantheon Books.
Conlisk, John. 1967. "Some Cross-State Evidence on Income Inequality," *The Review of Economics and Statistics* 49, no. 1, pp. 115-18.
Cooper, George. 1979. *A Voluntary Tax? New Perspectives on Sophisticated Estate Tax Avoidance*. Washington, DC: The Brookings Institution.
Creedy, John. 1985. *Dynamics of Income Distribution*. Oxford: Basil Blackwell.
Cue, Felix M. 1988. "Income Distribution and Economic Development: A Case Study of the Kuznets' Hypothesis Applied to Puerto Rico," *Review of Social Economy* 46, no. 1, (April), pp. 61-80.

Daly, Herman E., and Cobb, John B., Jr. 1989. *For the Common Good: Redirecting the Economy toward Community, the Environment, and a Sustainable Future.* Contributions by Clifford W. Cobb. Boston: Beacon Press.

Daniels, Norman, ed. 1975. *Reading Rawls: Critical Studies on Rawls' Theory of Justice.* New York: Basic Books.

Danziger, Sheldon, and Gottschalk, Peter. 1985a. "How Have Families with Children Been Faring?" Prepared for the Joint Economic Committee of the Congress. Mimeo, 54 pp.

———. 1985b. "The Impact of Budget Cuts and Economic Conditions on Poverty," *Journal of Policy Analysis and Management* 4, pp. 587-93.

———. 1986. "Do Rising Tides Lift All Boats? The Impact of Secular and Cyclical Changes on Poverty," *American Economic Review* 76, no. 2, (May), pp. 405-10.

———. 1988-1989. "Increasing Inequality in the United States: What We Know and What We Don't," *Journal of Post-Keynesian Economics* 11, no. 2 (Winter), pp. 174-95.

Danziger, Sheldon, and Haveman, Robert. 1981. "The Reagan Budget: A Sharp Break with the Past," *Challenge* (May-June), pp. 5-13.

Danziger, Sheldon, and Weinberg, Daniel H., eds. 1981. *Fighting Poverty: What Works and What Doesn't.* Cambridge, MA: Harvard University Press.

Dardanoni, V., and Lambert, P. 1988. "Welfare Ranking and Income Distributions: A Role for the Variance and Some Insights for Tax Reform," *Social Choice and Welfare* 5, nos. 2–3, pp. 1-17.

David Martin. 1985. "The Distribution of Income in the United States: Implications for the Design of the SIPP Model," *Journal of Economic and Social Measurement* 13, pp. 305-17.

Dixon, Robert. 1981. "A Model of Income Distribution," *Journal of Post Keynesian Economics* 3, no. 3 (Spring), pp. 383-402.

Djilas, Milovan. 1957. *The New Class.* New York: Praeger.

Donahue, John D. 1989. *The Privatization Decision: Public Ends, Private Means.* New York: Basic Books.

Dovring, Folke. 1959. "The Share of Agriculture in a Growing Population," *FAO Monthly Bulletin of Agricultural Economics and Statistics* 8, nos. 8–9 (August-September), pp. 1-11.

———. 1965. "Bondage, Tenure, and Progress," *Comparative Studies in Society and History* 7, no. 3 (April), pp. 309-23.

———. 1968a. "Aid by Dumping?" *International Development Review* 10, no. 3 (September), pp. 2-5.

———. 1968b. "Land Reform and Productivity in Mexico," *Land Economics* 46, no. 3 (August), pp. 264-74.

———. 1973. "Distribution of Farm Size and Income," *Land Economics* 49, no. 2 (May), pp. 133-47.

———. 1974. "Land Reform: A Key to Change in Agriculture." In *Agricultural Policy in Developing Countries: Proceedings of a Conference,* edited by Nurul Islam, pp. 509-21. London: Macmillan.

———. 1979. "The Two Faces of Economic Distributions: Population and Distributed Good." University of Illinois, Dept. of Agricultural Economics, staff paper 79E-97.

——. 1983. "Concepts of Land, Value and Wealth." In *Land—Something of Value, Proceedings*, edited by Gene Wunderlich, pp. 11-19. Cambridge, MA: Lincoln Institute.

——. 1984a. "Interest Rates: A Form of Inflation?" *Illinois Business Review* 41, no. 2, (April), pp. 4-5, 12.

——. 1984b. *Riches to Rags: The Political Economy of Social Waste*. Cambridge, MA: Schenkman.

——. 1987a. "By Faith and Credit: Economic Growth in the 1980s," *Illinois Business Review* 44, no. 5, (October), pp. 10-13.

——. 1987b. *Productivity and Value: The Political Economy of Measuring Progress*. New York: Praeger.

——. 1988. *Farming for Fuel: The Political Economy of Energy Sources in the United States*. New York: Praeger.

——, and Dovring, Karin. 1971. *The Optional Society: An Essay on Economic Choice and Bargains of Communication in an Affluent World*. The Hague: Martinus Nijhoff.

Dovring, Folke, Leuthold, Raymond M., and Karr, Gerald L. 1974. "Distributive Equity of Income in Rural Illinois." In *Rural Community and Regional Development*, edited by John T. Scott, pp. 41-52. University of Illinois at Urbana-Champaign, AE 4336, June.

Drucker, Peter F. 1989. *The New Realities: In Government and Politics/In Economics and Business/In Society and World View*. New York: Harper and Row.

Duesenberry, James S. 1967. *Income, Saving, and the Theory of Consumer Behavior*. New York: Oxford University Press.

Dugger, William M. 1987. "Three Modes of Income Distribution: Market, Hierarchy, and Industry," *Journal of Economic Issues* 21, no. 2, (June), pp. 723-31.

Duignan, Peter, and Rabushka, Alvin, eds. 1988. *The United States in the 1980's*. Foreword by W. Glenn Campbell. Stanford, CA: The Hoover Institution.

Duncan, Greg J., with Coe, Richard D., Corcoran, Mary E., Hill, Martha S., Hoffman, Saul D., and Morgan, James N. 1984. *Years of Poverty, Years of Plenty: The Changing Economic Fortunes of American Workers and Families*. Foreword by Lee Rainwater. Ann Arbor: Survey Research Center, Institute for Social Research, University of Michigan.

Durden, Garey C., and Schwarz-Miller, Ann V. 1982. "The Distribution of Individual Income in the U.S. and Public Sector Employment," *Social Science Quarterly* 63, no. 1, (March), pp. 40-47.

Ebert, Udo. 1988a. "A Family of Aggregate Compromise Inequality Measures," *International Economic Review* 29, no. 2, pp. 363-76.

——. 1988b. "Measurement of Inequality: An Attempt at Unification and Generalization," *Social Choice and Welfare* 5, nos. 2-3, pp. 147-69.

Ehrlich, Paul R., and Ehrlich, Anne H. 1990. *The Population Explosion*. New York: Simon and Schuster.

Eliot, Marc. 1989. *Rockonomics: The Money behind the Music*. New York and Toronto: Franklin Watts.

Esfahani, Hadi S. 1987. "Growth, Employment and Income Distribution in Egyptian Agriculture, 1964-79," *World Development* 15, no. 9, pp. 1201-17.

Esteban, J. 1966. "Income-Share Elasticity and the Size Distribution of Income," *International Economic Review* 27, no. 2, pp. 439-44.

Farbman, Michael. 1973. "Income Concentration in the Southern United States," *The Review of Economics and Statistics* 55, no. 2, pp. 333-40.

Fichtenbaum, Rudy. 1985. "Consumption and the Distribution of Income," *Review of Social Economy* 43, pp. 234-45.

Fields, G. S. 1987. "Measuring Inequality Change in an Economy with Income Growth," *Journal of Development Economics* 20, no. 2, pp. 357-74.

Finance and Development. A Quarterly Publication of the International Monetary Fund and the World Bank. Washington, DC.

Foley, John W. 1977. "Trends, Determinants and Policy Implications of Income Inequality in U.S. Counties," *Sociology and Social Research* 61, no. 4, pp. 441-61.

Gaffney, Mason. 1973. "Land Rent, Taxation and Public Policy," *American Journal of Economics and Sociology* 32 (January), pp. 17-34.

Gagliani, Giorgio. 1987. "Income Inequality and Economic Development," *Annual Review of Sociology* 13, pp. 313-34.

Galbraith, John Kenneth. 1958. *The Affluent Society*. Boston: Houghton Mifflin.

Gallardo, Julio López. 1983. "La distribución del ingreso en México: Estructura y evolución," *El Trimestre Económico* 40, no. 4, pp. 2227-56.

Geisler, Charles C., and Popper, Frank J., eds. 1984. *Land Reform, American Style*. Totowa, NJ: Rowman and Allanheld.

George, Henry. 1879. *Progress and Poverty*. San Francisco, CA: Wm. N. Hinton.

Gibrat, Robert. 1931. *Les inégalités économiques*. Paris: Receuil Sirey.

Gibson, Bill. 1984. "Profit and Rent in a Classical Theory of Exhaustible and Renewable Resources," *Zeitschrift für Nationalökonomie* (Vienna) 44, no. 2, pp. 131-49.

Gibson, Bill, and Esfahani, Hadi. 1983. "Nonproduced Means of Production: Fundamentalists vs. Sraffians," *Review of Radical Economics* 15, pp. 83-105.

Giersch, Herbert. 1983. "Arbeit, lohn und produktivität," *Weltwirtschaftliches Archiv* 119, no. 1, pp. 1-18.

Glendinning, Chellis. 1990. *When Technology Wounds: The Human Consequences of Progress*. New York: William Morrow.

Glewwe, Paul. 1986. "The Distribution of Income in Sri Lanka in 1969-70 and 1980-81," *Journal of Development Economics* 24, pp. 255-74.

Goldschmidt, Walter. 1978. *As You Sow*. Montclair, NJ: Allanheld, Osmun.

Gordon, Gregory, and Cohen, Ronald E. 1990. *Down to the Wire; UPI's Fight for Survival*. New York: McGraw Hill.

Grais, W. M. 1987. "Coping with a Decline in World Energy Prices. Macroeconomic and Income Distribution Effects in Thailand," *Journal of Development Economics* 26, pp. 235-255.

Grasso, Patrick G., and Sharkansky, Ira. 1980. "Economic Development and the Distribution of Income in the American States," *Social Science Quarterly* 61, no. 3-4 (December), pp. 446-57.

Greenhalgh, Susan. 1985. "Is Inequality Demographically Induced? The Family Life Cycle and the Distribution of Income in Taiwan," *American Anthropologist* 87, no. 3 (September), pp. 571-94.

Grosh, Margaret E., and Nafziger, E. Wayne. 1986. "The Computation of World Income Distribution," *Economic Development and Cultural Change* 34, no. 2, pp. 347-59.

Gross, Bertram. 1980. *Friendly Fascism: The New Face of Power In America*. New York: M. Evans.
Guha, Sunil. 1981. "Income Redistribution through Labour-Intensive Public Works: Some Policy Issues," *International Labour Review* 120, no. 1, pp. 67-82.
Gyimah-Brempong, Kwabena. 1988. "Agricultural Development and the Size Distribution of Personal Income: The Tropical African Experience," *World Development* 16, no. 4, pp. 483-88.
Harrington, Michael. 1989. *Socialism Past and Future*. New York: Arcade Publishing, Little, Brown and Co.
Harris, Donald J. 1978. *Capital Accumulation and Income Distribution*. Stanford, CA: Stanford University Press.
Harrison, Bennett, Tilly, Chris, and Bluestone, Barry. 1986. "Wage Inequality Takes a Great U-Turn," *Challenge* (March-April), pp. 26-32.
Haworth, Charles T., Long, James E., and Rasmussen, David W. 1978. "Income Distribution, City Size, and Urban Growth," *Urban Studies* 15, pp. 1-7.
Heller, Robert. 1989. *The Decision Makers. The Men and the Million-Dollar Moves Behind Today's Great Corporate Success Stories*. New York: Truman Talley Books, E.P. Dutton.
Heroles, Jesús Reyes. 1988. "Las politicas financieras y la distribución del ingreso en México," *El Trimestre Económico* 55, no. 3, (July-September), pp. 649-702.
Hirsch, Fred. 1976. *Social Limits to Growth*. Cambridge, MA: Harvard University Press.
Hoggart, K. 1987. "Income Distribution, Labor Market Sectors and the Goldschmidt Hypothesis—The Nonmetropolitan United States in 1970 and 1930," *Journal of Rural Studies* 3, no. 3, pp. 231-45.
Horowitz, Grace. 1974. "Wage Determination in a Labor Surplus Economy: The Case of India," *Economic Development and Cultural Change* 22, no. 4, pp. 666-72.
Ikemoto, Yukio. 1985. "Income Distribution in Malaysia: 1957-80," *The Developing Economies* 23, no. 4, (December), pp. 347-67.
Ioannides, Yannis M. 1986. "Heritability and Ability, Intergenerational Transfers and the Distribution of Wealth," *International Economic Review* 27, no. 3, pp. 611-23.
Ireson, W. Randall. 1987. "Landholding, Agricultural Modernization, and Income Concentration: A Mexican Example," *Economic Development and Cultural Change* 35, no. 2, pp. 351-65.
Irvine, Ian. 1980. "The Distribution of Income and Wealth in Canada in a Life Cycle Framework," *Canadian Journal of Economics* 13, no. 3, (August), pp. 455-74.
Ishizaki, Tadeo. 1986. "Is Japan's Income Distribution Equal? An International Comparison," *Japanese Economic Studies* (Winter), pp. 30-55.
Jacoby, Henry. [1969] 1973. *The Bureaucratization of the World*. Translated from German. Berkeley, CA: University of California Press.
Jain, Shail. 1975. *Size Distribution of Income: A Compilation of Data*. Washington, DC: The World Bank.
Jencks, Christopher; Smith, Marshall; Acland, Henry; Bane, Mary Jo; Cohen, David; Gintis, Herbert; Heyns, Barbara; and Michelson, Stephan. 1972.

Inequality: A Reassessment of the Effect of Family and Schooling in America. New York and London: Basic Books.

Jonish, James E., and Kau, James B. 1973. "State Differentials in Income Inequality," *Review of Social Economy* 31, no. 2, (October), pp. 179-90.

Jorgenson, D.W., and Slesnik, David. 1984. "Inequality in Distribution of Individual Welfare," *Advances in Econometrics* (February), pp. 67-130.

Kahn, Herman, with the Hudson Institute. 1979. *World Economic Development 1979 and Beyond.* Boulder, CO: Westview Press.

Kaiser, Helmut, and Spahn, Bernd. 1989. "On the Efficiency and Distributive Justice of Consumption Taxes: A Study of VAT in West Germany," *Journal of Economics—Zeitschrift für Nationalökonomie* 49, no. 2, pp. 199-218.

Kakwani, Nawak C. 1980. *Income Inequality and Poverty: Methods of Estimation and Policy Applications.* New York: Oxford University Press for the World Bank.

———. 1986. *Analyzing Redistribution Data: A Study Using Australian Data.* Cambridge: Cambridge University Press.

———. 1988. "Income Inequality, Welfare and Poverty in a Developing Economy with Application to Sri Lanka," *Social Choice and Welfare* 5, nos. 2-3, pp. 199-222.

King, Willford Isbell. 1915. *The Wealth and Income of the People of the United States.* New York: Macmillan Company.

Kolko, Gabriel. 1962. *Wealth and Power in America: An Analysis of Social Class and Income Distribution.* New York, Washington, DC, and London: Praeger.

Kozol, Jonathan. 1985. *Illiterate America.* Garden City, NY: Anchor Press/Doubleday.

Kravis, Irving B., Heston, Alan W., and Summers, Robert. 1978a. *International Comparisons of Real Product and Purchasing Power.* Baltimore and London: Johns Hopkins Press.

———. 1978b. "Real GDP *per Capita* for More Than One Hundred Countries," *The Economic Journal* 88 (June), pp. 215-42.

Kregal, J. A. 1979. "The Relation of Distribution to Growth," *World Development* 7, no. 10, (October), pp. 933-41.

Krelle, Wilhelm, ed. 1989. *The Future of the World Economy: Economic Growth and Structural Change.* Berlin: Springer-Verlag.

Krongkaew, Medhi. 1985. "Agricultural Development, Rural Poverty, and Income Distribution in Thailand," *The Developing Economies* 23, no. 4, (December), pp. 325-46.

Kuo, Shirley W. Y., Ranis, Gustav, and Fei, John C. H,. 1981. *The Taiwan Success Story: Rapid Growth with Improved Distribution in the Republic of China, 1952-1979.* Boulder, CO: Westview Press.

Kuznets, Simon. 1953. *Shares of Upper Income Groups in Income and Saving.* New York: National Bureau of Economic Research.

———. 1955. "Economic Growth and Income Inequality," *American Economic Review* 45, no. 1, (March), pp. 1-28.

———. 1963. "Quantitative Aspects of the Economic Growth of Nations: VIII, Distribution of Income by Size," *Economic Development and Cultural Change* 11, no. 2, (January), pp. 1-80.

———. 1965. *Economic Growth and Structure: Selected Essays.* New York: Norton.

———. 1976. "Demographic Aspects of the Size Distribution of Income," *Economic Development and Cultural Change* 25, no. 1, pp. 1-99.

Lane, Frederic C. 1979. *Profits from Power: Readings in Protection Rent and Violence-Controlling Enterprises.* Albany, NY: State University of New York Press.

Lasswell, Harold D. [1936] 1950. *Politics: Who Gets What When, How.* New York: Peter Smith.

Layard, Richard, and Zabalza, Antoni. 1979. "Family Income Distribution: Explanation and Policy Evaluation," *Journal of Political Economy* 87, no. 5, pt. 2, pp. S133-S161.

Lecaillon, Jacques, and Germidis, Dimitri. 1977, avec le concours de Jean-Pierre Kerneis. *Inégalité des revenus et développement économique: Cameroun, Côte-d'Ivoire, Madagascar, Sénégal.* Paris: Presses Universitaires de France.

Leontief, Wassily. 1983. "Technological Advance, Economic Growth, and the Distribution of Income," *Population and Development Review* 9, no. 3 (September), pp. 403-10.

Leven, Maurice, Moulton, Harold G., and Warburton, Clark. 1934. *America's Capacity to Consume.* Washington, DC: The Brookings Institution.

Levy, A. 1987. "Income Inequality and the Distribution of Ownership of Productive Resources," *Journal of Policy Modeling* 9, no. 2, pp. 321-36.

Lilla, Mark. 1984. "Why the 'Income Distribution' Is So Misleading." *The Public Interest* 77 (Fall), pp. 62-76.

Lillard, Lee A. 1977. "Inequality: Earnings vs. Human Wealth," *American Economic Review* 67, no. 2, pp. 43-54.

Lin, Tzong-biau. 1985. "Growth, Equity and Income Distribution in Hong Kong," *The Developing Economies* 23, no. 4, (December), pp. 391-413.

Lindert, Peter H. 1986. "Unequal English Wealth since 1670," *Journal of Political Economy* 94, no. 6, pp. 1127-62.

Loehr, William. 1980. "Economic Growth, Distribution and Incomes of the Poor," *Journal of Economic Studies* 7, no. 3, pp. 127-139.

Long, James E., Rasmussen, David W., and Haworth, Charles T. 1977. "Income Inequality and City Size," *The Review of Economics and Statistics* 59, no. 2, pp. 244-46.

Lorenz, M. O. 1905. "Methods of Measuring the Concentration of Wealth," *Quarterly Publications of the American Statistical Association* 9, pp. 205-19.

Lucas, R. E. B. 1977. "Is There a Human Capital Approach to Income Inequality?" *Journal of Human Resources* 31 (Summer), pp. 387-95.

Lydall, H. F. 1968. *The Structure of Earnings.* Oxford: Clarendon Press.

McGreevey, William Paul, ed. 1980. *Third-World Poverty: New Strategies for Measuring Development Progress.* Lexington, MA: Lexington Books, D.C. Heath and Company.

McLean, Ian, and Richardson, Sue. 1986. "More or Less Equal? Australian Income Distribution in 1933 and 1980," *The Economic Record* 42, no. 176, pp. 67-81.

Magaziner, Ira C., and Patinkin, Mark. 1989. *The Silent War: Inside the Global Business Battles Shaping America's Future.* New York: Random House.

Marglin, Stephen A. 1984. *Growth, Distribution, and Prices.* Cambridge, MA, and London: Harvard University Press.

Midlarsky, Manus I. 1982. "Scarcity and Inequality: Prologue to the Onset of the Mass Revolution," *Journal of Conflict Resolution* 26, no. 1 (March), pp. 3-38.

Miller, Herman P. 1966. *Income Distribution in the United States: A 1960 Census Monograph*. Washington, DC: U.S. Department of Commerce, Bureau of the Census.

Miller, Lawrence M. 1989. *Barbarians to Bureaucrats: Corporate Life Cycle Strategies. Lessons from the Rise and Fall of Civilizations*. New York: Clarkson N. Potter.

Mizoguchi, Toshiyuki. 1985. "Economic Development Policy and Income Distribution: The Experience in East and Southeast Asia," *The Developing Economies* 23, no. 4, (December), pp. 307-24.

Montani, G. 1975. "Scarce Natural Resources and Income Distribution," *Metroeconomica* 27, no. 1, pp. 68-101.

Morley, Samuel A. 1988. "Relative Wages, Labor Force Structure, and the Distribution of Income in the Short and Long Run," *Economic Development and Cultural Change* 36, no. 4, pp. 651-68.

Morris, Charles R. 1990. *The Coming Global Boom: How to Benefit from Tomorrow's Dynamic World Economy*. New York: Bantam Books.

Moss, Milton. 1978. "Income Distribution Viewed in a Lifetime Perspective," *Review of Income and Wealth* 24, no. 2, (June), pp. 119-36.

Moss, Ralph W. 1989. *The Cancer Industry: Unraveling the Politics*. Photographs by Peter Barry Chowka. New York: Paragon House.

Moyes, P. 1988. "A Note on Minimally Progressive Taxation and Absolute Income Inequality," *Social Choice and Welfare* 5, nos. 2-3, pp. 227-34.

Muller, Edward N. 1988. "Democracy, Economic Development, and Income Inequality," *American Sociological Review* 53, no. 1, (February), pp. 50-68.

Murray, Charles. 1984. *Losing Ground: American Social Policy, 1950-1980*. New York: Basic Books.

Myint, Hla. 1958. "The Classical Theory of International Trade and the Underdeveloped Countries," *The Economic Journal* 68, no. 270 (June), pp. 311-37.

Naisbitt, John, and Aburdene, Patricia. 1990. *Megatrends 2000*. New York: William Morrow.

Nelson, Joel I. 1984. "Income Inequality: The American States," *Social Science Quarterly* 65, pp. 854-60.

Nerlove, Marc; Razin, Assaf; and Sadka, Efraim. 1987. *Household and Economy: Welfare Economics of Endogenous Fertility*. Boston: Academic Press.

Nolan, Brian. 1988-89. "Macroeconomic Conditions and the Size Distribution of Income: Evidence from the United Kingdom," *Journal of Post-Keynesian Economics* 11, no. 2, (Winter), pp. 196-221.

Nozick, Robert. 1974. *Anarchy, State and Utopia*. New York: Basic Books.

O'Connell, Philip J. 1982. "The Distribution and Redistribution of Income in the Republic of Ireland," *The Economic and Social Review* 13, no. 4 (July), pp. 251-78.

O'Higgins, Michael, Schmaus, Guenther, and Stephenson, Geoffrey. 1989. "Income Distribution and Redistribution: A Microdata Analysis for Seven Countries," *Review of Income and Wealth* 35, no. 2 (June), pp. 107-31.

Okner, Benjamin A. 1975. "Taxes and Income: A Microunit Analysis," *The Review of Income and Wealth*, 21, no. 3 (September), pp. 279-99.

Okun, Arthur. 1975. *Equality and Efficiency: The Big Tradeoff*. Washington, DC: The Brookings Institution.

O'Neill, June Ellenhoff. 1987. "Discrimination and Income Inequality," *Social Philosophy and Policy* 5, no. 1, pp. 170-87.

Orsatti, Alvaro. 1983. "La nueva distribución funcional del ingreso en la Argentina," *Desarrollo Económico* 23, no. 91 (October-December), pp. 315-39.

Osberg, Lars. 1984. *Economic Inequality in the United States*. Armonk, NY, and London: M. E. Sharpe.

Oshima, Harry. 1962. "The International Comparison of Size Distribution of Family Incomes with Special Reference to Asia," *Review of Economics and Statistics*. 44, no. 3, (November), pp. 439-45.

Özbudun, Ergun, and Ulusan, Aydin, eds. 1980. *The Political Economy of Income Distribution in Turkey*. New York and London: Holmes and Meier.

Packard, Vance. 1989. *The Ultra Rich: How Much Is Too Much?* Boston, Toronto, and London: Little, Brown and Co.

Papanek, Gustav F., and Kyn, Oldrich. 1986. "The Effect on Income Distribution of Development, the Growth Rate and Economic Strategy," *Journal of Development Economics* 23, pp. 55-65.

Pasinetti, L., ed. 1980. *Lectures on the Theory of Joint Production*. New York: Columbia University Press.

Pastore, José. 1982. *Inequality and Social Mobility in Brazil*. Translated by Robert M. Oxley. Madison: University of Wisconsin Press.

Paukert, Felix, Skolka, Jiri, and Maton, Jef. 1981. *Income Distribution, Structure of Economy and Employment: The Philippines, Iran, the Republic of Korea and Malaysia. A Study Prepared for the International Labour Office within the Framework of the World Employment Programme*. London: Croom Helm.

Peters, Thomas J., and Waterman, Robert H., Jr. 1982. *In Search of Excellence: Lessons from America's Best-Run Companies*. New York: Harper and Row.

Pettengill, John S. 1980. *Labor Unions and the Inequality of Earned Income*. Amsterdam, New York, and Oxford: North-Holland.

———. 1981. "Firearms and the Distribution of Income: A Neo-Classical Model," *The Review of Radical Political Economics* 13, no. 2 (Summer), pp. 1-10.

Pfeffermann, Guy, and Webb, Richard. 1983. "Pobreza e distribuição de renda no Brazil: 1960-1980." *Revista brasileira de economia* 37, no. 2, (April/June), pp. 147-75.

Phelps, E. S., comp. 1973. *Economic Justice: Selected Readings*. Middlesex, UK: Penguin.

Pigou, C. A. [1920], 1932. *Economics of Welfare*. 4th ed. London: Macmillan.

Plotnick, Robert D., and Skidmore, Felicity. 1975. *Progress against Poverty: A Review of the 1964-1974 Decade*. New York: Academic Press.

Pomanskiĭ, A. B. 1985. "An Analysis of the Incentive Model and the Log-Normal Distribution of Income," *Matekon* 22, no. 1, (Fall), pp. 86-104.

Porter, Philip K., and Slottje, Daniel J. 1985. "A Comprehensive Analysis of Inequality in the Size Distribution of Income for the United States, 1952-1981," *Southern Economic Journal* 52, no. 2, (October), pp. 412-21.

Powell, Irene. 1987. "The Effect of Reductions in Concentration of Income-Distribution," *Review of Economics and Statistics* 69, no. 1, pp. 75-82.

Psacharopoulos, George. 1990. "Poverty Alleviation in Latin America," *Finance and Development* 27, no. 1 (March), pp. 17-19.

Radner, Daniel B. 1985. "Family Income, Age, and Size of Unit: Selected International Comparisons," *The Review of Income and Wealth*, 31, no. 2 (June), pp. 103-26.

Rainwater, Lee. 1974. *What Money Buys: Inequality and the Social Meanings of Income*. New York: Basic Books.

Ram, Rati. 1988. "Economic Development and Income Inequality: Further Evidence on the U-Curve Hypothesis," *World Development* 16, no. 11, pp. 1371-76.

Ranis, Gustav. 1981. "Technology Choice and the Distribution of Income," *Annals of the American Academy of Political and Social Science* 458, (November), pp. 41-53.

Rawls, John. 1971. *A Theory of Justice*. Cambridge, MA: Belknap Press of Harvard University Press.

Regan, Donald T. 1988. *For the Record: From Wall Street to Washington*. San Diego, CA: Harcourt Brace Jovanovich.

Reich, Michael. 1981. *Racial Inequality: A Political-Economic Analysis*. Princeton, NJ: Princeton University Press.

Reynolds, Lloyd G. 1974. *Labor Economics and Labor Relations*. 6th ed. Englewood Cliffs, NJ: Prentice-Hall.

Reynolds, Morgan O. 1987. *Making America Poorer: The Cost of Labor Law*. Washington, DC: Cato Institute.

Reynolds, Morgan O. and Smolensky, Eugene. 1977. *Public Expenditures, Taxes, and the Distribution of Income*. New York, San Francisco, and London: Academic Press.

Ricardo, David. [1817], 1951. *On the Principles of Political Economy and Taxation. The Works and Correspondence of David Ricardo*, vol. 1, ed. Piero Sraffa with the collaboration of M. H. Dobb. Cambridge: Cambridge University Press.

Rice, G. Randolph, and Sale, Tom S., III. 1975. "Size Distribution of Income in Louisiana and Other Southern States," *Growth and Change* 6, pp. 26-33.

Rivera-Batiz, Francisco L. 1983. "Trade Theory, Distribution of Income, and Immigration," *American Economic Review* 73, no. 2 (May), pp. 183-87.

Robinson, Joan. 1933. *The Economics of Imperfect Competition*. New York: Macmillan.

———. 1961. "Equilibrium Growth Models," *American Economic Review* 51, no. 3, pp. 360-69.

Roemer, John E. 1979. "The Real Distribution of Current Goods and Services," *Journal of Post-Keynesian Economics* 2, no. 2, pp. 212-22.

———. 1987. "History's Effect on the Distribution of Income," *Social Science Information* 26, no. 2, pp. 403-15.

Rothman, Robert A. 1978. *Inequality and Stratification in the United States*. Englewood Cliffs, NJ: Prentice-Hall.

Ruthenberg, David, and Stano, Miron. 1977. "The Determinants of Interstate Variations in Income Distribution," *Review of Social Economy* 35, no. 1 (April), pp. 55-65.

Rytina, Nancy F. 1982. "Earnings of Men and Women: A Look at Specific Occupations," *Monthly Labor Review* 105 (April), pp. 25-31.

Sahota, G. S. 1978. "Theories of Personal Income Distribution: A Survey," *Journal of Economic Literature* 16, no. 1 (March), pp. 1-57.

Sahota, G. S., and Rocca, Carlos A. 1985. *Income Distribution: Theory, Modeling and Case Study of Brazil*. Ames: Iowa State University Press.

Saith, A. 1983. "Development and Distribution: A Critique of the Cross-Country U-Hypothesis," *Journal of Development Economics* 13, no. 3, pp. 367-82.

Sale, Tom S. 1974. "Interstate Analysis of the Size Distribution of Family Income 1950-1970," *Southern Economic Journal* 41, pp. 434-41.

Sampson, A. A. 1984. "Unemployment and the Distribution of Income," *Australian Economic Papers* 23, no. 43 (December), pp. 249-58.

Saposnik, Subin. 1988. "The Distribution of Income, Incomplete Information and the Rank and Pareto Criteria," *Public Choice* 59, pp. 195-202.

Sarantides, S. A. 1987. "International Income Inequality and Per-Capita Income Rates of Growth," *International Journal of Social Economics* 14, no. 7, pp. 195-210.

Satchell, D. E. 1987. "Sources and Subgroup Decomposition Inequalities for the Lorenz Curve," *International Economic Review* 28, no. 2, pp. 323-29.

Sawyer, Malcolm. 1976. "Income Distribution in OECD Countries," *OECD Economic Outlook, Occasional Studies* (July), pp. 3-36.

Schnitzer, Martin. [1974], 1975. *Income Distribution: A Comparative Study of the United States, Sweden, West Germany, East Germany, the United Kingdom, and Japan*. New York, Washington, DC, and London: Praeger.

Schultz, T. P. 1972. "Long-Term Change in Personal Income Distribution," *American Economic Review* 62, no. 2 (May), pp. 361-62.

Schultz, Theodore W. 1968. "Institutions and the Rising Economic Value of Man," *American Journal of Agricultural Economics* 50, no. 5 (December), pp. 1113-22.

———. 1980. "Nobel Lecture: The Economics of Being Poor," *Journal of Political Economy* 88, no. 4, pp. 639-51.

Schumpeter, Joseph A. 1951. *Imperialism and Social Classes*. Translated by Heinz Norden, edited with an introduction by Paul M. Sweezy. New York: Augustus M. Kelley.

Segal, Harvey H. 1989. *Corporate Makeover: The Reshaping of the American Economy*. New York: Viking.

Seligson, Mitchell A., ed. 1984. *The Gap between Rich and Poor: Contending Perspectives on the Political Economy of Development*. Boulder, CO, and London: Westview Press.

Sen, Amartya K. 1973. *On Economic Inequality*. Oxford: Clarendon Press.

Serrón, Luis A. 1980. *Scarcity, Exploitation, and Poverty: Malthus and Marx in Mexico*. Foreword by Irving M. Zeitlin. Norman: University of Oklahoma Press.

Shand, R. T. 1987. "Income Distribution in a Dynamic Rural Sector: Some Evidence from Malaysia," *Economic Development and Cultural Change* 36, no. 1, pp. 35-50.

Shepherd, William G. 1989. "Capital Gain as Economic Rent," *Review of Social Economy* 47, no. 2 (Summer), pp. 155-72.

Shorrocks, Anthony F. 1982. "Inequality Decomposition by Factor Components," *Econometrica* 50, no. 1 (January), pp. 193-211.

———. 1984. "Inequality Decomposition by Population Subgroups, *Econometrica* 52, no. 6 (November), pp. 1369-85.

Silber, Jacques. 1989. "Factor Components, Population Subgroups and the Computation of the Gini Index of Inequality," *The Review of Economics and Statistics* 71, no. 1, pp. 107-15.

Silber, John. 1989. *Straight Shooting: What's Wrong with America and How To Fix It*. New York: Harper and Row.

Slesnick, Daniel T. 1989. "Specific Egalitarianism and Total Welfare Inequality: A Decompositional Analysis." *Review of Economics and Statistics* 71, no. 2, pp. 116-27.

Slottje, Daniel J. 1984. "A Measure of Income Inequality in the U.S. for the Years 1952-1980 Based on the Beta Distribution of the Second Kind," *Economics Letters* 15, pp. 369-75.

Smeeding, Timothy N. 1988-1989. "Poverty, Affluence, and the Income Costs of Children: Cross-National Evidence from the Luxembourg Income Study (LIS)." *Journal of Post-Keynesian Economics* 11, no. 2 (Winter), pp. 222-39.

Soltow, Lee 1984. "Wealth Inequality in the United States in 1798 and 1860," *Review of Economics and Statistics* 66, no. 3, pp. 444-51.

———. 1985. "Egalitarian America and its Inegalitarian Housing in the Federal Period," *Social Science History* 9, no. 2 (Spring), pp. 199-213.

———. 1987. "The Distribution of Income in the United States in 1798," *Review of Economics and Statistics* 69, no. 1, pp. 181-85.

Spahr, Charles B. [1896], 1970. *An Essay on the Present Distribution of Wealth in the United States [:] America's Working People*. New York and London: Johnson Reprint Company.

Sraffa, Piero. [1960] 1975. *Production of Commodities by Means of Commodities*. London: Cambridge University Press.

Steindl, Joseph. 1965. *Random Processes and the Growth of Firms: A Study of the Pareto Law*. London: Griffin.

Sterling, Claire. 1990. *Octopus: The Long Reach of the Sicilian Mafia*. New York and London: W. W. Norton.

Stewart, Charles T., Jr., and Lee, Jin-shia. 1986. "Urban Concentration and Income Distribution," *The Journal of Developing Areas* 20 (April), pp. 357-68.

Stewart, Frances, and Streeten, Paul. 1976. "New Strategies for Development: Poverty, Income Distribution, and Growth," *Oxford Economic Papers* 28, no. 3, pp. 381-405.

Summers, Robert, and Heston, Alan. 1984. "Improved Comparisons of Real Product and Its Composition, 1950-80," *The Review of Income and Wealth* 30, no. 2 (June), pp. 207-62.

———. 1988. "A New Set of International Comparisons of Real Product and Price Levels. Estimates for 130 Countries, 1950-1985," *The Review of Income and Wealth* 34, no. 1 (March), pp. 1-25.

Sundrum, R. M. 1987. *Growth and Income Distribution in India: Policy and Performance since Independence*. New Delhi, Newbury Park, CA, and London: Sage Publications.

Suppes, P. 1988. "Lorenz Curves for Various Processes: A Pluralistic Approach to Equity," *Social Choice and Welfare* 5, nos. 2-3, pp. 89-101.

Terasaki, Yasuhiro. 1985. "Income Distribution and Development Policies in the Philippines," *The Developing Economies* 23, no. 4 (December), pp. 368-90.

Theil, Henri. 1988. "Income Inequality and the Progressivity of the Income Tax," *Review of Social Economy* 46, no. 3 (December), pp. 252-54.
Thurow, Lester C. 1970. "Analyzing the American Income Distribution," *American Economic Review* 60, no. 2 (May), pp. 261-69.
———. 1975. *Generating Inequality: Mechanism of Distribution in the U.S. Economy.* New York: Basic Books.
———. 1987. "A Surge in Inequality," *Scientific American* 256, no. 5 (May), pp. 30-37.
Tilak, Jandhyala B. G. 1987. *The Economics of Inequality in Education.* New Delhi, Beverly Hills, Newbury Park, CA, and London: Sage Publications.
Tinbergen, Jan. 1975. *Income Distribution: Analysis and Policies.* Amsterdam, Oxford, and New York: North-Holland, American Elsevier.
Tomes, Nigel. 1981. "The Family, Inheritance, and the Intergenerational Transmission of Inequality," *Journal of Political Economy* 89, no. 5, pp. 928-58.
Tool, Marc R., and Samuels, Warren J., eds. [1980], 1989. *The Economy as a System of Power.* 2d ed., rev. New Brunswick, NJ, and Oxford: Transaction Publishers.
Treas, Judith. 1983. "Trickle Down or Transfers? Postwar Determinants of Family Income Inequality," *American Sociological Review* 48, no. 4, (August), pp. 546-49.
———. 1987. "The Effect of Women's Labor Force Participation on the Distribution of Income in the United States," *Annual Review of Sociology* 13, pp. 259-88.
Tuckman, Barbara. 1976. "The Green Revolution and the Distribution of Agricultural Income in Mexico," *World Development* 4, no. 1, pp. 17-24.
United Nations. Secretariat of the Economic Commission for Europe. 1967. *Incomes in Postwar Europe: A Study of Policies, Growth and Distribution.* Economic Survey of Europe 1965, Part 2. Geneva: United Nations.
United Nations Development Programme. Annual. *World Development Report.* New York: United Nations Development Programme.
United States Department of Commerce. 1974. "Consumer Income," *Current Population Reports,* P-60, no. 92 (March).
———. 1980. *Current Population Reports* P-60, no. 122 (March).
———. "Consumer Income," *Current Population Reports* P-60, no. 162 (1988).
United States Department of Commerce. Bureau of the Census. 1975. *Historical Statistics of the United States Colonial Times to 1970.* Bicentennial ed. Washington, DC.: U.S. Department of Commerce.
United States Department of the Treasury. Internal Revenue Service. *SOI Bulletin.* Washington, DC.
Vatter, Harold C. 1982. "The Atrophy of Net Investment and Some Consequences for the U.S. Mixed Economy," *Journal of Economic Issues* 16, no. 1 (March), pp. 237-53.
Veblen, Thorstein. 1899. *The Theory of the Leisure Class: An Economic Study of Institutions.* New York: Macmillan.
Venables, A. J. 1983. "Random Job Prospects and the Distribution of Income," *Quarterly Journal of Economics* 98, no. 4, pp. 637-57.
Venieris, Yiannis P., and Gupta, Dipak K. 1986. "Income Distribution and Sociopolitical Instability as Determinants of Savings: A Cross-Sectional Model," *Journal of Political Economy* 94, no. 4, pp. 873-84.

Viscusi, W. Kip. 1978. "Wealth Effects and Earnings Premiums for Job Hazards," *Review of Economics and Statistics* 60, no. 3 (August), pp. 408-16.

Wallace, Phyllis A., and LaMond, Annette M., eds. 1977. *Women, Minorities, and Employment Discrimination.* Lexington, MA: Lexington Books.

Ward, Michael Don. 1978. *The Political Economy of Distribution: Equality versus Inequality.* New York and Oxford: Elsevier.

Waring, Marilyn. 1988. *If Women Counted: A New Feminist Economics.* Introduction by Gloria Steinem. San Francisco and New York: Harper and Row.

Waterman, Robert H., Jr. 1987. *The Renewal Factor: How the Best Get and Keep the Competitive Edge.* Toronto, New York, London, Sydney, and Auckland: Bantam Books.

Weede, Eric. 1981. "Income Inequality, Average Income, and Domestic Violence," *Journal of Conflict Resolution* 25, no. 4 (December), pp. 639-54.

Weil, Gordon. 1984. "Cyclical and Secular Influences on the Size Distribution of Personal Income in the UK: Some Econometric Tests," *Applied Economics* 16, pp. 749-755.

Weinberg, D. H. 1987. "The Distributional Implications of Tax Expenditures and Comprehensive Income Taxation," *National Tax Journal* 40, no. 2, pp. 237-53.

Weiss, Y. 1972. "The Risk Element in Occupational and Educational Choice," *Journal of Political Economy* 80, no. 6, pp. 1203-13.

Williamson, Jeffrey G., and Lindert, Peter H. 1980. *American Inequality: A Macroeconomic History.* New York: Academic Press.

Winegarden, C. R. 1984. "Income Redistribution versus Accelerated Economic Growth: A Comparison of Demographic Effects," *Oxford Bulletin of Economics and Statistics* 46, no. 3, pp. 255-71.

Wolff, Edward N. 1979. "The Rate of Surplus Value, the Organic Composition, and the General Rate of Profit in the U.S. Economy, 1947-67," *American Economic Review* 69, no. 3 (June), pp. 329-42.

Wolfson, Michael. 1986. "Stasis and Change: Income Inequality in Canada 1965-1983," *The Review of Income and Wealth* 32, no. 4 (December), pp. 337-70.

Women: A World Report. 1985. A New Internationalist Book. London: Methuen.

Wright, Charles L. 1978. "Income Inequality and Economic Growth: Examining the Evidence," *The Journal of Developing Areas* 13 (October), pp. 49-66.

Yamane, Linus. 1986. "Relative Price Changes and the Real Distribution of Income: The Case of Brazil," *Economics Letters* 20, pp. 217-20.

Yoneda, Kinimaru. 1985. "A Note on Income Distribution in Indonesia," *The Developing Economies* 23, no. 4 (December), pp. 414-22.

Young, Ruth C., and Moreno, José A. 1965. "Economic Development and Social Rigidity: A Comparative Study of Forty-Eight States," *Economic Development and Cultural Change* 13, no. 5:1 (July), pp. 439-52.

Index

adversary trade, 26
after-tax income, 65, 72, 76
AID (Agency for International Development) Review, Spring 1970, 99, 111
AIDS epidemic, 91
aid to dependent children, 113
allocations familiales (in France), 93, 113
asbestos, 138
Associated Press, 137

black-market trading, 71
business mergers, 132

campaign "handlers," 19
capital bias, 108-9
caste, 136
Catholic bishops' letter (in the United States), 74
Catholic Christianity, 119
cattle kingdoms, 121
Chayanov, A. V., 79
Civil Code (Code Napoléon in France) 93, 113
cohort fertility, 45
comparative advantage, 24-25
conspicuous consumption, 106-7

contrived scarcity, 4
Corn Laws (in England), 75
corporate culture, 133
corporate power, 121
cyclical variation, 71

death duties, 76
demographic transition, 92, 112
discontinuous distributions, 41-42
discrimination, 20-22
Disraeli, Benjamin, 106
distribution of total income, 40-41
distributive functions, 30-31
Djilas, Milovan, 21
domestic violence, 120
Douglas, Paul, 122
dualistic growth model, 94
dumping, 26

economic rent, 10-13, 20
Einstein, Albert, 138
enclosures, 75, 89
entailed estates, 76
entrepreneurial earnings, 20
Erhard, Ludwig, 144
estate or inheritance taxes, 66, 128, 143, 147

exponential function, 34–36, 151–58, 159–61
exurban settlements, 59

factor shares, 7, 64
family cycle, 79
farm-size distributions, 42
farm versus nonfarm income disparity, 57–58
Federal Reserve System, 142
female occupations, 120
free rider problem, 27
"friendly fascism," 124

Galsworthy, John, 119
General Accounting Office, 147
gentrification, 107
Georgist taxation, 13
"ghost town" syndrome, 118
Gibrat, Robert, 31
Gini, Corrado, 32
Gini index, 32–34
"golden parachutes," 20, 132
"golden rule," 6
graduated income tax, 20
"green giant," 145
"green revolution," 81–82
Grotius, Hugo, 119

Head Start, 116
hexachlorophene, 139
higher order equations, 36
homeless people, 136
Hoover Institution, 3, 20, 124
hostile takeovers, 132–33
housework as income in-kind, 43, 67
housing values, 51
human capital, 15, 17–19, 96, 116, 130

immigration laws, 114
industry bias, 108
infant industry, 133
insider trading, 123
interest rates, 55
Islam, 119

Jefferson, Thomas, 10
junk bond financing, 123

Junker estates (in Prussia), 111, 114
justice, 5–8

Keynes, John Maynard, 131
Kuznets, Simon, 2, 55, 59, 77, 84, 87–89, 96, 101, 148

labor unions, 136
Ladejinsky, Wolf, 111
land reform, 77–78, 79, 81, 84, 98–100, 109–112, 145
Lasswell, Harold D., 3, 18
Lenin, Vladmir I., 99, 106
lifetime incomes, 45, 60–62
LIS (Luxembourg Income Study), 74
location rents, 100
location values, 13
lognormal function, 31
Lorenz's curve, 32–33
Luddites, 28
Luxembourg Income Study (LIS), 74

McCarthyism, 111–12
Madison, James, 2, 10
Mafia, 2, 8, 21
Malthus, Thomas R., 93, 113
margin theory, 142
market mechanisms, 26–27
market power, 20
Marx, Karl, 3, 14
mass transit, 131
"mechanizator cadres" (in the Soviet Union), 108
median/average ratio, 36–40
medical professions, 23
methanol industry, 146
migrant farm workers, 24
mode, 38–40
monopoly rent, 14, 18, 19, 93, 102, 129, 130
multinational corporations, 121, 142, 144
multiple lock-in system, 131
Muslims, 93, 119

nonmarket goods, 68

overpopulation, 11

INDEX

Pareto, Vilfredo, 30
Pareto function, 30, 35
parliamentary enclosures, 75
patronage, 18
pension funds, 8
perquisite incomes, 71
Pigou, C. A., 6, 7, 101
pilot reform, 112
plantations, 47, 55, 58, 97–98, 100, 102, 109–10, 114, 117–18, 121
plutocracy, 4, 106, 121–22
police state, 106
Poor Laws (in England), 93, 113
population growth rates, 92–93
positional goods, 18
power of the purse, 121
PPP (Purchasing Power Parity), 68–69, 82, 86
price bias, 44
primogeniture, 93, 113
privatization, 142, 147
production function, 22
productivity paradox, 7, 27
protection rent, 11, 26
public works, 146
Purchasing Power Parity (PPP), 68–69, 82, 86
Puzo, Mario, 21

qualified labor, 15
quasi rent, 12

race discrimination, 58–59, 117–19
Rand, Ayn, 20
Reagan, Ronald W., 128–29, 137
Reagan budget, 66
rent, 8–13
returns to size or scale, 98
Ricardo, David, 3, 9–11, 75
risky occupations, 17
Robinson, Joan, 11

savings-and-loan associations, 123
savings-in-kind, 95
scarce occupations, 17–19
school taxes, 116
Schumpeter, Joseph A., 131
Schutz index, 33

sector proportions, 89–92, 93, 101
sex discrimination, 56, 61
site value, 13
size group frequencies, 38
slavery, 3, 54, 109, 117
slum formation, 58, 100, 118
Smith, Adam, 139
snapshot data, 45, 60
social Darwinism, 123, 127
social waste, 4, 26, 130, 146
sperm whale oil, 144
stagflation, 130
Stalin, Joseph, 142
star effect, 18, 96, 129
statutory adjustments, 49
suburbanization, 59
sunk costs, 12
surplus value, 14
sweatshops, 17

tax avoidance, 51
tax incidence, 72
technology fatigue, 139
telephone switchboard operators, 120
terms of trade, 28, 94
Theil index, 33
transition theory, 45
trickling down, 80, 127
truncating effect, 52
Tudor enclosures, 75

U-curve, inverted, 55, 77, 88–89, 97, 101–3, 148
underclass, 58, 118, 146
United Fruit Company, 111
United Press International, 137
urban sprawl, 59, 131
utopia, 122

valuation problems, 43
variable proportions, law of, 126
Veblen, Thorstein, 104, 128
vent for surplus, 24–25, 85, 94
Viet Cong movement, 112

war on poverty, 56
welfare programs, 54

ABOUT THE AUTHOR

FOLKE DOVRING was raised and educated in Sweden, studying first the humanities and social sciences and then economic history at Lund University. He went on to teach there before joining the United Nations' Food and Agriculture Organization (FAO) as a statistician and economist for several years. Since 1960, Professor Dovring has taught land economics and economic development at the University of Illinois College of Agriculture. He has published many books on a variety of topics ranging from land tenure in medieval Europe to energy economics. Recent Praeger publications by Dovring are *Productivity and Value* (1987), *Farming for Fuel* (1988), and *Progress for Food or Food for Progress?* (1988).